Fodor's Inside

Paris

CONTENTS

ABOUT THIS GUIDE

Inside Paris is the City of Light like you've never seen it. Written entirely by Parisians, it includes features on the city's neo-bistro and wine movements; and plenty of insider tips. The result is a curated compilation infused with authentic Parisian flavor, accompanied by easy-to-use maps and transit information. Whether you're visiting Paris for the first time or a seasoned traveler looking to explore a new neighborhood, this is the guide for you.

We've handpicked the top things to do and rated the sights, shopping, dining, and nightlife in the city's most dynamic, up-and-coming neighborhoods. Truly exceptional experiences in all categories are marked with a ★.

Restaurants, bars, and cafés are a huge part of Paris's appeal, of course, and you'll find plenty to savor in its diverse neighborhoods. We cover cuisines in all price points, and everything from enduring institutions and groundbreaking chefs to the fixings for the perfect picnic. We cover hotels in the Experience section at the front of this guide.

Use the $ to $$$$ price charts below to estimate meal and room costs. We list adult prices for sights; ask about discounts when purchasing tickets.

Paris is constantly changing. All prices, opening times, and other details in this guide were accurate at press time. Always confirm information when it matters, especially when making a detour to a specific place.

Visit Fodors.com for expanded restaurant and hotel reviews, additional recommendations, news, and features.

WHAT IT COSTS: Restaurants

$	$$	$$$	$$$$
Under €18	€18–€24	€25–€32	Over €32

Prices are the average cost of a main course at dinner or, if dinner is not served, at lunch.

WHAT IT COSTS: Hotels

$	$$	$$$	$$$$
Under €121	€121–€175	€176–€250	Over €250

Prices are the lowest cost of a standard double room in high season.

LES PUCES

ÉPINETTES

CLIGNAN-COURT

LA CHAPELLE

LA VILLETTE

LES BATIGNOLLES

MONTMARTRE

TERNES

MONCEAU

PIGALLE

LES GRANDS BOULEVARDS

SENTIER

CANAL ST-MARTIN

BELLEVILLE

CHAILLOT

CHAMPS-ÉLYSÉES

TROCADÉRO

BOIS DE BOULOGNE

PASSY

PALAIS-ROYAL

LES HALLES

LE MARAIS

OBERKAMPF

MÉNILMONTANT

PÈRE-LACHAISE

LES INVALIDES

AUTEUIL

VAUGIRARD

ST-GERMAIN-DES-PRÉS

LES ÎLES

QUARTIER LATIN

BASTILLE

BERCY

CHARONNE

BEL-AIR

JAVEL

MONTPARNASSE

ST-LAMBERT

BUTTE-AUX-CAILLES

AUSTERLITZ

BOIS DE VINCENNES

MONTROUGE

MAISON BLANCHE

WELCOME
TO PARIS

It's easy to place Paris in the past, an echo of its former Belle Époque or 1920s self. But Paris is a living, thriving city, teeming with a new wave of neo-bistros, trendy nightlife spots, and innovative culture. Today, this combination of classic Paris and a youthful, authentic capital is certainly worth a visit.

PARIS TODAY

Paris has always been a city divided by its river. The Left Bank, historically, has been the thinking man's bank, home to the medieval Sorbonne University and, later, to the cafés where Existentialist, Surrealist, and Lost Generation writers came together to debate and share their ideas. The Right Bank, meanwhile, has long been defined by grand palaces: not just the Louvre, but also palace hotels like the Crillon or the Ritz and grand squares like Place Vendôme or Place des Vosges.

But this dichotomy has started to change. Hemingway's cheap sixth-story apartment overlooking Place de la Contrescarpe is now the expensive stomping grounds of France's *gauche caviar*: intellectual, left wing–thinkers with quite a bit of money to burn. And while the immediate Right Bank is still a living museum to the aristocracy of yore, journey a bit farther north (especially into eastern Paris), and you'll find an enclave of artists, hipsters, and students who have added

their own brand of innovation and vibrancy to the capital.

REVOLUTIONARY HISTORY

Paris may be more than 2,000 years old, but as it stands today, Paris is defined by its more recent Revolutionary past. The first French Revolution took place in 1789 and not only positioned France as the nation of the *Rights of Man* but also indirectly brought about Napoléon Bonaparte's Empire. Napoléon immediately began making changes to the cityscape, building the four major cemeteries at each of its cardinal points (including Père Lachaise) and installing a number of fountains and two triumphal archways along the central historic axis connecting the Louvre to the Champs-Élysées.

But it was truly the Revolution of 1848 that would change the face of Paris forever. Following this Revolution, Napoléon III came to power and founded the Second Empire. In cooperation with city planner Georges-Eugène Haussmann, Napoléon demolished the narrow medieval streets, replacing them with the wide avenues, expansive green spaces, and cream-colored Haussmannian buildings one still sees throughout Paris today. Despite these major changes, certain neighborhoods, like Belleville, Montmartre, Butte-aux-Cailles, and parts of the Marais, escaped renovation and remain a testament to pre-19th-century Paris today.

CULINARY EVOLUTION

Paris has long been seen as an epicenter of haute cuisine, but the quality of much of the food served in the capital had been going slowly but surely downhill until the late 1990s. It was then that several major changes began to occur on the culinary scene.

The French government introduced a decree in 1993 that formally defined what ingredients could be used in a *baguette de tradition française* (yes, they're regulated by law!), marking the final straw in the dissatisfaction with the industrially produced bread products that had become the norm in the city. At around the same time, chef Yves Camdeborde became the founder of the neo-bistro movement, also known as *bistronomie* in French. This movement takes the classic Parisian bistro, which traditionally served hearty comfort food (and had unfortunately evolved to serve mainly reheated frozen food), and turns it on its head. Today, chefs at neo-bistros show off their creativity and innovation with dishes inspired by the classics and made with simple, seasonal ingredients—no Michelin-star-worthy plating (or prices) needed.

FRENCH CULTURE

The stereotype of French "rudeness" is largely a matter of a misunderstanding of differences between French and American culture. First, all French interactions begin with an exchange of *bonjour*. It's inappropriate, in France, to tack a request onto your "hello" before the person you're speaking to has returned your bonjour in kind. If you learn one French word before your trip, learn this one, and say it to every shopkeeper, waiter, and bus driver you meet.

Waiters bear the brunt of the French "rudeness" stereotype, due to their perceived pushiness. Many are those who have asked for their *steak-frites* well done only to be asked to choose something else. This is not necessarily a question of pushiness, but rather the server attempting to guide the customer toward the best possible dining experience. French waiters can also seem as though they're ignoring you, particularly once you've finished your meal. This is because most restaurants don't expect to "turn over" tables, and a server doesn't want to rush you by hovering. This does mean that it can take a long time to get the check, but it also means that you won't be kicked to the curb the second you swallow your last mouthful of crème brûlée.

WHAT'S WHERE IN PARIS

Paris is organized into 20 arrondissements, or districts, that spiral out like a snail shell from the 1er in the center to the 20e in the east, each with its own personality and character. To help you choose how to organize your visit, here's a rundown of the areas we cover in detail. The numbers refer to chapter numbers.

2. LES HALLES AND PALAIS-ROYAL

Predominantly known for the Louvre, the imposing former palace and largest art museum in the world, these areas in the 1er arrondissement also have a rich connection with France's culinary history, as the home of the bustling Les Halles market. That heritage continues today with an innovative food scene, not to mention chic boutiques that are definitely worth a visit.

3. SENTIER AND LES GRANDS BOULEVARDS

Sentier was once Paris's garment district, but it has since evolved into the tech center of Paris and is home to one of the city's top market streets, Rue Montorgueil, and some of the best restaurants. The Grands Boulevards and their gorgeous 19th-century covered passageways, meanwhile, are filled to the brim with shops and boutiques.

4. LE MARAIS

A large neighborhood spanning the 3e and 4e, the historic Jewish district of Paris is now divided in two: the South Marais, with the famous Rue des Rosiers, still retains many elements of its Jewish heritage and more than its fair share of vintage shops. The North Marais, meanwhile, has become a foodie mecca, with a superb concentration of restaurants and cocktail bars. The nightlife in both is worth the trip.

5. QUARTIER LATIN

The Latin Quarter gets its name from the imposing Sorbonne University, founded in the Middle Ages, when teaching was conducted in Latin. Today, it is still the student district, with cheap bars and restaurants galore. It's also a great spot for delving into some of Paris's lesser-known historical sites, including some of its only remaining Roman ruins.

6. ST-GERMAIN-DES-PRÉS AND LES INVALIDES

These ritzy areas between the Latin Quarter and the Eiffel Tower have long been boutique central, and while you'll see more big-brand stores than you might have in the past, it's still a great spot for fashionistas. This area is also home to some of the illustrious cafés once frequented by Paris's literary intelligentsia.

7. TROCADÉRO AND CHAMPS-ELYSÉES

Along the right bank from Trocadéro to Triangle d'Or and to Place de la Concorde, vistas over museums and palaces can be found at every turn. This neighborhood is the prime spot for feeling pampered, whether it's at a fancy restaurant, a glitzy hotel or spa, or an exclusive cocktail bar.

8. LES BATIGNOLLES AND LES PUCES

Bargain hunters will love the northern limit of Paris, where the imposing Marché aux Puces (flea market) draws collectors and sellers of antiques and trinkets every week. To the west in the 17e, in Batignolles, you'll encounter a completely different atmosphere: that of a small village within the city.

9. MONTMARTRE AND PIGALLE

While Montmartre has been part of Paris since 1860, it still retains the picturesque small-town appeal that clearly shows why artists like van Gogh and Picasso chose to live here. While Montmartre and Pigalle (in the 18e and 9e) have also historically been linked to the red light district in Paris, what remains of these cabarets is a bit more Epcot-esque these days.

10. CANAL ST-MARTIN

The area around the Canal St-Martin connecting the Seine to the Canal de l'Ourcq is hipster central, with Anglo-style coffee shops, natural wine bars, and dance clubs galore. Use the Canal as your central artery to explore this hip neighborhood in the 10e.

11. OBERKAMPF AND BASTILLE

Foodies need look no further than the neighborhoods of the 11e to get a glimpse of the culinary revolution currently taking place in Paris. Down every street in Oberkampf, you'll find a new, exciting restaurant to try. Bastille has historically been the stomping ground of students out for a night on the town, but this culinary revolution is arriving at the former site of the French Revolution too.

12. BELLEVILLE AND MÉNILMONTANT

These multicultural neighborhoods welcomed waves of Chinese immigrants and artists in the 1980s, changing them forever. Gentrified nearly beyond recognition, Belleville and Ménilmontant are inhabited by hipsters, with a lively nightlife and a superb street art scene.

13. BUTTE-AUX-CAILLES AND BERCY

The former village of Butte-aux-Cailles has a Revolutionary streak, as one of the last bastions of the 1871 Commune of Paris. Today it has an eccentric vibe and a vibrant street art scene. At the riverbanks, this bohemian spirit is replaced by imposing monuments to culture like the Bibliothèque Nationale François Mitterrand and Cinémathèque Française.

TOP EXPERIENCES IN PARIS

It's impossible to see and do everything in one trip to Paris, but there are some local traditions you simply shouldn't miss. Our top experiences will guide you to the best of the city.

SIPPING COFFEE AT A CAFÉ

While it might seem that there's nothing more Parisian than sipping coffee on a sidewalk terrace, the truth is that most of the espressos at your average café range from ho-hum to barely drinkable. But these days, there are a handful of truly great coffee spots, especially near **Oberkampf** and **Bastille.** The best part? There's no rent due on your seat in Paris, so one coffee, whether it's at a typical sidewalk café or a hipster coffee shop, earns you the right to camp out and people-watch for as long as you like. Check out some of the big name roasters in town, including **The Beans on Fire, Ten Belles,** and **Belleville Brûlerie.**

EXPLORING PARKS AND GARDENS

Paris is home to more than 400 green spaces, from manicured royal gardens like the **Jardin des Tuileries** to more rustic spots like the **Jardin Naturel** in Belleville. Take some time to discover your favorite: sprawl out near the Eiffel Tower on the **Champ de Mars,** check out the views from the hill overlooking the man-made lake in beautiful Buttes-Chaumont, or pull up a chair and read near the fountains at **Jardin du Luxembourg.** One of our favorite spots to stroll is the former railway turned promenade, **Coulée Verte René-Dumont,** running from Bastille to Bercy.

LOOKING WITH THE EYE OF AN ARTIST

Paris's history as a center for the arts is long and well earned. But museums like the **Louvre** and the **Musée d'Orsay** are just the beginning. Explore some of the lesser-known museums like the **Jacquemart-André,** home to Uccello's famed *Saint George and the Dragon* or the **Musée Marmottan Monet,** home to an impressive array of Impressionist pieces by the artist, including *Impression Soleil Levant.* And Paris's art isn't limited to museums. See the former neighborhood of some of Paris's best-loved artists, including Salvadore Dalí, with a stroll through **Montmartre,** or discover what its newest artists are up to with a wander through the galleries in the Marais or **Les Frigos** in Bercy. Street art has also taken Paris by storm; you'll find it in spades in the **13e**

arrondissement (see **Street Art 13** in our Butte-aux-Cailles and Bercy chapter) as well as in **Belleville,** particularly on Rue Dénoyez.

THE WORLD OF APÉRO

To feel like a real local, you'll need to get on board with *apéro*. Short for aperitif, apéro is an essential part of any Parisian evening, a time for drinking, noshing, and socializing before digging into dinner. Choose a sidewalk café, an up-and-coming cocktail bar, or even the restaurant where you plan to dine, and order a Parisian favorite: the spritz has become a popular choice of late, though traditionally, whiskey, pastis, or a kir do the trick nicely. Simple snacks will often be served, but at our favorite wine bars like **Le Barav** or **Septime la Cave,** you could just as easily opt for a shared charcuterie board or a delicious assortment of small plates to whet your appetite before dinner.

MARKET SHOPPING

Gone are the days when all Parisians shop at outdoor markets, though their popularity is certainly making a comeback. With nearly 100 weekly markets within the city limits, including the **Marché d'Aligre** and the **Marché des Enfants Rouges,** it's likely there will be a market near you—the only thing to consider is what you're looking for. Unlike the United States, France doesn't have many farmers' markets; there might only be one producer or two among market vendors. One of the top markets for buying from actual farmers is the covered **Marché Biologique des Batignolles.** If you're in for a flea market dive, head to the sprawling **Marché aux Puces de St-Ouen** to browse more than 1,700 arts and antiques vendors.

WALKING ALONG THE WATERFRONT

Paris is, indeed, land-locked, but with a river and two canals running through it, it has more than its share of waterfront fun. A walk along **Les Berges de Seine** on the Left Bank and **Parc Rives de Seine** on the Right Bank will not only allow you to partake in the floating gardens, sports facilities, and exhibition areas installed there, but will also give you a view of most of Paris's major monuments. Walking west from **Notre-Dame,** you'll encounter the **Louvre, Musée d'Orsay,** the **Grand and Petit Palais, Invalides,** and the **Eiffel Tower,** not to mention several of the city's most beautiful bridges, like **Pont Neuf** and **Pont des Arts.** To the northeast, the city's two canals, **Canal St-Martin** and **Canal de l'Ourcq,** offer a slightly different vibe. St-Martin is a picnicker's dream, and when the locks open, it's always a delightful show. Ourcq has wider banks, perfect for a game of pétanque (lawn bowling) or sunbathing when it's nice. It also plays host to an outdoor swimming pool every summer as part of **Paris Plages.** *Check our Events section for more info.*

PARIS WITH KIDS

It can be a challenge to discover Paris with kids. Lines are long, dinner is later, and kids' menus are often nonexistent. But if you play your cards right, there are tons of ways to have family fun.

CAROUSELS

Paris is home to several old-fashioned carousels, including one right across from the Eiffel Tower and another at the base of Montmartre. These can afford a great pause for kids and parents alike.

PUPPET SHOWS

Guignols are old-fashioned marionettes that used to pop up in nearly every park in Paris and put on a show. There are still a handful of regular guignol shows in the capital, including ones at **Parc Georges Brassens** and the **Jardin du Luxembourg.**

SAILING TOY BOATS

A most idyllic scene greets families in the **Jardin du Luxembourg**: scores of families sailing 100-year-old toy boats on the pond in the center of the garden. Rent one and you'll find they're not motorized; a push stick keeps them from the borders of the pond.

ANIMAL-ORIENTED ATTRACTIONS

Paris does have a large zoo on its outskirts, in the **Bois de Vincennes,** but there's also a small menagerie—the second-oldest in the world—at the **Jardin des Plantes,** There are no large animals here, but kids can encounter red pandas, flamingos, and more. The Jardin des Plantes is also home to the **Galerie de Paléontologie,** a hit with dinosaur fans.

THE CATACOMBS

Mature kids might enjoy the thrill of Paris's Catacombs. Dug as mines for sourcing the limestone used to build Paris's most emblematic buildings, the Catacombs were filled with the remains of 6 million Parisians beginning in the 18th century. Today, 1 mile of the underground tunnels are open to exploration, featuring skeletons arranged into strange, macabre designs.

MUSEUM SCAVENGER HUNTS

Visiting a major museum like the **Louvre** or **Musée d'Orsay** with little ones might seem like an exercise in futility, but thanks to a number of tour companies, it's possible to find tours that cater to children. Many of these tours, like those from **That Muse,** offer scavenger hunts to make exploring an interactive experience. *See Tours Worth Taking for more info.*

MADE IN PARIS

Paris's fashion has deviated from its haute couture past to welcome small makers and creators. Here's a short list of local makers to look for when you're browsing.

···

CLOTHING AND ACCESSORIES

Shoppers used to stick to the Champs-Élysées and the Boulevard St-Germain, but local fashion boutiques have popped up all over the city. Check out **Rue Oberkampf, Rue Keller,** and **Rue Charonne** in the 11e arrondissement and **Rue Beaurepaire, Rue Bichat,** and **Quai Valmy** in the 10e for some of the newest and trendiest, including concept stores like **Centre Commercial.** Wander around near **Rue Ste-Croix de la Bretonnerie** in the Marais for some of the best vintage shops, and don't forget about the Grands Magasins, the big department stores in central Paris. Items there might be a bit less unique, but it's an experience just to explore these gorgeous buildings—take the escalator to the top of the **Galeries Lafayette** for a beautiful view over the city.

BEAUTY PRODUCTS

Pharmaciennes have begun to grow accustomed to American women entering with a shopping list a mile long: French beauty products are some of the best, and you can get them much more inexpensively at local Parisian pharmacies. Try Caudalie's resveratrol creams or anything from La Roche Posay.

HOME DECOR

Concept shops like **Merci** will lead you toward some of the funkiest decor and home goods in Paris, but you'll also have quite a bit of luck at *brocantes*. These markets, a bit more elegant than your run-of-the-mill flea markets, are the best places for seeking out antique Limoges porcelain, enamelware, or even small furniture. The famous flea market, **Marché aux Puces de St-Ouen,** is also worth a dive.

EDIBLES

Bringing home an edible treat from Paris will make you a friend for life. Seek out MOF producers for the very best: chocolates and candies travel quite well. You could also opt for jarred treats like mustard (try **Le Jeune Homme**) or regional French honey from specialty store **Les Abeilles,** in Butte-aux-Cailles. While you can't bring cured meats across the border, most cheeses are allowed—just ask your cheesemonger to vacuum seal them (*sous vide,* in French) so they don't stink up your flight.

FOOD AND DRINK IN PARIS

Paris's culinary scene has become a bit divided of late. On one hand, there are classic bistros steeped in tradition; on the other, there are exciting neo-bistros that revisit the authentic dishes of yore with an innovative spin.

TRADITIONAL BISTROS

While many old-school bistros are catering mainly to tourists these days, there are a few fantastic options that continue to live up to the hype. Be sure to sample *steak-frites* with creamy pepper sauce or a perfectly crisp roast chicken. More adventurous diners may prefer garlicky escargots or the offal meats the French so love: veal sweetbreads, tripe sausage, and blood pudding are all local favorites.

NEO-BISTROS

At Paris's contemporary neo-bistros, you'll encounter *bistronomie*. First coined in the 1990s, the term refers to a movement that revisits the old-fashioned bistro staple with smaller portions, fresher flavors, and more innovative plating style. Many of our favorite restaurants in Paris play into this trend, from those looking merely to update the bistro and those who want to turn it on its head.

COFFEE

The café is an integral part of Paris culture—in fact, it's a way of life. Despite its ubiquity, the actual coffee served at many of these classic spots has long been underwhelming at best. But a new wave of coffee shops, often with American or Australian co-owners, has brought the flat white and the cold brew to Paris. Just don't expect to take your coffee to go—Parisians prefer to linger.

BRUNCH

Traditionally, a croissant and a coffee would do for French *petit déjeuner* (breakfast)–but oh, how times have changed. Parisians line up on weekends for the American-style pancakes at Holybelly, treat themselves to American Southern recipes and boozy teatime at Treize au Jardin, and tuck into some seriously photogenic avocado toast at Café Oberkampf.

HEALTHY OPTIONS

Yes, the Paris of the past seems to have been built solely on butter and carbs. But these days the capital city is taking a cue from the kitchens of California, offering more gluten-free, vegetarian, and vegan options than ever before. Start your day with a fresh juice at Bob's Juice Bar, dig into an açai bowl from Echo Deli, or grab a late-night "burger" at Super Vegan.

INTERNATIONAL CUISINE

Paris is a truly multicultural city, and both Asian and Italian cuisines are well represented. A host of Japanese restaurants can be found in the heart of Paris near Les Halles and Palais-Royal, as well as authentic Chinese in the 13e arrondissement near Butte-aux-Cailles, with more choices in Belleville. Italian spots are also trending in part thanks to the Big Mamma Group, who have opened a host of hip trattorias and bars around the city.

MODERN CRÊPERIES

You can't leave the city without trying this delectable specialty. Although the treat has made its way around the world (let's face it, you're probably no stranger to these thin pancakes, often stuffed with melty Nutella and bananas or savory meat and cheese) there's something to be said about trying one in its home country. Spots like Breizh Café and Brutus are sure-fire bets for a modern take.

SWEETS AND BAKED TREATS

In the 19th century, Parisians were eating about a pound of bread per person per day, and while the average today is quite a bit less, the bakery remains an integral part of the Parisian landscape. That said, not all bakeries are created equal: estimates point to about half of croissants sold in Parisian boulangeries being frozen. To find a great bakery, keep an eye out for decals showing the bakery has won the *Meilleur Baguette de Paris* (best baguette in Paris) or *Meilleur Croissant en Île de France* (best croissant in Île de France) contests. You'll also find delicious sweets at any bakery, pâtisserie, chocolatier, or candy shop that displays the blue, white, and red *Meilleur Ouvrier de France* (MOF) label. Top choices include macarons, *choux à la crème* (cream puffs), and the stacked, cream-filled *Paris-Brest*.

NATURAL WINE BARS

Things are changing for Paris's traditional drink of choice, as well. A new trend toward organic, bio-dynamic, and natural, sulfite-free wines is sprouting up across the city. The *cave à vin* wine bar has also truly come into its own, with many of these cozy establishments offering small plates that rival dishes at the city's top restaurants.

BEER AND COCKTAILS

Wine has long been the pride of France, but Paris has joined the beer and cocktail scene, too. Locally brewed beers can be found around town, especially in Les Batignolles and around the student-heavy area of the Latin Quarter. Tons of exciting cocktail choices abound in the ritzy hotel bars and speakeasies near the Champs Élysées and in the artsier neighborhoods of Montmartre and Pigalle.

WHAT TO WATCH AND READ

To learn more about Paris, before or after you visit, consider these movies, TV shows, books, blogs, and podcasts.

MOVIES

As the birthplace of cinema, it's no surprise that Paris as a city stars in more than its fair share of films. Catch a glimpse of Paris's past from director François Truffaut via his Antoine Doinel arc, beginning with the internationally acclaimed coming-of-age story *The 400 Blows* (1959). The lesser-known *Stolen Kisses* (1968) follows the same character upon his release from the army, as he works as a private detective in Paris. Truffaut's desire to film on-location, a staple technique of New Wave film, allows him to offer a true glimpse of Parisian life through both films. *Breathless* (1960) is yet another New Wave staple, this time from Jean-Luc Godard. The fast pace of the film as the characters whirl through Paris offers a different glimpse of the city as a place to flee from, rather than to.

At the opposite end of the spectrum, *Amélie* (2001) portrays a whirlwind romance with Paris, Montmartre specifically. The film, tinged with fantasy, is a wonderful romp through the 18e arrondissement, with more than a handful of nods at its red light district past. Paris is no stranger to having its neighborhoods appear as characters in films. In fact, that's the whole concept behind *Paris Je T'Aime* (2006), which features 18 vignettes, each from a different director, representing 18 of the 20 arrondissements of Paris. Directors Joel and Ethan Coen, Gus Van Sant, Alfonso Cuarón, and Wes Craven all lent their talents to the ensemble. Also based in Paris, *Les Intouchables* (2011) tells the story of an unlikely friendship that forms between a quadriplegic man and his live-in caretaker. American filmmakers show Paris through their own lens. For instance, Woody Allen's *Midnight in Paris* (2011) evokes a longing and nostalgia for a bygone era of the city. Film can be a great way to introduce children to Paris as well: try the *Madeline* series or *Linnea in Monet's Garden* (1992).

TV SHOWS

There aren't many English TV shows that take place entirely in Paris, but there are more than a few very special episodes that sent our favorite characters here. Eternal New Yorker Carrie Bradshaw left her city behind for Paris in the final two episodes of *Sex and the City*, and season four of *Gossip Girl* also saw New Yorkers trade

Manhattan for Paris. Both shows depicted a slightly romanticized version of Paris, nevertheless incorporating the city as a proper character in the show, as is only apt for series so focused on setting. One French television show, aptly named *Paris,* shows the lives of several strangers in the city over 24 hours, exploring how their lives will cross paths with Paris as a looming backdrop. Netflix is also a good source for modern-day French language shows: the french drama series *Call My Agent!* (*Dix Pour Cent* in French) follows a group of movie-star agents based in Paris; *The Returned* (*Les Revenants* in French) is about locals from a small mountain town who come back from the dead.

BOOKS

The 19th century was the prime period for French writers to pen novels about Paris, with authors such as Victor Hugo and Emile Zola setting some of their most famous works in the city. Try Hugo's *The Hunchback of Notre-Dame,* set at the famous cathedral during the Middle Ages; *Les Misérables,* which charts the years leading up to the 1830 Revolution; or Zola's *The Belly of Paris,* which revolves around the Les Halles market.

Ernest Hemingway explored his own experience in Paris in the 1920s in his memoir *A Moveable Feast.* The same period is illustrated quite deftly in *Sylvia Beach and the Lost Generation* (and wonderfully fictionalized from Hemingway's

wife's point of view in *The Paris Wife*). More recently, former *New Yorker* writer Adam Gopnik penned his experiences as an American in the City of Light in *Paris to the Moon.* Another American writer and humorist, David Sedaris, recounts his experiences trying to learn French in Paris in *Me Talk Pretty One Day.* Fiction writers also spend quite a bit of time capturing Paris. *The Elegance of the Hedgehog* follows the life events of a concierge in Paris, offering a glimpse into modern daily life in the city, while *Anna and the French Kiss* offers a wonderful romantic romp through the capital.

BLOGS AND PODCASTS

Quite a few American bloggers living in Paris offer a peek into Parisian life that can be helpful before your arrival. Lindsey Tramuta's *Lost in Cheeseland* is a fan favorite, as is David Lebovitz's self-titled food blog (he also wrote *The Sweet Life in Paris* about his experience moving to Paris). Meg Zimbeck's *Paris by Mouth* offers some of the top English-language restaurant reviews anywhere around. The *HiP Paris* blog, written in English, is a good one to follow to keep up with the coolest restaurants, bars, and shopping. For news in Paris, France, and around the globe, France24 has an English version of its French news site ⊕ *www.france24.com/fr/en.* The *Earful Tower* podcast and the YouTube series *What the F**k France?!* both offer deft social commentary on life and culture in the city.

PARIS TIMELINE

So much has happened on this plot of land that is today called Paris. These are just some of the game-changing events that have made the city what it is today.

250–52 BC: Settlement of the Parisii Celts on Île de la Cité and the banks of the Seine.

52 BC: Parisii settlement is invaded by Julius Caesar and redubbed Lutetia (Lutèce in French).

481: Following the fall of the Roman Empire, Clovis becomes King of the Franks and makes Paris his capital.

481–639: Paris is ruled by the Merovingian kings, who settle in the Latin Quarter; none of their city remains today.

1163: Ground is broken on the construction of Notre-Dame Cathedral, an imposing Gothic structure championed by Bishop Maurice de Sully. The Cathedral will not be finished until 1260.

1190: King Philippe-Auguste builds a wall around the city of Paris to protect it from foreign invaders while he is on Crusade. He also builds the original Louvre fortress, the remains of which can still be seen in the basement of the modern museum.

1257: The Sorbonne University building is erected in the Latin Quarter, though the university has been recognized officially since 1200 and existed unofficially since the mid-12th century. It is considered the second-oldest university in Europe.

1337–1453: A dispute between the House of Plantagenet and the House of Valois over who can rightfully rule over France results in the Hundred Years' War. Five generations of kings fight over the throne.

1356: Charles V replaces one of Philippe-Auguste's fortifications with his own and transforms the Louvre into a royal residence for the first time.

1418: The future King Charles VII, then Dauphin, is forced to flee Paris, which is taken by John the Fearless, Duke of Burgundy.

1429: Charles VII, with help from Joan of Arc, sieges and attempts to reclaim Paris from the English. He will not succeed until the 1430s.

1528: King Francis I orders the demolition of the former Louvre Palace and begins the construction of a Renaissance palace that will house the ever-growing royal art collection.

1562–98: The Wars of Religion take place, with an estimated 3 million casualties, including 3,000 in Paris alone during the Saint Bartholomew's Day massacre, which occurs several days after Henri III of Navarre (the future Henri IV of France) is married to Henri II's daughter Margaret.

1589: Henri IV becomes King of France. He begins work to remove the remnants of the medieval fortress and link the Tuileries Palace to the Louvre. He also builds what is now Paris's oldest bridge, Pont Neuf.

1609: King Louis XIII creates the Louvre Galerie, which hosts painters and sculptors in workshops.

1643: Louis XIII dies, leaving five-year-old Louis XIV to become king. He is kept safe at the Palais-Royal, but he grows up with a strong dislike of Paris.

1671: Louis XIV moves the royal residence to Versailles and begins renovating the palace. His royal gardener, André Le Nôtre, designs these gardens as well as those at the Tuileries Palace and creates the Champs-Élysées.

1755–63: The Seven Years' War, which breaks out over colonial disputes between France and England, drains most of the royal treasury.

1789: Due in part to growing discontent with high taxes and in part to a wave of Enlightenment writers promoting free thought, the French Revolution begins. The French citizens storm the Bastille, publish the *Declaration of the Rights of Man and of the Citizen* and the first Constitu-

tion, and assassinate King Louis XVI and Queen Marie-Antoinette.

1793: The Louvre opens to the public, making it the first public art museum in the world.

1804–15: Napoléon Bonaparte is Emperor of France. He builds four major cemeteries, including Père Lachaise.

1815–30: Monarchy is restored.

1830: The second French Revolution is fought, and a new king—no longer King of France but King of the French—is placed on the throne: Louis-Philippe I.

1848: The third French Revolution is fought, and the Second French Republic is founded.

1852: Louis-Napoléon Bonaparte, nephew of Napoléon I and president of the French Republic, founds the Second French Empire. Working with Prefect of Paris Georges Eugène Haussmann, he completely revitalizes Paris, widening its streets, adding green spaces, installing a sewer system, and building monuments including the Opéra building.

1870: The Franco-Prussian War results in the siege of Paris. The Commune of Paris rises up against the (mostly monarchist) government, eventually resulting in the Bloody Week, when the Commune is quashed and its members are killed or deported. The Third French Republic is now in power.

1914–18: World War I claims the lives of about 1.7 million French people.

1921: Ernest Hemingway moves to Paris, where he will be part of a thriving community of Lost Generation writers and jazz musicians from the United States, France, and the British Isles.

1939–45: World War II breaks out. Paris is occupied from 1940 until 1944. During the Occupation, strict rations are imposed and Jewish residents are targeted. On the night of July 16, 1942, 13,152 Jews are rounded up by the French police on orders of the Germans and sent to Auschwitz.

1954–62: The Algerian National Liberation Front rises up against France for the decolonization of Algeria. In 1961, the French National Police attack a demonstration of 30,000 Algerians, killing an estimated 100–300 people, many by drowning in the Seine.

1968: Student occupations and generalized strikes paralyze the city for the month of May. Many participants in this social revolution remain defined by it to this day.

1993: President François Mitterand's Grand Louvre project is completed. The project not only saw the famous glass pyramid installed in the Louvre's courtyard but also revealed portions of the medieval Louvre to the public.

2001: The first annual Nuit Blanche takes place, opening museums and galleries to the public during a free all-night festival.

2002: The first euro coins and bills are used in France, replacing the franc as currency. The same year, temporary beaches called Paris Plages are installed along the Seine; they return every summer.

2007: Paris Mayor Bertrand Delanoë introduces Vélib' bike-sharing to reduce traffic within the city limits.

2015: A new symphony hall with avant-garde architecture, the Philharmonie de Paris, opens in Parc de la Villette.

2017: Emmanuel Macron starts his term as president of France. Paris wins a bid to host the summer Olympic Games in 2024.

2018: France wins the FIFA World Cup for the first time since 1998 and celebrates with a victory parade down the Champs-Élysées.

TOURS
WORTH TAKING

Whether you want to skip the line at a major monument or learn a bit more about a particularly intriguing neighborhood, enlisting the help of a local professional is often a good idea. A well-trained tour guide will help you get to know the true history and culture of Paris.

Localers

As its name suggests, this tour company focuses on opening up local experiences to visitors. With tours focusing on essential or eccentric elements of Parisian history like the Revolution, the Occupation, or royal scandals, as well as unique Parisian experiences like playing *pétanque* (lawn bowling) or making pastries with locals, this is one of the best ways to get a firmer grasp on local culture. ⊠ *Paris* ☎ *01-83-64-92-01.*

Paris by Mouth

This tour company started as an Anglophone restaurant review site. Today, they offer small-group tasting tours of a variety of Paris neighborhoods, complete with wine, cheese, and charcuterie pairings. They also offer more intensive wine- and cheese-tasting courses, for the true oenophile or turophile. The English tours last three hours and start at €110. ⊠ *Paris* ⊕ *parisbymouth.com.*

Paris Muse

Paris is home to dozens of museums, including some must-sees like the Louvre. But with more than 30,000 works of art (and lines out the door), visiting these major museums can seem overwhelming. With a professional guide from Paris Muse, museum visits are a breeze: expert guides get you in to see the essentials while also ensuring that you don't stay trapped in the museum longer than needed. Prices for the Louvre are €115 per person. ⊠ *Paris* ☎ *06-73-77-33-52* ⊕ *parismuse.com.*

Street Art Tours Paris

Explore the towering murals of the 13e arrondissement and Butte-aux-Cailles or the colorful, hip streets of Belleville with this tour company, founded by a local artist. Tours start at €22 per person for two hours and are a great introduction to the city's coolest neighborhoods of the moment. ⊠ *Paris* ☎ *06-52-63-97-59* ⊕ *streetarttourparis.com.*

That Muse

Turning museum visits into a treasure hunt is one of the best ways to add a touch of excitement to your experience. The team at That Muse seeks to make your Louvre or d'Orsay visit memorable *and*educational, with scavenger hunts starting at €25 that encourage you to see what lies beyond the typical tourist path. ⊠ *Paris* ☎ *06-86-13-32-12* ⊕ *thatmuse.com.*

BEST PARIS EVENTS

You can always find something special to do in Paris, but these are the standouts that locals plan their calendars around.

JANUARY AND FEBRUARY

Paris Fashion Week

Fashion Week (also in September) brings big crowds to Paris, not just in hopes of attending some of the top shows, but also to take in the street style (and hopefully get invited to one of the major parties). Hang out near the Louvre, the Grand Palais, or the Marais for a chance to glimpse top models. ⊠ *Paris* ⊕ *fashionweekonline.com/fashion-week-dates.*

Les Soldes

Huge retail sales called "soldes" take place after the holidays through February. You can find discounts at the Grand Magasins, the famous department stores in the city center, including Galeries Lafayette and Au Printemps ⊠ *Paris.*

MAY

Belleville Open Studios

Artists first began gravitating toward Belleville in the 1980s, and today, the neighborhood has become a vibrant, exciting artists' haven. Every year in May, more than 200 of these artists open their studios to the public, free of charge, over a period of several days. ⊠ *Belleville* ☎ *01–73–74–27–67* ⊕ *ateliers-artistes-belleville.fr.*

JUNE

Fête de la Musique

Every June 21, the streets of Paris come alive with music. During this festival every street corner, bar, and restaurant welcomes a different musician or band. Wandering the streets, you'll encounter all different genres; try the Irish Cultural Center for the excellent ambience complete with a pop-up craft beer bar. ⊠ *Paris* ⊕ *fetedelamusique.culture.gouv.fr.*

JULY

Bastille Day

French people don't actually call July 14 Bastille Day, but they do celebrate it. In honor of *Le Quatorze*, also known as *Fête de la Fédération* (Federation Day), the French celebrate liberty and equality. It's the French equivalent of July 4, with a magnificent fireworks display at the Eiffel Tower with musical accompaniment and a parade down the Champs-Élysées. Firehouses all over the city open their doors for festive firemen's balls. (Search for *bal des pompiers* a few weeks in advance for the full list of participating firehouses.) ⊠ *Paris.*

Paris Plages

In July, the rivers and canals become beaches with the arrival of Paris Plages. Chaise longues, water misters, and games are set up at the Quais de Seine, while a free outdoor pool and paddle boats are installed at the Canal de l'Ourcq. ⊠ *Paris*.

Tour de France

The Tour de France bike race takes all of France by storm every year, but the finish on the Champs-Élysées is uniquely Parisian. People line up along the famous avenue early in the day to get the chance to see the cyclists arrive after three weeks of cycling across France. ⊠ *Champs-Élysées, Champs-Élysées* ⊕ *www.letour.fr/en*.

Fermeture Exceptionnelle

August is defined not by its events, but rather by the absence of them: almost all locals flee Paris in August thanks to French policies granting workers five weeks of paid vacation, so many top restaurants and shops shutter for the whole month. Be sure to check in advance and make sure the spots you want to visit will remain open. ⊠ *Paris*.

Rock-en-Seine

This massive rock festival draws big crowds to the outskirts of the city for three days of music every year. Past headliners have included the Arctic Monkeys, the Foo Fighters, and Lana Del Rey. A three-day pass is €159. ⊠ *Domaine National de St-Cloud, Parc de St-Cloud, Paris* ⊕ *www.rockenseine. com* Ⓜ *Boulogne-Pont de Saint-Cloud*.

European Heritage Days

Every year, the French Minister of Culture organizes special events for European Heritage Days. These may include opening to the public monuments that one usually can't visit, like the École Militaire, or waiving entrance fees for museums. Lines can get long, but often, accessing unique spots is worth the wait. ⊠ *Paris*.

Nuit Blanche

Literally "white night," Nuit Blanche is an annual all-night festival in early October. Museums open their doors to nighttime visitors, and special concerts take place throughout Paris. Notably, the line 14 métro runs all night long to cater to revelers. ⊠ *Paris* ⊕ *www.paris.fr/nuitblanche*.

Beaujolais Nouveau

Every third Thursday of November, the *primeurs* of the Beaujolais region, the very first young wines of the year that are ready to be drunk, are released. While opinions on the quality of Beaujolais Nouveau are mixed (and are, in all honesty, mostly negative), it's still a fun evening to spend at your favorite wine bar—even if you're not drinking Beaujolais at all. ⊠ *Paris*.

Christmas Markets

Drink some *vin chaud* (mulled wine) and shop for gifts at the local markets that pop up around the holidays at Champs-Élysées, Place St-Sulpice, and Trocadéro, which also has an ice-skating rink.

BEST BETS

With so many places to go and things to do in Paris, how will you decide? Fodor's writers and editors have chosen our favorites to help you plan. Search the neighborhood chapters for more recommendations.

ACTIVITIES AND SIGHTS

ARCHITECTURE

Arènes de Lutèce, Quartier Latin

Cité de la Mode et du Design, Bercy

The Hoxton Paris, Sentier

La Grande Mosquée de Paris, Quartier Latin

Palais-Royal, Les Halles and Palais-Royal

Panthéon, Quartier Latin

Place des Vosges, Le Marais

MUSEUMS AND GALLERIES

Atelier des Lumières, Oberkampf

Galerie Véro-Dodat, Les Halles and Palais-Royal

Ground Effect, Les Grands Boulevards

Les Frigos, Bercy

Maison Européenne de la Photographie, Le Marais

Musée d'Orsay, Les Invalides

Musée Jacquemart-André, Les Grands Boulevards

Musée Marmottan Monet, Trocadéro and Champs-Élysées

Musée Rodin, Les Invalides

Musée Yves Saint Laurent Paris, Trocadéro and Champs-Élysées

Street Art 13, Bercy

PARKS AND GREEN SPACES

Canal St-Martin, Canal St-Martin

Coulée Verte René Dumont, Bastille

Jardin des Plantes, Quartier Latin

Parc Clichy-Batignolles–Martin-Luther-King, Les Batignolles

Parc de la Villette, Belleville

Promenade des Berges de la Seine, Les Invalides

VIEWS

Arc de Triomphe, Trocadéro and Champs-Élysées

Basilique du Sacré-Coeur, Montmartre

Eiffel Tower, Les Invalides

Notre-Dame Cathedral, Quartier Latin

Parc de Belleville, Belleville

SHOPPING

PARIS-MADE

Empreintes, Le Marais

French Touche, Les Batignolles

Fromagerie Laurent Dubois, Quartier Latin

Gab & Jo, St-Germain-des-Prés

Les Abeilles, Butte-aux-Cailles

Merci, Le Marais

Artazart, Canal St-Martin

Shakespeare and Company, Quartier Latin

Amélie Pichard, Bastille

The Broken Arm, Le Marais

Centre Commercial, Canal St-Martin

L'Appartement Sézane, Les Grands Boulevards

L'Exception, Les Halles and Palais-Royal

Marché aux Puces de St-Ouen, Les Puces

Marché Biologique Batignolles, Les Batignolles

Marché d'Aligre, Bastille

Marché des Enfants Rouges, Le Marais

Rue Mouffetard, Quartier Latin

Free 'P' Star, Le Marais

Kilo Shop, Le Marais

La Boutique Sans Argent, Bercy

FOOD

Boulangerie l'Essentiel, Butte-aux-Cailles

Carl Marletti, Quartier Latin

Du Pain et Des Idées, Canal St-Martin

Pain Pain, Montmartre

Stoney Clove Bakery, Sentier

Vandermeersch, Bercy

Le Baratin, Belleville

La Bourse et la Vie, Les Grands Boulevards

Le Buisson Ardent, Quartier Latin

Les Papilles, Quartier Latin

Juvéniles, Les Halles and Palais-Royal

Clamato, Bastille

Comme Chez Maman, Les Batignolles

Coretta, Les Batignolles

Ellsworth, Les Halles and Palais-Royal

Gare au Gorille, Les Batignolles

Hugo & Co, Quartier Latin

Le Comptoir, Belleville

Le Coq Rico, Montmartre

Le Galopin, Canal St-Martin

Mensae, Belleville

Pirouette, Les Halles and Palais-Royal

Quinsou, St-Germain-des-Prés

Tomy & Co, Les Invalides

Sellae, Bercy

Semilla, St-Germain-des-Prés

Café Oberkampf, Oberkampf

Hardware Société, Montmartre

Holybelly, Canal St-Martin

Treize au Jardin, St-Germain-des-Prés

Daroco, Sentier

Mio Posto, Bastille

Ober Mamma, Oberkampf

Passerini, Bastille

Pizza Rossi, Sentier

ASIAN

Cô My Cantine, Ménilmontant

Dersou, Bastille

Dong Huong, Belleville

Hiramatsu, Trocadéro and Champs-Élysées

Le Rigmarole, Oberkampf

Matsuhisa, Trocadéro and Champs-Élysées

Miss Kô, Banks of the Seine

Pierre Sang Signature, Oberkampf

WenZhou, Belleville

MICHELIN-STAR DINING

Frenchie, Les Grands Boulevards

Il Carpaccio, Trocadéro and Champs-Élysées

L'Arcane, Montmartre

La Tour d'Argent, Quartier Latin

Saturne, Sentier

Septime, Bastille

Sola, Quartier Latin

CRÊPES

Breizh Café, St-Germain-des-Prés

Brutus, Les Batignolles

HEALTHY AND GLUTEN-FREE

Clover Green, St-Germain-des-Prés

Echo Deli, Sentier

Interfabric, Les Batignolles

Kitchen, Le Marais

NoGlu, St-Germain-des-Prés

Wild & The Moon, Oberkampf

QUICK BITES

L'As du Fallafel, Le Marais

Mokonuts, Bastille

Mr.T, Le Marais

DRINK

COFFEE

The Beans on Fire, Oberkampf

Belleville Brûlerie, Belleville

Café Coutume, St-Germain-des-Prés

Café Kitsuné, Les Halles and Palais-Royal

Café Lai'Tcha, Les Halles and Palais-Royal

Café Lomi, Montmartre

Honor, Banks of the Seine

La Caféothèque, Le Marais

Loustic, Le Marais

Peonies, Canal St-Martin

Ten Belles, Canal St-Martin

COCKTAILS

Comptoir Général, Canal St-Martin

Dirty Dick, Pigalle

Glass, Montmartre

Harry's New York Bar, Les Grands Boulevards

Le Bar Botaniste, Trocadéro and Champs-Élysées

Le Bar at Hotel George V, Trocadéro and Champs-Élysées

Sherry Butt, Le Marais

Tiger, St-Germain-des-Prés

CRAFT BEER

Académie de la Bière, Quartier Latin

Brewberry, Quartier Latin

La Robe et La Mousse, St-Germain-des-Prés

Paname Brewery Company, Belleville

Société Parisienne de Bière, Les Batignolles

ROOFTOP BARS

Khayma Rooftop Generator Paris, Canal St-Martin

Le Perchoir, Ménilmontant

Le Petit Bain, Bercy

WINE

Au Passage, Oberkampf

Compagnie de Vins Surnaturels, St-Germain-des-Prés

La Buvette, Oberkampf

La Cave de Belleville, Belleville

Le Barav, Le Marais

Les Caves Populaires, Les Batignolles

Septime la Cave, Bastille

Verjus Wine Bar, Les Halles and Palais-Royal

NIGHTLIFE AND PERFORMING ARTS

CABARET

Au Lapin Agile, Montmartre

Crazy Horse, Trocadéro and Champs-Élysées

Lido, Trocadéro and Champs-Élysées

CINEMA

Cinémathèque Française, Bercy

Le Champo, Quartier Latin

Le Grand Rex, Les Grands Boulevards

Le Louxor, Montmartre

DANCING

Badaboum, Bastille

Ground Control, Bercy

Wanderlust, Bercy

LIVE MUSIC

Bataclan, Oberkampf

Caveau de la Huchette, Quartier Latin

Fréquence, Bastille

La Maroquinerie, Ménilmontant

PEOPLE WATCHING

Aux Folies, Bellveille

La Perle, Le Marais

Le Nemours, Les Halles and Palais-Royal

Les Ambassadeurs, Trocadéro and Champs-Élysées

Les Bains, Le Marais

SPEAKEASIES AND HIDDEN BARS

Ballroom du Beef Club, Les Halles and Palais-Royal

Candelaria, Le Marais

Castor Club, St-Germain-des-Prés

Prescription Cocktail Club, St-Germain-des-Prés

THEATER AND PERFORMANCE

Comédie Française, Les Halles and Palais-Royal

La Cigale, Pigalle

Opéra Bastille, Bastille

Théâtre de Ménilmontant, Ménilmontant

CAN'T-MISS TOURIST SPOTS

Paris welcomes tens of millions of tourists every year, many of them toting the same list of must-see spots to visit. This means that some travelers, hoping to avoid the crowds, will occasionally blacklist these locales entirely—and that's a shame. Even if you want to skip waiting in long lines, there are a few can't-miss experiences that should be part of everyone's Paris trip. Here's our short list, along with a few ways to make their popularity a touch more tolerable.

EIFFEL TOWER

Built in 1889 for the World's Fair, the Eiffel Tower is a feat of modern engineering that's well worth a visit. There are three different observation decks to explore, not to mention Gustave Eiffel's top-floor apartment, complete with mannequins representing the engineer entertaining Thomas Edison at his exclusive address.

In recent years, however, increased security measures have meant that accessing the world-famous tower can be a painful experience, so be sure to plan ahead. Booking tickets online or through a tour operator grants you a guaranteed entry time, skipping to the front of the longest portion of the line. And if any waiting at all sounds like a less-than-ideal way to spend your time in Paris, you may wish to forego climbing entirely, opting instead to photograph the tower from the Trocadéro palace across the river to the north or from the end of the Champ de Mars park to the south. (St-Germain-des-Prés and Les Invalides)

ARC DE TRIOMPHE AND CHAMPS-ÉLYSÉES

"The World's Most Famous Avenue" runs for more than a mile through the 8e arrondissement, linking the Place de la Concorde, at the end of the Louvre's Tuileries Gardens, with Napoléon I's triumphal archway at Place Charles de Gaulle. Known mainly for luxury shopping, the avenue nevertheless draws even those not looking for designer boutiques: the Tour de France, Bastille Day parade, and yearly Christmas market make this a popular locale, as does the Arc itself.

While Napoléon conceived of and commissioned the Arc, he never got the chance to see it: he was exiled from France in 1814, and the structure wasn't completed until 1836. Today, visitors to Paris are drawn to it both for the eternal flame flickering beneath it and for the birds-eye views of the Étoile—or star—of avenues branching out from it, including the Champs-Élysées. *(The Banks of the Seine)*

BASILIQUE DU SACRÉ-CŒUR

At the top of Paris's tallest hill, Montmartre, sits a stark white basilica. The church, named Sacré-Coeur, was built in the late 19th century and is the centerpiece of the most touristic part of the former village. Climb to the top of the steps in front of Sacré-Coeur for some of the most beautiful views of the city below before visiting the church itself, including its dome, which affords more spectacular views. Then, with your back to the basilica, follow the path to the right, passing by one of the best views of the Eiffel Tower, toward Place du Tertre. This square is known for welcoming a variety of artists and caricaturists in spring and summer months. *(Montmartre and Pigalle)*

MUSÉE DU LOUVRE

The world's largest and most-visited art museum, the Louvre is an essential stop on any Parisian tour. Rather than letting yourself get overwhelmed by the 38,000 items on display, however, make a plan in advance and stick to it: maps of the various rooms and exhibits are available online, so you can chart out a path to take you past the works you most want to see. The top hit list for most visitors usually includes the *Mona Lisa, Winged Victory of Samothrace, Venus de Milo,* and Delacroix's *Liberty Leading the People.* Other sites not to miss include Louis IV's gilded Apollo Gallery as well as the underground traces of the medieval fortress that once stood at the site of the Renaissance palace-turned-museum. *(Les Halles and Palais-Royal)*

NOTRE-DAME

Notre-Dame was once Paris's tallest building, and while it has since lost that honor, it's still one of the city's most impressive. Built in 1163, the famous home of (fictional) hunchback Quasimodo boasts three 12th-century rose windows and several important Catholic relics, including the Crown of Thorns. The view from the top is incredible, but there's usually a bit of a wait, so buy a ticket from the machines just outside the north wall of the cathedral before visiting the breathtaking ground floor to "kill time" before your climb. *(Quartier Latin)*

JARDIN DU LUXEMBOURG

This beautiful garden behind the 17th-century Luxembourg Palace is known for its beautiful flowerbeds and picturesque fountains. Chairs placed throughout the park make this a fantastic place to enjoy the sunshine in warmer months. Of note is the large pond in the center where toy sailboats can be rented—a particularly big hit with kids. Don't miss the monumental Medici fountain and its Italian Renaissance–inspired details. *(St-Germain-des-Prés and Les Invalides)*

JARDIN DES TUILERIES

These manicured gardens were once attached to a magnificent palace of the same name, built under the orders of Queen Catherine de Medici. While the palace was destroyed by the Paris Commune in 1870, the gardens remain a testament to the symmetry and order so prized in the French aesthetic. Of special note is the Orangerie, previously a shelter for orange trees and now home to a large Impressionist collection, including eight large-format water lily paintings by master Claude Monet. *(Les Halles and Palais-Royal)*

MUSÉE D'ORSAY

Just across the river from the Louvre sits the Musée d'Orsay, a former Beaux Arts railway station that now houses the largest Impressionist and Postimpressionist collection in the world. Start your visit on the top level, where you'll find most of these famed works, and be sure to walk behind the enormous clock face that stands out as an emblem of the museum. The ground floor is notably home to a scale model of the Garnier Opera House, including the underground lake of Phantom of the Opera fame. *(St-Germain-des-Prés and Les Invalides)*

OPÉRA GARNIER

This 19th-century opera building is more often home to ballet performances than operas these days, but even if you're not seeing a show of any kind, the monument is worth a visit. Built in the late 19th century in the eclectic Napoléon III style, the opera house effortlessly blends a variety of building materials and styles to make up a thoroughly impressive whole. While no Phantom lives inside (we think!) there is an underground lake where the Parisian fire department trains for water rescues. *(Sentier and Les Grands Boulevards)*

CENTRE POMPIDOU

The Pompidou Center is a multifaceted structure housing a public library, music research center, and the largest modern art museum in Europe. Known for its high-tech design, the Pompidou Center boasts visible piping as part of its exterior: green pipes are for plumbing, blue for climate control, yellow for electric, and red for safety elements. The escalators taking you to the top afford stunning views of the city below. Don't miss the nearby Stravinsky fountain, featuring 16 moving aquatic sculptures. *(Le Marais)*

MUSÉE NATIONAL PICASSO-PARIS

After reopening in 2014 after a five-year renovation, this popular museum, home to the largest public collection of works from Pablo Picasso, is going strong. Even though it packs more than its fair share of tourists, the museum's collection of the Spanish artist's paintings, sculptures, and prints (there are more than 200,000 works on display!) is unrivaled. Beat the crowds by planning your visit on a weekday; crowds are thickest on weekends. *(Le Marais)*

COOL PLACES TO STAY

Paris is a city defined by its neighborhoods; when choosing a place to stay, bear in mind where you'd like to spend most of your time. While fantastic hotels can be found in the historic center, you may lose out on experiencing Paris like a local. These hotels each offer a great neighborhood locale and a little something extra to make them stand out from the crowd.

BELLEVILLE AND MÉNILMONTANT

Hôtel Mama Shelter

$$ | Hotel. Located in the up-and-coming 20e arrondissement, just steps from Père-Lachaise Cemetery, this hotel is known for its modern, hipster vibe. **Pros:** rooftop bar; in-house DJ; great restaurant with a menu from Michelin-starred Guy Savoy. **Cons:** frequently overbooked; can be noisy; restaurant service occasionally slow. *Rooms from: €159 ⊠ 109 rue de Bagnolet Belleville ☎ 08–25–00–62–62 ⊕ mamashelter. com ⇗ 170 rooms ⊚ breakfast, lunch, and dinner available ⓜ Gambetta, Porte de Bagnolet.*

OBERKAMPF AND BASTILLE

Eden Lodge

$$$ | Hotel. Set back in a hidden tree-shaded courtyard off an uninspiring street minutes from Père Lachaise cemetery, no lodging in the capital is quite as unobtrusively fabulous as this trailblazing, 100% sustainable, five-room eco-lodge. **Pros:** 100% sustainable; tons of great restaurants in the neighborhood; lovely terraces in all rooms.

Cons: low-key neighborhood; no in-house bar; not on the prettiest street. *Rooms from: €225 ⊠ 175 rue de Charonne Bastille ☎ 01–43–56–73–24 ⊕ www.edenlodgeparis.net ⇗ 5 rooms ⊚ free breakfast ⓜ Alexandre Dumas, Charonne.*

Hôtel Fabric

$$ | Hotel. This urban-chic hotel tucked away on an old artisan street is fully in tune with the pulse of the lively Oberkampf neighborhood, close to fabulous nightlife, cocktail bars, restaurants, bakeries, and shopping (and the Marais and Canal St-Martin). The funky mix-and-match interior crosses industrial-loft style with eclectic antiques and still manages to be warm and welcoming. **Pros:** all-you-can-eat breakfast for €17; lots of great sightseeing within walking distance; warm and helpful staff. **Cons:** rooms can be noisy; very popular so book well in advance; might be too party-focused for some. *Rooms from: €153 ⊠ 31 rue de la Folie Méricourt Oberkampf ☎ 01–43–57–27–00 ⊕ www.hotelfabric.com ⇗ 33 rooms ⓜ Saint-Ambroise, Oberkampf.*

CANAL ST-MARTIN
Generator Hostel Paris
$ | Hostel. For an inexpensive stay with loads of charm, the Generator Hostel, located in the hip 10e arrondissement, ticks all the boxes. **Pros:** private and shared rooms available; rooftop bar; views over Sacré-Coeur. **Cons:** no kitchen; not always spotless; staff can be impolite. *Rooms from: €60 ⊠ 9–11 pl. du Colonel Fabien Canal St-Martin ☎ 01–70–98–84–00 ⊕ generatorhostels.com ⤳ 199 rooms ⊚ breakfast, lunch, and dinner available Ⓜ Colonel Fabien.*

Le Citizen Hôtel
$$$ | Hotel. Overlooking the trendy Canal St-Martin, Le Citizen embraces a minimalist, Scandinavian style uniting light wood and splashes of color. **Pros:** several apartment-like suites, perfect for families; delicious lunch and evening tapas; wonderful view of the Canal. **Cons:** smaller rooms; can be loud; a bit pricey. *Rooms from: €199 ⊠ 96 quai de Jemmapes Canal St-Martin ☎ 01–83–62–55–50 ⊕ lecitizenhotel.com ⤳ 12 rooms ⊚ breakfast and lunch available Ⓜ Jacques-Bonsergent.*

LE MARAIS
Hôtel Jules & Jim
$$$ | Hotel. Named for Truffaut's 1962 cinematic masterpiece, this ultracontemporary hotel in the Marais manages to cultivate a bohemian aesthetic at a price that won't break the bank. **Pros:** cozy, book-lined bar and outdoor courtyard; contemporary decor; funky, artsy spirit. **Cons:** smaller rooms; service can be aloof; no minibars or

fridges in rooms. *Rooms from: €240 ⊠ 11 rue des Gravilliers Le Marais ☎ 01–44–54–13–13 ⊕ hoteljulesetjim. com 23 rooms ⊚ breakfast available Ⓜ Arts et Métiers.*

Les Jardins du Marais
$$ | Hotel. The centerpiece of the Jardins du Marais hotel is an enormous, 16,000-square-foot courtyard around which the rooms are organized. **Pros:** on-site spa with sauna; on-site parking garage; the namesake gardens. **Cons:** on-site restaurant closed Sunday and Monday; rooms could use a spruce; noisy at night (even overlooking the courtyard). *Rooms from: €160 ⊠ 74 rue Amelot Le Marais ☎ 01–40–21–20–00 ⊕ lesjardinsdumarais.com ⤳ 265 rooms ⊚ breakfast, lunch, and dinner available Ⓜ Filles du Calvaire, Saint-Sébastien–Froissart.*

SENTIER AND LES GRANDS BOULEVARDS
Hôtel Scribe
$$$$ | Hotel. This five-star hotel managed by Sofitel is located not far from the famous Garnier Opera House, in the same building where,

in the late 19th century, the Lumière brothers first showed off their brand-new invention: film. **Pros:** the romantic Lumière restaurant, with its gorgeous glass ceiling; free access to gym and spa; ultraprofessional staff. **Cons:** some rooms are beginning to show their age; breakfast varies in quality; standard rooms are on the small side. *Rooms from: €290 ✉ 1 rue Scribe Grands Boulevards ☎ 01–44–71–24–24 ⊕ hotel-scribe.com/en ⥲ 213 rooms ⏐◯⏐ breakfast, lunch, and dinner available Ⓜ Opéra.*

The Hoxton Paris

$$$ | Hotel. Located just steps from Paris's gorgeous 19th-century covered passageways, this trendy hotel offers everything you need for a successful stay in Paris, including a hip bar on-site. **Pros:** located in a historic 18th-century building; delicious in-house brasserie; tons of light. **Cons:** can be noisy; service sometimes slow; smoking allowed on terraces. *Rooms from: €200 ✉ 30 rue du Sentier Grands Boulevards ☎ 01–86–76–06–49 ⊕ thehoxton.com ⥲ 173 rooms ⏐◯⏐ breakfast, lunch, and dinner available Ⓜ Grands Boulevards, Bonne Nouvelle.*

LES HALLES AND PALAIS-ROYAL

Hôtel du Continent

$$ | Hotel. You'd be hard-pressed to find a budget hotel this stylish anywhere in Paris, let alone in an upscale neighborhood close to many of the city's top attractions. The travel-themed boutique hotel is in an elegant building, has luxe decor, and has a deeply Parisian location just steps from Place de la Concorde, Place de la Madeleine, and Rue St-Honoré, arguably the city's best shopping street. **Pros:** superfriendly staff; all modern amenities; location, location, location. **Cons:** no lobby; tiny bathrooms; bold decor not for everyone. *Rooms from: €150 ✉ 30 rue du Mont-Thabor Palais-Royal ☎ 01–42–60–75–32 ⊕ www.hotelcontinent.com ⥲ 25 rooms Ⓜ Concord, Tuileries.*

MONTMARTRE AND PIGALLE

Hôtel Terrass

$$ | Hotel. If you feel like being away from it all, but in a reasonably priced, fairly self-sufficient setting with a good on-site restaurant and a chic bar with stupendous views, this is the place. **Pros:** panoramic views of all Paris; awesome terrace bar; welcoming common areas with complimentary coffee. **Cons:** basic rooms are small; restaurant could be better; some street noise. *Rooms from: €140 ✉ 12–14 rue Joseph de Maistre Montmartre ☎ 01–46–06–72–85 ⊕ www.terrass-hotel.com ⥲ 92 rooms Ⓜ Blanche, Abbesses.*

Le Relais Montmartre

$$ | Hotel. Located down a quiet side street in Montmartre, this charming boutique hotel is homey and warm. **Pros:** the beautiful courtyard patio; the location just steps from bustling Rue Lepic; lovely staff. **Cons:** a bit far from the center; can be noisy; requires a walk up or down a steep hill to get to the métro. *Rooms from: €120 ✉ 6 rue Constance Montmartre ☎ 01–70–64–25–25 ⊕ hotel-relais-*

montmartre.com ⤴ *26 rooms*
Ⓜ *Abbesses, Blanche.*

ST-GERMAIN-DES-PRÉS AND LES INVALIDES

Hôtel Max

$$ | **Hotel.** A sleek Scandinavian design with lively splashes of color, bright comfortable rooms, and a warm and welcoming atmosphere make this 19-room hotel one of Paris's best-kept secrets. **Pros:** excellent prices; intimate feel; quiet residential neighborhood. **Cons:** rooms on the small side; a walk or métro ride to most sights; no bathtubs. *Rooms from: €126* ✉ *34 rue d'Alésia Montparnasse* ☎ *00-43-27-60-80* ⊕ *www.hotel-max.fr* ⤴ *19 rooms* Ⓜ *Alésia.*

Relais Christine

$$$$ | **Hotel.** This gorgeous five-star hotel on a tiny street not far from St-Germain-des-Prés offers a luxury experience in an authentic Old Parisian locale. **Pros:** wonderful spa; calm, relaxing interior courtyard; professional, helpful concierges. **Cons:** narrow staircases; beehives in the garden (allergic folks, beware!); no on-site restaurant. *Rooms from: €375* ✉ *3 rue Christine St-Germain-des-Prés* ☎ *01-40-51-60-80* ⊕ *relais-christine.com* ⤴ *48 rooms* ⏐❍⏐ *breakfast available* Ⓜ *Odéon.*

QUARTIER LATIN

Hôtel Monge

$$$ | **Hotel.** Chic, cozy, and welcoming, you couldn't land in a more charming—and reasonably priced—small boutique hotel in Paris. **Pros:** excellent neighborhood close to sights and legendary markets; great views from balconies; lovely spa **Cons:** not all rooms have balconies; open-design showers; quiet neighborhood with few restaurants. *Rooms from: €250* ✉ *55 rue Monge Quartier Latin* ☎ *01-43-54-55-55* ⊕ *www.hotel-monge.com* ⤴ *30 rooms* Ⓜ *Jussieu, Cardinal Lemoine, Place Monge.*

TROCADÉRO AND CHAMPS-ÉLYSÉES

Pavillon des Lettres

$$$ | **Hotel.** This boutique hotel not far from the Champs-Élysées has a literary slant: every one of the 26 rooms is assigned a letter of the alphabet and then named after an author. A passage of the chosen author's work is reproduced on the wall. **Pros:** cool literary bent with lending library in the lobby; gorgeous shared spaces; complimentary cheese and charcuterie every evening in the cozy bar area. **Cons:** small rooms, especially for a four-star hotel; some street noise; spa off-site. *Rooms from: €190* ✉ *12 rue des Saussaies Champs-Élysées* ☎ *01-49-24-26-26* ⊕ *pavillondes-lettres.com* ⤴ *26 rooms* Ⓜ *Madeleine, Miromesnil.*

QUICK SIDE TRIPS

VERSAILLES

For most of history the kings of France lived at the Louvre, but in 1682, Louis XIV moved the royal residence to Versailles, converting the former hunting lodge into an ostentatious, opulent palace. Inside, be sure to stop in the Hall of Mirrors, where the Treaty of Versailles was signed, ending World War I. The Grands Appartements (State Apartments) are whipped into a lather of decoration, with painted ceilings, marble walls, parquet floors, and canopy beds topped with ostrich plumes. The Petits Appartements (Private Apartments), where the royal family and friends lived, are on a more human scale, lined with 18th-century gold and white rococo boiseries. Completed in 1701 in the Louis XIV style, the Appartements du Roi (King's Apartments) comprise a suite of 15 rooms set in a "U" around the east facade's Marble Court. The Chambre de la Reine (Queen's Bed Chamber)—once among the world's most opulent—was updated for Marie-Antoinette in the chicest style of the late 18th century.

The château itself is just the beginning: visit the geometric flower-beds and fountains of the gardens created by André Le Nôtre, as well as Marie-Antoinette's "hamlet," where she and her ladies-in-waiting would pretend to be shepherdesses. Just 21 km (13 miles) from Paris, Versailles is accessible from the Château de Versailles stop on RER line C. Leave the better part of a day to explore the grounds: the château (open from 9 am to 6:30 pm) is made up of a whopping 2,300 rooms. ⊠ Pl. d'Armes ⊕ en.chateauversailles. fr ⊗ Closed Mon. 🎫 Palace ticket €18.

CHARTRES

The small city of Chartres, just 96 km (60 miles) from Paris, is known mainly for its imposing cathedral, an early-13th-century Gothic marvel. The stained-glass windows feature a unique shade of blue that has since been dubbed bleu de Chartres or Chartres blue; it remains impossible to reproduce. Chartres is also home to a museum devoted to stained glass, and a wander through the center will take you over charming bridges that span the Eure River. Both Transilien and main-line (Le Mans–bound) trains leave Paris's Gare Montparnasse for Chartres (50–70 mins, €15). The train station on Place Pierre-Sémard puts you within walking distance of the cathedral.

CHAMPAGNE

Just under 160 km (100 miles) from Paris is the city of **Reims**, the heart of the Champagne region. Scattered throughout the surrounding countryside, you'll encounter all of the great Champagne houses, from Moët & Chandon to Veuve Clicquot to Dom Perignon. Most of the houses big and small offer tours, visits, and tastings, but be sure to book in advance. The city of Reims is worth a visit as well: it's home to the Gothic Reims Cathedral, the site where 37 French kings were crowned. Exploring Champagne is best with a car, though tour companies also run day tours of the region.

GIVERNY

Claude Monet moved to Giverny, in Normandy, in 1883, and over the course of more than 40 years, he built the home and extensive gardens that he would later render famous in his paintings. Visiting Giverny allows you to explore the home where Monet worked and lived with his family, the walls of which are blanketed in art. Outside, wander through the gardens to see the rowboat, Japanese bridge, and water lilies that Monet so loved to paint. Regular trains depart for Vernon from St-Lazare station in Paris; from there, it's a quick bus ride to Giverny. ⊠ *84 rue Claude Monet Giverny.* ☉ *Closed Nov. 2–Mar. 23.* ⊕ *Fondation-monet.com*

LOIRE VALLEY CASTLES

Renaissance castles are scattered through the Loire Valley, each with its own personality and draw. **Château de Chenonceau**, one of the most famous, spans the Loire River with a grand gallery that doubles as a bridge. Also known as the Ladies' Castle, Chenonceau was at the heart of a power struggle between King Henri II's long-time mistress, Diane de Poitiers, and his widow, Catherine de Medici. Also worth a trip is **Château de Chambord,** the largest of the castles, which was originally built as a hunting lodge for King Francis I. It notably features a double-spiral staircase that has been attributed to Leonardo da Vinci. The Italian Renaissance master was brought to France in 1516, where he spent the last three years of his life. He is buried at the Amboise Château. Reaching the Loire Valley castles is easiest by car, though trains to Chenonceaux do run, albeit with an interchange. Tour companies also run day trips to the Loire Valley.

NORMANDY'S D-DAY BEACHES

Head toward the Atlantic coast and you'll encounter one of the most important modern historical sites in France. The beaches of the Cotentin Peninsula were code-named Utah, Omaha, Gold, Sword, and Juno during World War II, and it is here that the Allied soldiers invaded France to begin the fight for freedom. Stop by the impressive military museum at the American Utah Beach before heading toward Omaha, where you'll be able to visit the American cemetery. Don't miss Pointe du Hoc, an important strategic point between the two. It was bombed out and remains littered with craters and former bunkers to this day. To visit the beaches from Paris, it's easiest to rent a car, but a number of tour companies run bus tours there as well. It's about a four-hour drive to Utah.

HOW TO SPEND A LONG WEEKEND IN PARIS

DAY 1

Get your bearings in the south **Marais,** the heart of Paris's historic Jewish quarter and one of the best vintage shopping areas in the capital. Start by fueling up at the **Caféothèque,** one of Paris's top coffee spots, before venturing north along the historic streets of the Marais: Rue des Rosiers and Rue des Francs-Bourgeois effortlessly combine bakeries and falafel shops with top friperies (secondhand shops) where you might uncover anything from Chanel to silk scarves to awesome costume jewelry.

Slowly make your way north along the Rue de Turenne toward the north Marais, where you'll encounter the **Picasso museum** as well as the **Marché des Enfants Rouges,** the oldest covered market in the city. Meander over to the Boulevard Beaumarchais to visit concept store **Merci**, then wind northwest to the Rue Dupetit-Thouars, home to an assortment of fantastic coffee shops and around the corner from concept store **The Broken Arm.**

Traverse Place de la République toward the beautiful (and hip) **Canal St-Martin** in the 10e arrondissement, and stroll along the canal's banks toward **Oberkampf** for lunch at **Robert** or **Clamato**—these spots can be pricier at night, but their lunchtime menus are a true steal. After refueling, head east toward **Ménilmontant** for an afternoon of shopping and people-watching, and then loop north toward **Belleville,** where you can take in local street art on Rue Denoyez. Grab a drink at local fave **Aux Folies** (or wine bar **La Cave de Belleville**) before dinner at **Mensae** or **Le Baratin.** Finish off the evening by visiting one of Belleville's many cultural venues such as the **Théâtre de Ménilmontant**—a larger selection can be found in our Belleville chapter.

DAY 2

Spending a long weekend in Paris means you'll have at least one Paris Sunday. Labor laws in France mean that many shops will be closed, so take a page out of the books of the locals and become a *flâneur,* a wanderer. **Montmartre** is an excellent neighborhood for this: as a recognized touristic center, more shops will be open here than in many other neighborhoods, but there's also a ton to see whether you're shopping or not. Get off the métro at Blanche, in front of the famed **Moulin Rouge** cabaret. Continue up Rue Lepic, the local market street, to Rue des Abbesses, home to a park featuring a wall reading "I love you" in more than 300 languages. Wind up the hill along Rue Lepic, where you'll pass the last remaining windmill of this former small village. Hang a left on Rue Girardon and follow Rue de l'Abreuvoir, which will take you past the **Clos de Montmartre** vineyard, an ancestral patch of vines dating back hundreds of years and still used to make wine today. Continue up toward **Sacré-Coeur** and snap a picture of the view before leaving the touristy pinnacle in favor of brunch at **The Hardware Société.** There will likely be a line, but it's worth the wait.

Meander north toward the **Marché aux Puces de St-Ouen** flea market to uncover some fantastic finds: the market is made up of several individual markets dedicated to furniture, deco objects, and more. Don't miss the covered **Marché Serpette,** a favorite of market regulars. When you've had your fill of shopping, head west toward **Les Batignolles,** home to the pretty **Square des Batignolles** and a variety of fantastic spots for dinner, like modern crêpe and cider bar **Brutus** or gorgeous neo-bistro **Gare au Gorille.** Grab a nightcap at local wine bar **Les Caves Populaires** before heading home.

DAY 3

Don't leave Paris without taking in some of its most famous sites. This can be done easily with a simple stroll along the banks of the Seine. Start by taking in the majesty of the **Eiffel Tower** from the Champ de Mars below. No need to actually climb it—as writer Guy de Maupassant used to say, the only place you can't see the Eiffel Tower is from the Eiffel Tower.

Next, begin walking eastward along the banks of the Seine. You'll pass the impressive gilded Alexandre III bridge connecting the **Grand Palais,** a 19th-century exhibition center, with **Invalides,** a former military hospital built by Louis XIV; it has since been converted into a military museum and is the burial place of Napoléon I and Napoléon III. Continuing east, you'll soon pass the **Louvre,** directly across the river from the **Musée d'Orsay.** Together, these imposing museums are home to a large portion of the national art collection of France, with art produced before 1848 located within the Louvre and works produced between 1848 and 1914 displayed in the former Orsay railway station, which was converted into a museum in the 1980s. Stop for lunch behind the Louvre at **Ellsworth** or **Juvéniles** before popping into either (or both) of the museums, then cross the Pont des Arts to return to the Left Bank, where you'll see the impressive Institut de France, home to the Académie française, which has been tasked with maintaining the French dictionary since 1635.

Meander away from the banks of the Seine to explore the quaint streets of **St-Germain-des-Prés** and the **Latin Quarter** before moving back toward the river to take in the majestic **Notre-Dame Cathedral.** Pop into **Shakespeare and Company** for a book or a coffee, then double back toward **l'Avant Comptoir du Relais,** a tapas and wine bar known for its modern French fare. Finish the day with dinner at neo-bistro **Hugo & Co.**

2

Les Halles and Palais-Royal

LES PUCES
CLIGNAN-COURT
ÉPINETTES
LA CHAPELLE
LA VILLETTE
LES BATIGNOLLES
MONTMARTRE
TERNES
MONCEAU
PIGALLE
CANAL ST-MARTIN
BELLEVILLE
LES GRANDS BOULEVARDS
CHAMPS-ÉLYSÉES
SENTIER
CHAILLOT
MÉNILMONTANT
BOIS DE BOULOGNE
PASSY
TROCADÉRO
PALAIS-ROYAL
LES HALLES
LE MARAIS
OBERKAMPF
PÈRE-LACHAISE
LES INVALIDES
LES ÎLES
BASTILLE
CHARONNE
AUTEUIL
VAUGIRARD
ST-GERMAIN-DES-PRÉS
QUARTIER LATIN
BERCY
BEL-AIR
JAVEL
MONTPARNASSE
BUTTE-AUX-CAILLES
SEINE
BOIS DE VINCENNES
ST-LAMBERT
AUSTERLITZ
MONTROUGE
MAISON BLANCHE

The heart of Paris and the most central of its arrondissements, the 1er is chock-full of heavy-hitter iconic sights no first-time visitor should miss, yet among its tourist-saturated streets are still a few surprises for the discerning traveler. Though the neighborhood has changed drastically over the years, its regal essence remains. On the west end is the extensive complex of the Louvre, the former palace of the French royals and paragon of Parisian opulence and elegance, an air upheld today by the world-famous museum, neighboring Jardin des Tuileries, and the area's many luxury hotels and haute couture shops. A few blocks east is the antithesis of all this elegance: Les Halles, market halls that were once a boisterous, gritty food hub and have undergone many face-lifts over the years. In 2016, during the most recent renovation, its La Canopée structure was unveiled to mixed reviews from locals. Nevertheless, the overhaul is cleaning up Les Halles, bringing in hip shops and resurrecting its culinary traditions with the help of the city's top chefs, who are enticing savvy Parisian diners back to the "Belly of Paris."—*by Lily Heise*

Sights

Fontaine des Innocents

A convenient meeting or resting point after shopping at Les Halles, this graceful Renaissance fountain has remarkably escaped the many waves of destruction the neighborhood has faced. Designed by Louvre architect Pierre Lescot and sculptor Jean Goujon in 1549, it sat next to a large cemetery that was shut down in 1787, its bones transferred to the Catacombs. ⊠ *Pl. Joachim du Bellay, Les Halles* ✛ *Southeast of Forum des Halles* Ⓜ *Châtelet–Les Halles.*

★ Galerie Véro-Dodat

Tucked away on a side street near the Louvre is one of the city's prettiest covered passageways. Restored to maintain its original 19th-century black-and-white marble flooring and light fixtures, the arcade is lined with posh boutiques, antique shops, and art galleries. It is flanked on one end by the workshop of superstar shoe designer Christian Louboutin, and on the other, a boutique by cosmetics-maker Terry De Gunzburg. ⊠ *9 rue Jean-Jacques Rousseau, Palais-Royal* ☉ *Closed Sun.* Ⓜ *Louvre–Rivoli.*

★ Jardin des Tuileries

The quintessential French garden, with its verdant lawns, manicured rows of trees, and gravel paths, was designed by André Le Nôtre for Louis XIV. After the king moved his court to Versailles in 1682, the Tuileries became *the* place for stylish Parisians to stroll. (Ironically, the name derives from the decidedly unstylish factories, which once occupied this area: they produced *tuiles,* or roof tiles, fired in kilns called *tuileries.*) Monet and Renoir captured the garden with paint and brush, and it's no wonder the Impressionists loved it—the gray, austere light of Paris's famously overcast days make the green trees appear even greener.

The garden still serves as a setting for one of the city's loveliest walks. Laid out before you is a vista of must-see monuments, with the Louvre at one end and the Place de la Concorde at the other. The Eiffel Tower is on the Seine side, along with the Musée d'Orsay, reachable across a footbridge in the center of the garden. A good place to begin is at the Louvre end, at the Arc du Carrousel, a stone-and-marble arch ordered by Napoléon to showcase the bronze horses he stole from St. Mark's Cathedral in Venice. The horses were eventually returned and replaced here with a statue of a *quadriga,* a four-horse chariot. On the Place de la Concorde end, twin buildings bookend the garden. On the Seine side, the former royal greenhouse is now the exceptional Musée de l'Orangerie, home to the largest display of Monet's lovely *Water Lilies* series, as well as a sizable collection of early-20th-century paintings. On the opposite end is the Jeu de Paume, which has some of the city's best temporary photography exhibits.

Note that the Tuileries is one of the best places in Paris to take kids if they're itching to run around. There's a carousel, trampolines, and, in summer, an amusement park.

If you're hungry, look for carts serving gelato from Amorino or sandwiches from the chain bakery Paul at the eastern end near the Louvre. Within the gated part of the gardens are four cafés with terraces. Pavillon des Tuilleries near Place de la Concorde is a good place to stop for late-afternoon tea or an apéritif. ✉ *Bordered by Quai des Tuileries, Pl. de la Concorde, Rue de Rivoli, and the Louvre, Louvre* ☎ *01-40-20-90-43* 🎟 *Free* Ⓜ *Tuileries or Concorde.*

Jeu de Paume

Photography fans should not miss the modern Jeu de Paume at the west end of the Jardin des Tuileries. Constructed in 1861 during the reign of Napoléon III as a venue for stylish Parisians to play *le jeu de paume* (a French precursor of tennis), it was converted in 1922 into a contemporary art museum. Today it focuses exclusively on photography, video, and installation exhibits by top international artists like Diane

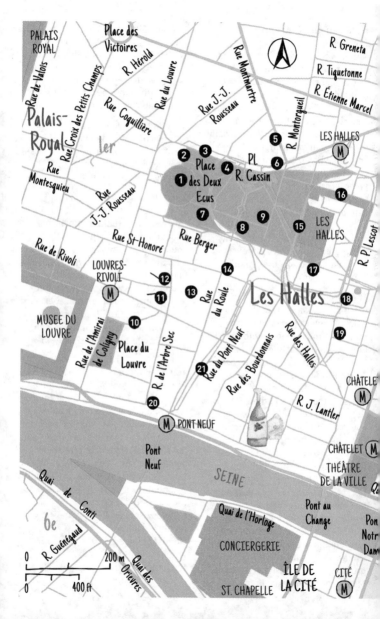

SIGHTS

SHOPPING

COFFEE & QUICK BITES

DINING

BARS & NIGHTLIFE

PERFORMING ARTS

Arbus, Richard Avedon, and Cindy Sherman. ⊠ *1 pl. de la Concorde, Concorde* ☎ *01–47–03–12–50* ⊕ *www. jeudepaume.org* ⊠ *€10* Ⓜ *Concorde.*

Les Arts Décoratifs

As the city's leading showcase of French design, Les Arts Décoratifs was rechristened the Musée des Arts Décoratifs—or MAD—in 2018 in an effort to better carve out a niche for itself in a city with many competitors for that title. Sharing a wing of the Musée du Louvre, but with a separate entrance and admission charge, MAD is actually three museums in one spread across nine floors. The stellar collection of decorative arts, fashion, and graphics includes altarpieces from the Middle Ages and furnishings from the Italian Renaissance to the present day. There are period rooms reflecting the ages, such as the early 1820s salon of the Duchesse de Berry (who actually lived in the building), plus several rooms reproduced from designer Jeanne Lanvin's 1920s apartment. Don't miss the gilt-and-green-velvet bed of the Parisian courtesan who inspired the boudoir in Émile Zola's novel *Nana*; you can hear Zola's description of it on the free English audioguide, which is highly recommended. The second-floor jewelry gallery is another must-see.

MAD is also home to an exceptional collection of textiles, advertising posters, films, and related objects that are shown in rotating exhibitions. The museum routinely makes headlines for crowd-pleasing temporary exhibits such as 2017's

GETTING HERE

The central district is highly walkable, but it's also well connected by public transportation and is home to the largest subway station in world: Châtelet–Les Halles (750,000 commuters pass through every weekday). Here you'll find métro lines 1, 4, 7, 11, and 14 as well as suburban RER lines A, B, and D. Line 1 runs along the district and can take you to most other places of interest.

Christian Dior show that broke records for attendance. Before leaving, take a break at the restaurant Le Loulou, where an outdoor terrace is an ideal spot for lunch or afternoon tea. Shoppers should browse through the on-site boutique as well. Stocked with an interesting collection of books, paper products, toys, tableware, accessories, and jewelry, it is one of the city's best museum shops. If you're combining a visit here with the Musée du Louvre, note that the two close on different days, so don't come on Monday or Tuesday. If you're pairing it with the exquisite Nissim de Camondo, joint tickets are available at a reduced cost. ⊠ *107 rue de Rivoli, Louvre* ☎ *01–44–55–57–50* ⊕ *madparis.fr* ⊠ *From €11* ⊗ *Closed Mon.* Ⓜ *Palais-Royal–Louvre.*

Les Caves du Louvre

At this unique wine experience venue in the beautifully restored cellars of the Louvre, visitors get a sensorial introduction to the winemaking process via clever interactive exhibits designed by the local

wine-tasting experts at O'Chateau. You can finish off your education by sampling wine at the bar or by creating your own blend during a wine-making workshop. ✉ *52 rue de l'Arbre Sec, Louvre* ☎ *01–40–28–13–11* ⊕ *www.cavesdulouvre.com* ✏ *Basic visit free, tours and workshops extra* Ⓜ *Louvre–Rivoli, Châtelet–Les Halles.*

Les Halles

Although it's impossible to bring back the gorgeous 19th-century market halls that were torn down in the 1960s, all Parisians would agree that something had to be done about the dilapidated state of this large market complex. A decade-long renovation project begun in 2007 has recently made it more inviting to visitors, refurbishing Europe's largest subway interchange station, the well-trodden Forum des Halles shopping center, and an adjacent park—while staying open to the public. Despite the fact that the popularity of the project's center-piece, a spaceship-like structure called La Canopée, has not taken off with locals, the new Les Halles is constantly abuzz with commuters and shoppers, who can also take a rest in the spruced-up park, renamed after Nelson Mandela. Luckily a few good nuggets of the Old Les Halles remain, including *Écoute* (*Listen*), a giant head sculpture by Henri de Miller sitting next to St-Eustache Church and the Bourse de Commerce (formerly the market's grain hall), which is being transformed into an art center to house the collection of French billionaire businessman François Pinault (scheduled to open in late 2019). ✉ *Forum des Halles, Les Halles* Ⓜ *Châtelet–Les Halles.*

★ The Louvre

Simply put, the Louvre is the world's greatest art museum—and the largest, with 675,000 square feet of works from almost every civilization on earth. The *Mona Lisa* is, of course, a top draw, along with the Venus de Milo and Winged Victory. These and many more of the globe's most coveted treasures are displayed in three wings—the Richelieu, the Sully, and the Denon—which are arranged like a horseshoe. Nestled in the middle is I.M. Pei's Pyramid, the giant glass pyramid surrounded by a trio of smaller ones that opened in 1989 over the new entrance in the Cour Napoléon. To plot your course through the complex, grab a color-coded map at the information desk. For an excellent overview, book a 90-minute English-language tour (€12, daily at 11 and 2); slick Nintendo 3DS multimedia guides (€5; pay for it when you buy your ticket), available at the entrance to each wing, offer a self-guided alternative.

Having been first a fortress and later a royal residence, the Louvre represents a saga that spans nine centuries. Its medieval roots are on display below ground in the Sully wing, where vestiges of the foundation and moat remain. Elsewhere in this wing you can ogle the largest display of Egyptian antiques outside of Cairo, most notably the magnificent statue of Ramses II (salle 12).

A LOCAL'S GUIDE TO THE LOUVRE

Attracting more than 7 million visitors each year, the Louvre can be a madhouse, especially in summer. Despite the crowds, the exceptional museum is still rightfully a bucket-list topper, and is home to incredible masterpieces including the Mona Lisa, the Venus de Milo, and the Winged Victory of Samothrace. If your trip to Paris isn't complete without the Louvre, follow these tips to help you navigate (and enjoy!) your visit.

To Beat the Crowds...

• Visit on Wednesday or Friday night when most tour groups are gone and the museum is open until 10 pm.

• Purchase skip-the-line tickets ⊕ www.ticketlouvre.fr or book a small group tour, such as those offered by Context Travel ⊕ www.contexttravel.com.

See This, Not That

• Instead of the Mona Lisa, turn around to admire the sensational sight of Veronese's The Wedding Feast at Cana, the largest painting in the museum.

• Instead of the Italian paintings in the cramped Grande Galerie, amble crowd-free through the glitzy Napoléon III apartments.

• Instead of the Venus de Milo and her constant stream of tour groups, gaze up at the gorgeous statues in the French sculpture atriums. Before leaving, don't miss out on walking around the moat of the former medieval fortress, uncovered during the 1980s restoration and located in the Sully wing.

Upstairs is the armless Venus de Milo, a 2nd-century representation of Aphrodite (salle 7). Highlights of the wing's collection of French paintings from the 17th century onward include the *Turkish Bath* by Jean-August-Dominique Ingres (salle 60). American Cy Twombly's contemporary ceiling in salle 32 adds a 21st-century twist. In the Denon wing, climb the sweeping marble staircase (Escalier Daru) to see the sublime Winged Victory of Samothrace, carved in 305 BC. This wing is also home to the iconic, enigmatic *Mona Lisa* (salle 6); two other Da Vinci masterpieces hang in the adjacent Grand Galerie. The museum's latest architec-

tural wonder is here as well—the 30,000-square-foot Arts of Islam exhibition space, which debuted in 2012. Topped with an undulating golden roof evoking a flowing veil, its two-level galleries contain one of the largest collections of art from the Islamic world. After admiring it, be sure to visit the Richelieu wing and the Cour Marly, with its quartet of horses carved for Louis XIV and Louis XV. On the ground floor, the centerpiece of the Near East Antiquities Collection is the Lamassu, carved 8th-century winged beasts (salle 4). The elaborately decorated Royal Apartments of Napoléon III are on the first floor. On the second floor, French and

Northern School paintings include Vermeer's *The Lacemaker* (salle 38). Note that crowds are thinner on Wednesday and Friday nights, when the museum is open late. Save queue time by purchasing online tickets for an additional fee; admission includes some temporary exhibitions and entry within 48 hours to the charming Musée Eugène-Delacroix. If you arrive without a ticket, you can buy one at the kiosks or automatic machines in a newly renovated space below the Pyramid. Avoid crowds by using the lesser-known entrance through the underground mall, Carrousel du Louvre. ⊠ *Palais du Louvre, Louvre* ☎ *01-40-20-53-17 for info* ⊕ *www. louvre.fr* ⌁ *€15, includes entry to Musée Eugène Delacroix (free 1st Sun. of month, Oct.–Mar.)* ⊙ *Closed Tues.* Ⓜ *Palais-Royal–Louvre, Louvre-Rivoli.*

Medici Column

Hiding in plain sight behind the Bourse de Commerce is this 92-feet-high column, which was built in 1575 at the request of Catherine de Medici. A small palace complex once stood here, the Hôtel de Soissons, where Queen de Medici temporarily lived after the death of her husband King Henri II. An avid fan of the occult, the queen had the column built as a lookout for her astrologers. While its 145 steps are now off-limits, you can spot the royal couple's emblem, an intertwined H and C, on its exterior. ⊠ *2 rue de Viarmes, Les Halles* Ⓜ *Châtelet–Les Halles, Louvre-Rivoli.*

Musée de l'Orangerie

Nestled in the corner of the Tuileries, skirting the Place de la Concorde, the Musée de l'Orangerie has a greenhouse-like facade with a glass wall facing the Seine. The side facing Rue de Rivoli is the opposite, almost windowless. Once used by the state to store orange trees, the 20th-century art museum is known today for its more famous Impressionist residents: Claude Monet's *Water Lilies*. ⊠ *Pl. de la Concorde, Concorde* ☎ *01-44-77-80-07* ⊕ *www.musee-orangerie. fr* ⌁ *€9, free 1st Sun. of month* ⊙ *Closed Tues.* Ⓜ *Concorde.*

★ Palais-Royal

Skip the crowds at the Tuileries and head instead to this exquisite palace and gardens. Built in the early 17th century as a home for Cardinal Richelieu, it was later gifted to Louis XIV's brother, who was known to throw wild parties here. Today, the quiet palace grounds are the perfect spot to spend an afternoon relaxing under the trees or taking quirky photos by the short black-and-white columns in the courtyard. ■TIP→ Enter the gardens through the passageway on Place Colette. ⊠ *8 rue de Montpensier, Palais-Royal* Ⓜ *Palais Royal–Musée du Louvre.*

Parc Rives de Seine

After the success of its Left Bank counterpart Les Berges, the Right Bank's expressway along the river was also converted into a permanent park in 2017. Spanning 3 1/3 km (2 miles) from the Pont de Sully to the Pont Neuf, the incredibly scenic walkway—with a backdrop

of top monuments like Notre-Dame and the Conciergerie—has become a hugely popular place to stroll, bike, or relax among its many outdoor cafés and inviting sitting areas. ⊠ *Parc Rives de Seine, Les Halles* ⊕ *en.parisinfo.com/transport/163277/Parc-Rives-de-Seine* Ⓜ *Châtelet–Les Halles*.

Place de la Concorde

This square at the foot of the Champs-Élysées was originally named after Louis XV. It later became the Place de la Révolution, where crowds cheered as Louis XVI, Marie-Antoinette, and some 2,500 others lost their heads to the guillotine. Renamed Concorde in 1836, it got a new centerpiece: the 75-foot granite Obelisk of Luxor, a gift from Egypt quarried in the 8th century BC. Among the handsome 18th-century buildings facing the square is the Hôtel Crillon, which was originally built as a private home by Gabriel, the architect of Versailles's Petit Trianon. After a massive renovation that spanned four years, the Crillon's scaffolding came down in summer 2017 to reveal a stunning face-lift. ⊠ *Rue Royale, Louvre* Ⓜ *Concorde*.

Place Vendôme

Jules-Hardouin Mansart, an architect of Versailles, designed this perfectly proportioned octagonal plaza near the Tuileries in 1702; and, to maintain a uniform appearance, he gave the surrounding *hôtels particuliers* (private mansions) identical facades. It was originally called Place des Conquêtes to extoll the military conquests of Louis XIV,

whose statue on horseback graced the center until Revolutionaries destroyed it in 1792. Later, Napoléon ordered his likeness erected atop a 144-foot column modestly modeled after Rome's Trajan Column. But that, too, was toppled in 1871 by painter Gustave Courbet and his band of radicals. The Third Republic raised a new column and sent Courbet the bill, though he died in exile before paying it. The Ritz, a longtime tenant, picked up the tab for a 2016 renovation teamed with the hotel's own four-year clean-up. Chopin lived and died at No. 12, which is also where Napoléon III enjoyed trysts with his mistress; since 1902 it has been home to the high-end jeweler Chaumet. ⊠ *Pl. Vendôme, Louvre* Ⓜ *Tuileries*.

🛍 Shopping

& Other Stories

H&M's latest upmarket "style-lab" covers all the major fashion bases while appealing to women of different tastes and ages. Unlike the minimalist COS—another H&M spawn—& Other Stories offers the kind of au courant looks and well-made basics that are beloved by urban sophisticates who wouldn't be caught dead buying the parent brand but still want style on a budget. The shoe collection downstairs is a serious draw all on its own. Accessories, lingerie, and makeup are also available. ⊠ *277 rue St-Honoré, 8e, Louvre* ☎ *01-53-32-85-05* ⊕ *www.stories.com* Ⓜ *Concorde*.

★ Chloé

Much like the clothes it sells, Chloé's flagship boutique is softly feminine and modern without being stark. Housed in an 18th-century mansion, its creamy-marble floors, gold sconces, and walls in the brand's signature rosy beige are the perfect backdrop for designer Clare Waight Keller's beautifully tailored yet fluid designs. Visitors are met with the kind of sincere attention that is all but extinct in most high-end Paris shops. Whether it's for a handbag or a whole new wardrobe, VIP rooms and professional stylists are available to assist anyone who calls for an appointment. ✉ *253 rue St-Honoré, 1e, Louvre* ☎ *01-55-04-03-30* ⊕ *www.chloe.com* Ⓜ *Franklin-D.-Roosevelt.*

Christian Louboutin

These shoes carry their own red carpet with them, thanks to their trademark crimson soles. Whether tasseled, embroidered, or strappy, in Charvet silk or shiny patent leather, the heels are always perfectly balanced. No wonder they set off such legendary legs as Tina Turner's and Gwyneth Paltrow's. The men's shop is next door at No. 17, and the women's pop-up store (Christian Louboutin Beauté, featuring his cosmetics line) is around the corner at Galerie Véro-Dodat. The glamorous No. 68 rue du Faubourg St-Honoré boutique carries a full line of women's shoes and accessories. ✉ *19 rue Jean-Jacques Rousseau, 1er, Louvre* ☎ *08-00-94-58-04* ⊕ *www.christian-louboutin.com* Ⓜ *Palais-Royal–Louvre.*

> ### ART IN THE WILD
>
> If the Mona Lisa isn't your idea of art, then wander through **59 Rivoli**, an alternative art space just a few blocks away from the imposing Louvre. One of the oldest artist squats in Paris, now legalized by City Hall, its six floors are overflowing with contemporary works that you can view on a donation basis. ⊕ www.59rivoli.org

Didier Ludot

The incredibly charming Didier Ludot inspired a fervent craze for vintage couture, and riffling through his racks of French-made pieces from the '20s to the '80s can yield wonderful Chanel suits, Balenciaga dresses, and Hermès scarves. Ludot has two boutiques in Galerie Montpensier: No. 20 houses his amazing vintage couture collection, while No. 24 has vintage ready-to-wear and accessories. ✉ *Jardins du Palais-Royal, 20–24 Galerie Montpensier, 1er, Louvre* ☎ *01-42-96-06-56* ⊕ *www.didierludot.fr* Ⓜ *Palais Royal–Musée du Louvre.*

E. Dehillerin

Never mind the creaky stairs: E. Dehillerin has been around for almost 200 years and clearly knows its business. The huge range of professional cookware in enamel, stainless steel, or fiery copper is gorgeous. During her years in Paris, Julia Child was a regular here. ✉ *18–20 rue Coquillière, 1er, Louvre* ☎ *01-42-36-53-13* ⊕ *www.edehillerin.fr* Ⓜ *Les Halles.*

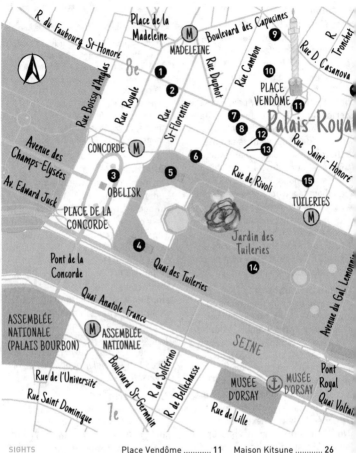

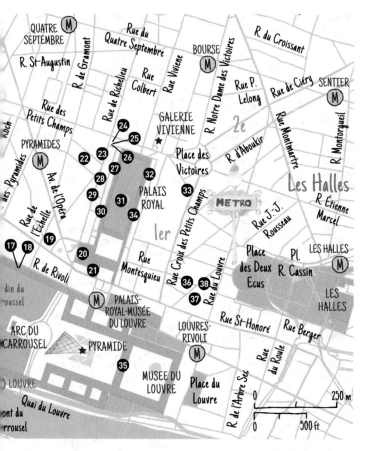

Ekyog

Amid the stock outlet shops clustered around Rue du Jour and Rue de Montmartre is this eco-friendly shop. Created in 2003, Ekyog was one of the first French fashion brands to adopt an environmental, sustainable, and ethical fashion manifesto. Their chic feminine basics are made with all-natural, organic, or recycled materials and are available here at excellent discounts. ⊠ *1 rue de Montmartre, Les Halles* ☎ *01-42-21-46-01* ⊕ *www. ekyog.com* ⊙ *Closed Sun. and Mon. morning, mid-Aug.* Ⓜ *Châtelet–Les Halles.*

Ladurée

Founded in 1862, Ladurée oozes period atmosphere—even at the big Champs-Élysées branch (No. 75)—but nothing beats the original tearoom on Rue Royale, with its pint-size tables and frescoed ceiling. Ladurée claims a familial link to the invention of the *macaron* and appropriately, there's a fabulous selection of these lighter-than-air cookies. Classic flavors include pistachio, salted caramel, and coffee; others, like violet–black currant, chestnut, and lime basil, are available seasonally. When you've worked your way through the macaron menu, try a cup of the famously rich hot chocolate with a flaky mille-feuille. Unfortunately, service has lagged at all three of the tearooms in recent years (including the charming upstairs room at 21 rue Bonaparte), and the crowded room feels ever more like an ersatz tourist destination than the historic tearoom that it is. Still, Ladurée's stylish boxes filled with sweet treats make memorable gifts. ⊠ *16 rue Royale, 8e, Louvre* ☎ *01-42-60-21-79* ⊕ *www.laduree.com* Ⓜ *Madeleine.*

★ Les Salons du Palais-Royal Serge Lutens

Every year Shiseido's creative genius, Serge Lutens, dreams up two new fragrances, which are then sold exclusively in this boutique. Each is compellingly original, from the strong *somptueux* scents (often with musk and amber notes) to intense florals (Rose de Nuit). Bottles can be etched and personalized for sumptuous gifts. ⊠ *Jardins du Palais-Royal, 142 Galerie de Valois, 1er, Louvre* ☎ *01-49-27-09-09* ⊕ *www.sergelutens.com* Ⓜ *Palais-Royal–Louvre.*

★ L'Exception

The Forum des Halles shopping mall got a lot cooler when the flagship of this online retailer took up residence in 2016. Representing more than 400 top contemporary French designers, the large concept store and café, with Coutume coffee and small bites by La Petite Table, is a one-stop shop for dressing like a hip *Parisien*. ⊠ *24 rue Berger, Les Halles* ☎ *01-40-39-92-34* ⊕ *www. lexception.com* Ⓜ *Châtelet–Les Halles.*

Maison Kitsuné

Pick up effortlessly cool casual wear for both men and women at the Palais-Royal fashion division of this hip electro music label, whose name means "fox" in Japanese. The modernity and simplicity of the East is blended with Parisian nonchalance in their T-shirts, hoodies, and jeans, emblazoned with their trademark fox logo. In addition to their boutique, Maison Kitsuné also has a stylish café. ⊠ *52 rue de Richelieu, Palais-Royal* ☎ *01-42-60-34-28* ⊕ *shop.kitsune.fr* Ⓜ *Palais Royal–Musée du Louvre, Pyramides.*

Nous

After the closure of Paris's most mythical concept store, Colette, in 2017, two of its former employees opened their own boutique on ultraposh Rue Cambon to keep the flame alive. A minimalist setting is the backdrop for a handpicked collection of young, hip streetwear and cool accessories (think sneakers and skateboard decks) that have younger Parisian fashionistas with large bank accounts flipping through the racks regularly. ⊠ *48 rue Cambon, Madeleine* ☎ *01-40-28-40-75* ⊕ *nous.paris* ⊘ *Closed Sun.* Ⓜ *Madeleine.*

W. H. Smith

This bookseller carries a multitude of travel and language books, cookbooks, plus fiction for adults and children. It also has the best selection of foreign magazines and newspapers in Paris (which you're allowed to flip through without interruption—many magazine dealers in France aren't so kind). ⊠ *248 rue de Rivoli, 1er, Louvre* ☎ *01-44-77-88-99* ⊕ *www.whsmith. fr* Ⓜ *Concorde.*

☕ Coffee and Quick Bites

Baguett's Café

$ | International. Conveniently located down the road from the Louvre, this contemporary café serves some of the best breakfast in town. Though its interior is simple (bare stone walls and pale wood furnishings), the menu is anything but: it's packed with Anglo-American breakfast classics with a contemporary twist, accompanied by fresh scones or, true to its name, a baguette. **Known for:** a heaping brunch; "Eggs & Go" eggs Benedict–style sandwich; gluten-free pastries. *Average main: €15* ⊠ *33 rue Richelieu, Palais-Royal* ☎ *09-54-83-04-86* ⊕ *ilovebaguetts. com* Ⓜ *Pyramides.*

Café Kitsuné

$ | Contemporary. The favorite coffee shop of Parisian fashionistas can be found behind this hip streetwear purveyor and electro music label's Palais-Royal outpost. Don't worry if you can't get a table on their prized terrace, overlooking a gorgeous garden—you might prefer to stroll through the park or window shop, coffee or cold-pressed juice in hand. **Known for:** dirty chai latte; trademark fox-shaped cookies; chic address. *Average main: €5* ⊠ *51 Galerie de Montpensier, Palais-Royal* ☎ *01-40-15-62-31* ⊕ *www.kitsune.fr* Ⓜ *Palais Royal–Musée du Louvre, Pyramides.*

★ Café Lai'Tcha

$ | French Fusion. You don't have to break the bank to taste the divine Franco-Chinese creations of Adeline Grattard, the talented chef behind Michelin-starred Yam'Tcha; all you have to do is stop in at her casual eatery, which opened in 2018. Pick up a portion of the regularly changing salads, hot dishes, and small bites to eat at the long bar in the Asian-inspired dining area or across the road in Jardin Nelson-Mandela. **Known for:** Asian tapas; crispy spring rolls with sweet and sour sauce; candied ginger cookies. *Average main: €15* ⊠ *7 rue du Jour, Les Halles* ☎ *01–40–26–05–05* ⊕ *www.yamtcha.com* ⊗ *Closed Sun.* Ⓜ *Châtelet–Les Halles.*

Claus

$$$ | Contemporary. Claus Estermann has redesigned the Parisian breakfast experience by weaving elements of his native Germany, his adopted city, and his experience working in the fashion world into a chic *épicerie du petit déjeuner* (breakfast grocery store) situated between Les Halles and Palais-Royal. Stock up on deluxe breakfast provisions, including fancy mueslis, pastries and jams, or enjoy an ultraposh brunch in their upstairs dining room. **Known for:** apple and almond Bavarian pancakes; inventive pastries like financiers with yuzu; stylish setting with prices to match. *Average main: €25* ⊠ *14 rue Jean-Jacques Rousseau, Palais-Royal* ☎ *01–42–33–55–10* ⊕ *www.clausparis.com* Ⓜ *Louvre–Rivoli, Châtelet–Les Halles.*

La Maison Plisson

$ | Contemporary. Riding on the success of their first restaurant and food shop in the Marais, this much-anticipated offshoot opened in 2018 in the classy Place du Marché St-Honoré. Have lunch outside on the sunny terrace, inside in the airy dining room, or pick up exquisite French produce, meats, and cheeses for a picnic in the nearby Jardin des Tuileries. **Known for:** seasonal dishes; ingredients exclusively from independent local producers; palate-popping fruit desserts. *Average main: €16* ⊠ *35 pl. du Marché St-Honoré, Place Vendôme* ☎ *01–71–18–19–09* Ⓜ *Pyramides, Tuileries.*

★ Maisie Café

$ | Vegetarian. Swap out heavy traditional French fare for a light meal at this excellent vegan café a block north of the Jardin des Tuileries. Their menu is small but packed with healthy snacks and salads that can be sampled in its bright dining room, adorned with pale greens and large leaf prints, or down the street in the Tuileries. **Known for:** quinoa bowls; organic nut shakes and juices; fruit-infused water. *Average main: €12* ⊠ *32 rue du Mont Thabor, Concorde* ☎ *01–40–39–99–16* ⊕ *www.maisiecafe.com* ⊗ *Closed Sun.* Ⓜ *Concorde, Tuileries.*

Marcelle

$ | Contemporary. Managed by three women, this little sister of the small chain of trendy Marcel restaurants features a more health-conscious menu than the other branches in Montmartre and the Canal St-Martin. The stylish and slender venue—spread over three floors and surrounded by the hip boutiques north of Les Halles—paired with its creative salads, seasonal dishes, and light snacks, perfectly embodies the modern *Parisien*. **Known for:** inventive salads; eccentric juice and lemonade combinations; fashionable diners. *Average main: €15 ⊠ 22 rue Montmartre, Les Halles* ☎ *01–40–13–04–04* ⊕ *www.restaurantmarcelle.fr* Ⓜ *Châtelet–Les Halles*.

Télescope

$ | Contemporary. A microscopic, minimalist venue of white walls and exposed wooden beams hides one of the city's most stellar coffee shops. A forerunner of Paris's flourishing coffee scene, Télescope boasts the first brews in the city to be made with the flavor-locking Über Boiler, and a co-owner who gained his know-how at the most buzzworthy roasters in Paris, Brûlerie de Belleville. **Known for:** some of Paris's best filtered coffee; no Wi-Fi (so you can concentrate on your phenomenal joe); ultrahip crowd. *Average main: €4 ⊠ 5 rue Villedo, Palais-Royal* ☉ *Closed Sun.* Ⓜ *Pyramides.*

🍴 Dining

Balagan

$$ | Israeli. Forget the Marais: Paris's most exciting taste of contemporary Israel is found not in its historically Jewish quarter, but at this stylish restaurant near the posh Rue St-Honoré and Place Vendôme. Meaning "joyful bazar," Balagan has a mouthwatering menu composed by some of Jerusalem's hottest chefs and serves dishes from all corners of the Jewish diaspora. **Known for:** sharing plates like Mahluta calamari with eggplant cream; inventive cocktails; lively ambience on weekends. *Average main: €18 ⊠ 9 rue d'Alger, Place Vendôme* ☎ *01–40–20–72–14* ⊕ *www.balagan-paris.com* Ⓜ *Tuileries.*

Baltard au Louvre

$$$ | Contemporary. Les Halles's renewed food scene took a step further in 2018 with the rebirth of this classic bistro, now under the command of rising Belgian chef Ewout Vranckx. The exceptionally creative and sophisticated small plates are stunningly presented in a luminous dining room with windows overlooking the Jardin Nelson-Mandela. **Known for:** Michelin-star quality at bistro prices; value lunch menu; tranquil terrace. *Average main: €30 ⊠ 9 rue Coquillière, Les Halles* ☎ *09–83–32–01–29* ⊕ *www.baltard.com* ☉ *Closed Sun., Aug.* Ⓜ *Châtelet–Les Halles, Louvre–Rivoli.*

Champeaux

$$ | French. Located within the new La Canopée building at Les Halles, Alain Ducasse's modern take on the traditional French brasserie has given new life to what was once the heart of gastronomic Paris. Don't expect to find his signature haute cuisine on the menu, but instead delight in high-quality, lighter versions of French classics served within a vast, light-filled dining room. **Known for:** savory and sweet soufflés; steak tartare; Michelin-starred chef at affordable prices. *Average main: €22* ⊠ *La Canopée, Forum des Halles, Les Halles* ☎ *01-53-45-84-50* ⊕ *www.restaurant-champeaux.com* Ⓜ *Châtelet–Les Halles.*

★ Chez La Vieille

$$ | French. American chef Daniel Rose has reinforced the pillars of French cuisine by reviving this legendary Les Halles bistro, which was managed for more than 30 years by the feisty Adrienne, nicknamed *La Vieille* (the old woman). Rose's team carries on in her footsteps, producing an exquisite menu of French classics from *terrine de canard* (duck pâté in a clay pot) to *tête de veau* (calf's head), reduced to their purest form with the occasional creative zest. **Known for:** acclaimed chef Daniel Rose; classic bistro experience; blanquette de veau (veal ragout). *Average main: €24* ⊠ *1 rue Bailleul, Les Halles* ☎ *01-42-60-15-78* ⊕ *www.chezlavieille.fr* ⊗ *Closed Sun. and Mon., end of July–Aug.* Ⓜ *Châtelet–Les Halles, Louvre–Rivoli.*

★ Ellsworth

$$ | Contemporary. Sample the superb cuisine of one of Paris's first neo-bistros, Verjus, at their more laid-back—and economical—small-plate venue located down the street from their original restaurant (around the corner from the Palais-Royal). Here, originality and finesse are applied to sophisticated seasonal dishes, served in a chic yet sober setting. **Known for:** legendary buttermilk fried chicken; great value

lunch menu; best contemporary cuisine near the Louvre. *Average main: €18* ⊠ *34 rue de Richelieu, Palais-Royal* ☎ *01-42-60-59-66* ⊕ *www.ellsworthparis.com* ⊗ *No dinner Sun., no lunch Mon., closed late July–Aug.* Ⓜ *Palais Royal–Musée du Louvre, Pyramides.*

★ Juvéniles

$$ | Wine Bar. A favorite with the French and the expat crowd, Juvéniles is the ideal kind of neighborhood outpost that mixes great dining with an inspired wine list, all at affordable prices. The lunch menu might start with velvety foie gras *maison* (paired with a crisp Riesling), followed by slow-braised beef with a tangy tarragon-and-dill sauce *ravigote*. **Known for:** prix-fixe lunch that's an outstanding bargain; bottles of wine also available to take home; small space so reserve in advance. *Average main: €21* ⊠ *47 rue de Richelieu, 1er, Louvre* ☎ *01-42-97-46-49* ⊗ *Closed Sun. No lunch Mon.* Ⓜ *Bourse, Pyramides.*

L'Ardoise

$$$ | Bistro. Despite the updated chic decor, this tiny, reliably good bistro has not sacrificed substance to style. This is first-rate dining, and the three-course dinner menu (you can also order à la carte, but it's less of a bargain) tempts with original dishes like mushroom-and-foie-gras ravioli with smoked duck; farmer's pork with porcini mushrooms; and red mullet with creole sauce. Just as enticing are the desserts, such as a superb *feuillantine au citron*—caramelized pastry leaves filled with lemon cream and lemon slices—and a boozy baba au rhum. **Known for:** good-value prix-fixe menus at lunch and dinner; traditional fare with a contemporary twist; noisy crowds. *Average main: €27* ⊠ *28 rue du Mont Thabor, 1er, Louvre* ☎ *01–42–96–28–18* ⊕ *www.lardoise-paris.com* ⊘ *No lunch Sun.* Ⓜ *Concorde.*

Les Fines Gueules

$$ | Bistro. Invest in good ingredients and most of the work is done: that's the principle of this wine bar–bistro that's developed a loyal following. The products are treated simply, often serving high-quality meats and vegetables raw alongside a salad or sautéed potatoes. **Known for:** good selection biodynamic and natural wines; fresh and succulent steak tartare; intimate atmosphere. *Average main: €20* ⊠ *43 rue Croix des Petits Champs, 1er, Louvre* ☎ *01–42–61–35–41* ⊕ *www.lesfinesgueules.fr* Ⓜ *Palais-Royal.*

Lou Lou

$$$ | Modern Italian. The style and elegance of the French Riviera grace the revamped restaurant of the Musée des Arts Décoratifs, overlooking the Jardin des Tuileries. Reinvented in 2016, the glamorous venue features Italian and southern French fusion dishes as beautiful as its fashionable clientele. **Known for:** one of the most coveted terraces in Paris; chic patrons and setting; Fashion Week hangout. *Average main: €30* ⊠ *107 rue de Rivoli, Louvre* ☎ *01–42–60–41–96* ⊕ *loulou-paris.com* Ⓜ *Palais Royal–Musée du Louvre.*

Margús

$ | South American. Colombia meets Paris at this excellent small-plate venue in the Les Halles area set in a gorgeously refurbished classic bistro complete with marble tabletops, a zinc bar, and large antique mirrors. Brothers Juan and Alexandre Quillet named the restaurant after their grandmother, who inspired the creative menu of contemporary South American tapas with a healthy dash of French and international influences. **Known for:** gourmet tacos; craft cocktails; lively vibe on weekends. *Average main: €12* ⊠ *1 rue des Prouvaires, Les Halles* ☎ *09–87–10–42–03* ⊕ *www.margus.fr* ⊘ *Closed Sun. and Mon.* Ⓜ *Châtelet–Les Halles.*

★ Pirouette

$$$ | Modern French. One of the earliest arrivals on the new restaurant scene at Les Halles, Pirouette marvels Parisian palates with its emblematic "bistronomie" cuisine, contemporary takes on traditional French bistro fare. Discreetly tucked away on a pedestrian street a stone's throw from La Canopée, the bright, contemporary space is the ideal backdrop for Pirouette's sensationally inventive and seasonal dishes. **Known for:** cutting-edge cuisine; prix-fixe menus at lunch and dinner; signature gnocchi. *Average main: €30* ⊠ *5 rue Mondétour, Les Halles* ☎ *01–40–26–47–81* ⊕ *www.restaurantpirouette.com* ⊘ *Closed Sun., Aug.* Ⓜ *Châtelet–Les Halles.*

★ Restaurant du Palais-Royal
$$$$ | Bistro. This stylish modern bistro serves stunning gastronomic cuisine to match its gorgeous location under the arcades of the Palais-Royal. Sole, scallops, and risotto—including a dramatic black-squid-ink-and lobster version, or an all-green vegetarian one—are beautifully prepared, but the grilled suckling pig and roasted carrots is also popular with expense-account lunchers. **Known for:** peerless setting in the Palais Royal gardens; outdoor dining in the garden in warm weather; reservations needed well in advance. *Average main: €35* ✉ *Jardins du Palais-Royal, 110 Galerie Valois, 1er, Louvre* ☎ *01–40–20–00–27* 🌐 *www.restaurantdupalaisroyal.com* ⏲ *Closed Sun. and Mon.* Ⓜ *Palais-Royal.*

Zen
$ | Japanese. There's no shortage of Japanese restaurants around the Louvre, but this one is a cut above much of the competition. The menu has something for every taste, from warming ramen soups (part of a €12 lunch menu that includes five pork dumplings) to sushi and sashimi prepared with particular care. **Known for:** quick, good-value lunch; great for vegetarians; friendly, helpful service. *Average main: €17* ✉ *8 rue de l'Echelle, 1er, Louvre* ☎ *01–42–61–93–99* ⏲ *Closed 10 days in mid-Aug.* Ⓜ *Pyramides, Palais-Royal.*

Bars and Nightlife

★ Ballroom du Beef Club
Unmarked black door, basement setting, pressed-tin ceilings, atmospheric lighting—did someone say "speakeasy"? All this and luscious libations draw a sophisticated crowd that appreciates the extra touches that make this cocktail bar a standout. ✉ *58 rue Jean-Jacques Rousseau, 1er, Louvre* ☎ *09–54–37–13–65* Ⓜ *Les Halles, Palais Royal–Musée du Louvre.*

Bar 8
Ever since the monolithic marble bar at the Mandarin Oriental Hotel opened its doors, it has been the "in" game in town. There's an extensive Champagne menu, and the terrace is especially busy during fashion weeks. ✉ *251 rue Saint-Honoré, 1er, Louvre* ☎ *01–70–98–78–88* 🌐 *www.mandarinoriental.com* Ⓜ *Concorde, Tuileries.*

Bar Hemingway
If you're going to treat yourself to a drink at one of the luxury hotel bars in the St-Honoré area, it should be at the legendary bar of the Ritz, famously "liberated" from the Nazis by its namesake Ernest Hemingway. The atmosphere of the historic bar thankfully remained unscathed during the hotel's vast overhaul, reopening in 2016 with its head barman Colin Field back in his usual position mixing impeccable classic cocktails like the Clean Dirty Martini and French 75. ✉ *15 pl. Vendôme, Place Vendôme* ☎ *01–43–16–33–74* 🌐 *www.ritzparis.com* Ⓜ *Opéra.*

Kong

This club is glorious not only for its panoramic skyline views but also for its exquisite manga-inspired decor and kooky, disco-ball-and-kid-sumo-adorned bathrooms. On weekends, top-shelf DJs keep patrons dancing. ⊠ *1 rue du Pont Neuf, 1er, Louvre* ☎ *01-40-39-09-00* ⊕ *www.kong.fr* Ⓜ *Pont Neuf.*

L'Entracte

With roots reaching back to 1614, this old-school watering hole behind the Palais-Royal is still a neighborhood favorite, evident from the festive crowds that overflow from it most nights. French for "intermission," (a name alluding to its location across from the historic Théâtre du Palais-Royal), it's also located next to the Verjus Wine Bar, making it easy for you to hop between old and new Paris. ⊠ *47 rue Montpensier, Palais-Royal* ☎ *01-42-97-57-76* Ⓜ *Palais Royal–Musée du Louvre.*

Le Fumoir

Fashionable neighborhood gallery owners and young professionals meet for late-afternoon wine, early-evening cocktails, or dinner at this oh-so-reliably ultrachic charmer across from the Louvre. It features a superstocked bar in the front, an ample multilingual library in the back, and chessboards for the clientele to use while sipping martinis. ⊠ *6 rue de l'Amiral-Coligny, 1er, Louvre* ☎ *01-42-92-00-24* ⊕ *www. lefumoir.com* Ⓜ *Louvre.*

Le Garde Robe

One of the first bars in Paris to highlight natural wines, Le Garde Robe is still the best bet for an excellent glass near Les Halles. As with most other *bars à vins* (wine bars), you can enjoy your wine with some nibbles, here in the form of more unusual cheeses and artisanal charcuterie. ⊠ *41 rue de l'Arbre Sec, Les Halles* ☎ *01-49-26-90-60* Ⓜ *Châtelet–Les Halles, Louvre–Rivoli.*

Le Nemours

With one of the city's ultimate people-watching terraces, this historic café on beautiful Place Colette has been turning heads itself thanks to a face-lift in 2016 by interior designer Michael Malapert. An Art Deco bar, sea-blue accents, funky decorative plates, and a wallpaper garden draw hip customers inside, and no matter where you sit, the café is a great place for a drink or light meal. ⊠ *2 pl. Colette, Palais-Royal* ☎ *01-42-61-34-14* ⊕ *www. lenemours.paris* Ⓜ *Palais Royal–Musée du Louvre.*

Le Sunset-Sunside

This two-part club hosts French and American jazz musicians: the Sunside upstairs is devoted mostly to acoustic jazz, while the Sunset downstairs features everything from electronic jazz, fusion, and groove to classic and swing. Jam sessions have been known to last well into the wee hours. ⊠ *60 rue des Lombards, 1er, Louvre* ☎ *01-40-26-46-60* ⊕ *www.sunset-sunside.com* Ⓜ *Châtelet–Les Halles.*

Maison Maison

This bar-restaurant is the best spot to enjoy the lively ambience along the western stretch of the Rives de Seine promenade. Order a crisp craft beer, glass of natural wine, or one of their tasty snacking plates, and sit back to admire the view of Pont Neuf, Pont des Arts, and the steady stream of evening strollers. ⊠ *16 quai du Louvre, (the Parc Rives de Seine Promenade), Louvre* ☎ *09–67–82–07–32* Ⓜ *Louvre–Rivoli, Pont Neuf.*

★ **Verjus Wine Bar**

Located on a quiet street behind the Palais Royal gardens, the renowned contemporary restaurant Verjus has an excellent wine bar, where exposed stone walls and a vaulted ceiling create a cozy ambience. Perch yourself on one of their dozen or so metal stools and try natural wines over snacks and cheese from the kitchen upstairs. ⊠ *47 rue Montpensier, Palais-Royal* ☎ *01–42–97–54–40* ⊕ *www.verjusparis.com* ⟳ *Closed weekends* Ⓜ *Palais Royal–Musée du Louvre.*

🎟 **Performing Arts**

★ **Comédie Française**

Founded in 1680, Comédie Française is the most hallowed institution in French theater. It specializes in splendid classical French plays by the likes of Racine, Molière, and Marivaux. Buy tickets at the box office, by telephone, or online. If the theater is sold out, the Salle Richelieu offers steeply discounted last-minute tickets an hour before the performance. ⊠ *Salle Richelieu, Pl. Colette, 1er, Louvre* ☎ *08–25–10–16–80 €0.15 per min* ⊕ *www.comedie-francaise.fr* Ⓜ *Palais-Royal–Musée du Louvre.*

Le Forum des Images

The Forum organizes thematic viewings in five state-of-the-art screening rooms, often presenting discussions with directors or film experts beforehand. Archival films and videos, workshops, and lectures are also on the schedule here. Movies cost €6, but roundtables and discussions are free; you can download the Forum app for smartphones. ⊠ *Forum des Halles, 2 rue du Cinéma, Louvre* ☎ *01–44–76–63–00* ⊕ *www. forumdesimages.fr* Ⓜ *Châtelet–Les Halles (St-Eustache exit).*

3

Sentier and Les Grands Boulevards

LES PUCES

ÉPINETTES

CLIGNAN-COURT

LA CHAPELLE

LA VILLETTE

LES BATIGNOLLES

MONTMARTRE

TERNES

MONCEAU

PIGALLE

CANAL ST-MARTIN

BELLEVILLE

LES GRANDS BOULEVARDS

CHAMPS-ÉLYSÉES

CHAILLOT

SENTIER

PASSY

TROCADÉRO

PALAIS-ROYAL

LES HALLES

LE MARAIS

OBERKAMPF

MÉNILMONTANT

PÈRE-LACHAISE

BOIS DE BOULOGNE

LES INVALIDES

LES ÎLES

BASTILLE

CHARONNE

AUTEUIL

VAUGIRARD

ST-GERMAIN-DES-PRÉS

QUARTIER LATIN

BERCY

BEL-AIR

JAVEL

MONTPARNASSE

ST-LAMBERT

BUTTE-AUX-CAILLES

AUSTERLITZ

SEINE

BOIS DE VINCENNES

MONTROUGE

MAISON BLANCHE

A stroll through the streets of the 2e arrondissement hints at its past as a working-class quartier and Paris's garment district. Today, numerous textile shops still call the district home, and you'll find some of the most famous Parisian shopping centers here. Aside from heavy hitters like Galeries Lafayettes and Au Printemps, the old-world Grands Boulevards boast 20-something passages and galeries (glass-and-iron-covered walkways) that can't be found in most other parts of Paris. More recently, the 2e arrondissement—and Sentier in particular—has evolved into a dynamic neighborhood, its hyper-central location making it a hotbed for Parisian startups and incubators, giving it the nickname "Silicon Sentier." You'll spot the tech crowd and bobos (short for bourgeois-bohème, the French equivalent of "hipster") at the trendy cafés in the area. It's also putting itself on Paris's food and drink map, with countless fast-casual and cocktail establishments choosing to open their doors in the 2e arrondissement in lieu of its popular neighbors.—*by Erin Dahl*

⊙ Sights

Bibliothèque nationale de France Richelieu

Parisian libraries are architectural masterpieces more often than not, but the Richelieu branch may just take the cake. The stunning space, which reopened its doors to the public in 2017 after being closed since 2009 for renovations, has soaring vaulted ceilings and an aura of literary excellence. Fashion fans will recognize the library as the setting for Rhianna's fall 2017 Fenty fashion show. ⊠ *58 rue de Richelieu, Bourse* ☎ *01-53-79-53-79* ⊕ *www. bnf.fr* ☉ *Closed Sun.* Ⓜ *Bourse.*

Ground Effect

Quite literally an underground art gallery, this funky subterranean space exhibits contemporary urban works from both visiting and resident artists. The gallery was founded in 2016 by three partners who work in the worlds of graffiti, fashion, and streetwear, and you'll see influences of each throughout the space. ⊠ *160 rue Montmartre, Grands Boulevards* ☎ *06-87-37-68-30* ⊕ *www.groundeffect.fr* Ⓜ *Grands Boulevards.*

Hôtel Drouot

Hidden away in a small antiques district, not far from the Opéra Garnier, is Paris's central auction house. With everything from old clothes to haute-couture gowns and from tchotchkes to ornate Chinese lacquered boxes, rare books, and wine, Drouot sells it all. Anyone can attend the sales and viewings, which draw a mix of art dealers, ladies who lunch, and art amateurs hoping to discover an unknown masterpiece. Check the website to see what's on the block. Don't miss the small galleries and antiques dealers in the Quartier Drouot, a warren of small streets around the auction house, notably on Rues Rossini and de la Grange-Batelière. ⊠ *9 rue Drouot, Grands Boulevards* ☎ *01–48–00–20–20* ⊕ *www.drouot.com* 🗺 *Free* 🕙 *Closed Sun.* Ⓜ *Richelieu-Drouot.*

★ The Hoxton Paris
The Brits are responsible for one of Sentier's most buzzworthy new hangouts. After the hip London-based boutique hotel brand launched its first Paris location in 2017, it quickly became the HQ for creative *bobos* and expats. Head to Moroccan-inspired Jacques' Bar for a craft cocktail, grab a bite at Rivié brasserie, or see what indie maker is selling their wares in the hotel's pop-up. For nomadic freelancers, this is also a prime spot to get work done. ⊠ *30–32 rue du Sentier, Sentier* ☎ *01–85–65–75–00* ⊕ *thehoxton.com* Ⓜ *Bonne Nouvelle.*

L'Oasis D'Aboukir
An undulating array of more than 200 plant species grace the building facade at this captivating vertical garden on Rue d'Aboukir. Created by botanist Patrick Blanc for Paris Design Week in 2013, the greenery is a welcome burst of vibrancy amid the building's muted Haussmannian neighbors. ⊠ *83 rue d'Aboukir,* *Sentier* ⊕ *www.verticalgardenpatrick-blanc.com/node/4676* Ⓜ *Sentier.*

★ Musée Jacquemart-André
Perhaps the city's best small museum, the opulent Musée Jacquemart-André is home to a huge collection of art and furnishings lovingly assembled in the late 19th century by banking heir Edouard André and his artist wife, Nélie Jacquemart. Their midlife marriage in 1881 raised eyebrows—he was a dashing bachelor and a Protestant, and she, no great beauty, hailed from a modest Catholic family. Still, theirs was a happy union fused by a common passion for art. For six months every year, the couple traveled, most often to Italy, where they hunted down works from the Renaissance, their preferred period. Their collection also includes French painters Fragonard, Jacques-Louis David, and François Boucher, plus Dutch masters Van Dyke and Rembrandt. The Belle Époque mansion itself is a major attraction. The elegant ballroom, equipped with collapsible walls operated by then-state-of-the-art hydraulics, could hold 1,000 guests. The winter garden was a wonder of its day, spilling into the *fumoir,* where André would share cigars with the *grands hommes* (important men) of the day. You can tour the separate bedrooms—his in dusty pink, hers in pale yellow. The former dining room, now an elegant café, features a ceiling by Tiepolo. Don't forget to pick up the free audioguide in English, and do inquire about the current temporary

GRANDS
BOULEVARDS Ⓜ

Rue Bergère

Rue du Faubourg Poissonnière

Rue d'Hauteville

Boulevard Poissonnière

Les
Grands
Boulevards

Rue Montmartre

2e

Rue d'Uzès

BONNE
NOUVELLE Ⓜ

❻ ❼

❽

R. St-Fiacre

Rue du Sentier

R. de la Lune

Squ
Jacq
Bida

❶

❺

R. Poissonnière

R. Beauregard

❷

Rue des Jeûneurs

Sentier

❹

❸

Rue du Croissant

R. St-Joseph

⓭

R. de Mulhouse

Rue de Ciéry

Rue d'Aboukir

BOURSE Ⓜ

R. Notre-Dame des Victoires

Rue Réaumur

⓮ ⓯

❶❻

R. Ste-Fo

Rue P. Lelong

SENTIER Ⓜ

⓱

⓴

R. Dussouds

⓲ ⓳

❿

⓬

R. Montorgueil

Rue de Ciéry

R. St-Sauveur

Sq. Pierre Laz

Rue d'Aboukir

⓫

Rue
Bachaumont
R. Mandar

㉚

㉛

Place des
Victoires

Rue du Louvre

R. Greneta

㉜

R. Hérold

Rue Montmartre

㉗

Passage du
Grand Cerf

㉖

R. Tiquetonne

㉘

㉔

㉕

R. Étienne Marcel

㉙

Rue J.-J. Rousseau

R. du Jour

Place
des Deux
Ecus

Rue de Turbigo

LES HALLES Ⓜ

ETIENNE
MARCEL Ⓜ

exhibition, which is usually top-notch. Plan on a Sunday visit and enjoy the popular brunch (€29.30) in the café from 11 am to 2:30 pm. Reservations are not accepted, so come early or late to avoid waiting in line. ⊠ *158 bd. Haussmann, Grands Boulevards* ☎ *01-45-62-11-59* ⊕ *www.musee-jacquemart-andre. com* 🖅 *From €14* Ⓜ *St-Philippe du Roule, Miromesnil.*

Parc Monceau

This exquisitely landscaped park began in 1778 as the Duc de Chartres's private garden. Though some of the land was sold off under the Second Empire (creating the exclusive real estate that now borders the park), the refined atmosphere and some of the fanciful faux ruins have survived. Immaculately dressed children play under the watchful eye of their nannies, while lovers cuddle on the benches. In 1797 André Garnerin, the world's first-recorded parachutist, staged a landing in the park. The rotunda—known as the Chartres Pavilion—is surely the city's grandest public restroom: it started life as a tollhouse. ⊠ *Entrances on Bd. de Courcelles, Av. Velasquez, Av. Ruysdaël, Av. van Dyck, Grands Boulevards* Ⓜ *Monceau.*

🛍 Shopping

Au Printemps

Encompassing a trio of upscale department stores (Printemps Mode, Printemps Beauté-Maison-Enfant, and Printemps Homme), this vast, venerable retailer has been

GETTING HERE

Paris's arrondissements twirl out from the city center like a snail, so it's no surprise that the 2e is particularly convenient—and accessible. It's within walking distance from the Seine and other major sites, and several major métro lines service the area. To access the Grands Boulevards, take line 8 or line 9 to the eponymous stop. For Sentier, exit at the Sentier stop on line 3. You can also take line 4 to Étienne Marcel or to Châtelet—a major métro hub—which is an eight-minute walk away.

luring shoppers since 1865. Besides the clothes, shoes, housewares, and everything else, there are appealing lunch options here. Two floors of the main building (Printemps Homme) have been completely renovated and are now home to Printemps du Goût, a celebration of French cuisine. If you are a do-it-yourselfer, you can find the best of French foodstuffs on the seventh floor. But if you want to eat in style while taking in spectacular views, either from inside via floor-to-ceiling windows or outside on the wraparound terrace, continue on to the eighth floor, where four noted chefs and food artisans—master cheesemaker Laurent Dubois, chef pâtissier Christophe Michalak, artisanal baker Gontran Cherrier, and master chef Akrame—oversee a gourmet cornucopia. ⊠ *64 bd. Haussmann, Grands Boulevards* ☎ *01-42-82-50-00* ⊕ *www.printemps. com* Ⓜ *Havre–Caumartin, St-Lazare.*

Galeries Lafayette

The stunning Byzantine glass *coupole* (dome) of the city's most famous department store is not to be missed. Amble to the center of the main store, amid the perfumes and cosmetics, and look up. If you're not in the mood for shopping, visit the (free) first-floor Galerie des Galeries, an art gallery devoted to fashion, applied arts, and design; or have lunch at one of the restaurants, including a rooftop bar and restaurant in the main store. On your way down, the top floor of the main store is a good place to pick up interesting Parisian souvenirs. Across the street in Galeries Maison, the excellent Lafayette Gourmet food hall has one of the city's best selections of delicacies. Try a green-tea éclair from Japanese-French baker Sadaharu Aoki—and don't miss the Bordeauxthèque on Galeries Maison's first floor, where €30,000 bottles of wine are on display. ⊠ *35–40 bd. Haussmann, Grands Boulevards* ☎ *01–42–82–34–56* ⊕ *www.galerieslafayette.com* Ⓜ *Chaussée d'Antin–La Fayette, Havre–Caumartin.*

Kiliwatch

This 20-year-old shop is something of an institution on the thrift scene, but it also sells new streetwear— the best of both fashion worlds. Inside the 6,500-square-foot industrial space, you'll find a curated mix of big-name designers, like Isabel Marant, and lesser-known makers for both men and women. Come prepared: the digging here is usually productive. ⊠ *64 rue Tiquetonne, Sentier* ☎ *01–42–21–17–37* ⊕ *kiliwatch.paris* ☉ *Closed Sun.* Ⓜ *Étienne Marcel.*

L'Appartement Sézane

If you want to achieve the classic French girl look, head to Sézane. The cult women's line created by Morgane Sézalory started as an online-only shop but transitioned to a brick-and-mortar showroom, much to the bliss of the brand's loyal followers. As its name suggests, the space feels a bit more like a pied-à-terre than a retail store. Understated clothing lines the walls, while front-and-center seating areas are neatly styled with for-purchase books, candles, and accessories. Aim to visit at off hours or risk waiting to get inside. ⊠ *1 rue St-Fiacre, Grands Boulevards* ⊕ *www.sezane.com* ☉ *Closed Sun.–Tues.* Ⓜ *Grands Boulevards.*

O'Kari

Of Paris's many hammams, this women-only location opened by Algerian-born Karima Lasfar is a favorite. Here, the self-care-focused rituals center on relaxation and purification. Basic entry (€59) will get you access to a eucalyptus steam bath, black-soap body exfoliation, natural soap and shampoo, and a glass of homemade lemonade. If that's not enough, try out one of the intriguing add-ons: wraps, massages, facials, and more. ⊠ *22 rue Dussoubs, Sentier* ☎ *01–42–36–94–66* ⊕ *www.o-kari.com* ☉ *Closed Sun.* Ⓜ *Réaumur–Sébastopol.*

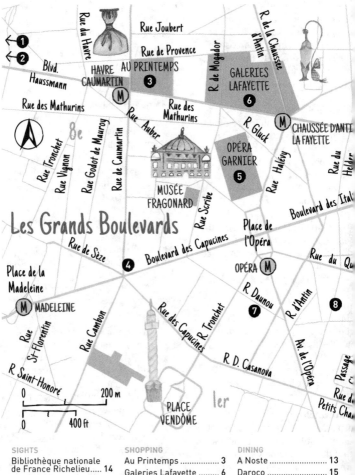

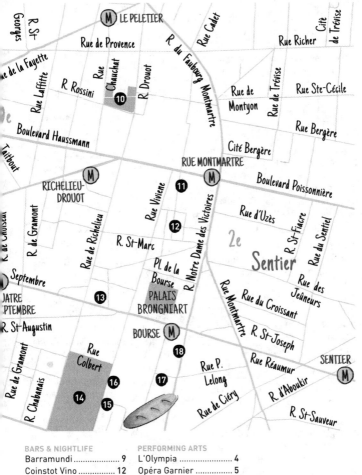

Nose

This concept store offers a personalized service to help you find your ideal fragrance. A bilingual specialist takes you through a seven-step diagnostic to identify your olfactory profile—then the smelling begins. With all there is to choose from, one never leaves unsatisfied. Hard-to-locate lines of luxe body lotions, face serums, bath gels, scented candles, and yummy laundry soaps are also stocked. Fans can keep up with promotions and in-store events via the monthly "noseletter." ⊠ *20 rue Bachaumont, 2e, Louvre* ☎ *01–40–26–46–03* ⊕ *www.nose.fr* Ⓜ *Etienne Marcel.*

Rue Montmartre

For those who consider shopping a sartorial necessity rather than a fun leisure activity, Rue Montmartre is an efficient destination. Located just north of Les Halles, the street has a concentration of go-to mid-range boutiques (think Zadig & Voltaire, Other Stories, Maje, COS, and Des Petits Hauts) that makes it almost impossible to head home empty-handed. ⊠ *Rue Montmartre, Sentier* Ⓜ *Sentier.*

Rue Montorgueil

Situated between Les Halles and Sentier, car-free Rue Montorgueil is a bustling street filled with some of the best food shopping around. Enter beneath the iconic green arch at Rue Réamur and stroll south, picking up whatever vittles most entice. For a full meal, try the snails at L'Escargot Montorgueil, a once-upon-a-time favorite of Marcel Proust and Sarah Bernhardt. ⊠ *Rue Montorgueil, Paris* ✛ *North of Les Halles* Ⓜ *Sentier.*

Tealer

Graphic tees with cheeky references to cannabis culture abound at this streetwear store and "tee-shirt dealer," but even non- *fumeurs* will enjoy the selection of fresh sweatsuits here. The brand also has a hand in the local music scene with their own music label, Tealer Records, and has hosted "Kush Parties" at clubs across the city. ⊠ *11 rue d'Alexandrie, Sentier* ☎ *01–42–36–07–46* ⊕ *tealer.fr* ☾ *Closed Sun.* Ⓜ *Sentier.*

🍵 Coffee and Quick Bites

Boneshaker

$ | **Bakery.** The true sweet tooth must stop for a doughnut at Boneshaker, a family-run confectionary with a signature recipe that blends American and French pastry techniques. Flavors range from classics to the creative. **Known for:** The O.G. (original glazed); Hoppy Days (chocolate-stout doughnut with glaze and toasted marshmallow); locally roasted coffee. *Average main: €4* ⊠ *77 rue d'Aboukir, Sentier* ☎ *01–45–08–84–02* ⊕ *www.boneshakerparis.com* ☾ *Closed Sun.* Ⓜ *Sentier.*

Chez Meunier

$ | **Bakery.** Award-winning boulanger Thierry Meunier serves up his organic baguettes and croissants at around €1 each, proving that the best things can come with small price tags. If you can take the somewhat lax service with a grain of salt, Chez Meunier also offers quick lunchtime bites, like omelets, salads, and sandwiches. **Known for:** classic baguette; éclairs; pain au chocolat. *Average main: €2* ✉ *181 rue St-Denis, Sentier* ☎ *01–42–33–16–12* 🚫 *No credit cards* Ⓜ *Réaumur–Sébastopol.*

⭐ Echo Deli

$ | American. Clean, oh-so-Cali foods are served up in a warm and inviting atmosphere at this new-to-the-scene deli and coffee shop in Sentier. The authentic California kitchen, headed by LA transplant Mailea Weger, makes it possible to feel sunny vibes even in the notoriously gray Parisian weather. **Known for:** almond and coconut lattes; vegan bacon; American-style sandwiches. *Average main: €12* ✉ *95 rue d'Aboukir, Sentier* ☎ *01–40–26–53–21* 🌐 *www.echo-paris.com* 🕙 *Closed Mon. and Tues.* Ⓜ *Bonne Nouvelle, Sentier.*

Frenchie To Go

$ | Modern French. The third outpost in Frenchie's Rue du Nil empire, Frenchie To Go capitalizes on three of the latest Paris food trends: breakfast, fast food, and takeaway. The hot dogs and tasty pastrami (almost unheard of in Paris) are meticulously sourced, as is pretty much everything else—Brittany lobster for the lobster rolls and line-caught hake for the scrumptious fish-and-chips. **Known for:** good value for top-quality ingredients; quick breakfasts or take-out lunches; homemade ginger beer. *Average main: €10* ✉ *9 rue du Nil, 2e, Louvre* ☎ *01–40–39–96–19* 🌐 *www. frenchietogo.com* Ⓜ *Sentier.*

Juicerie

$ | American. Juicerie's cold-pressed, bottled juices are a refreshing way to quench your thirst and your vitamin intake. Ideal for a healthy, grab-and-go snack or lunch, they are offered alongside a selection of house-made bites, including an organic açai bowl and granola. **Known for:** Icy Twist (fennel, kiwi, pineapple, mint, chia seeds); Hit Machine (spinach, pear, cucumber, lemon, matcha tea); Beet It (beet, apple, celery, lemon). *Average main: €7 ⊠ 2 rue de la Michodière, Opéra* ☏ *09–81–87–78–10* ⊕ *www.juicerie.fr* ☉ *Closed Sun.* Ⓜ *Opéra.*

Kodama

$ | Asian. Call it tea infusion or alchemy—either way this new-age teahouse is a hit. Kodama's innovative blends are made with high-quality tea leaves, flowers, and spices, and can be ordered hot or iced. **Known for:** floral green tea; strong black tea; sweet infusions. *Average main: €6 ⊠ 30 rue Tiquetonne, Sentier* ☏ *01–45–08–83–44* ⊕ *www.shop-kodama.com* Ⓜ *Étienne Marcel.*

Mr. Zhao

$ | Asian. The street-food sibling of beloved La Taverne de Zhao near the Canal St-Martin, Mr. Zhao is a must for Xi'an-inspired dishes. Much like the original, this quick-eats outpost serves up its Chinese specialties with a healthy dose of love. **Known for:** spicy biang biang noodles; stewed pork mo sandwiches; Chinese cookies. *Average main: €11 ⊠ 37 rue des Jeûneurs, Grands Boulevards* ☏ *01–73–74–94–05* ⊕ *mrzhao.fr* ☉ *Closed Sun.* Ⓜ *Grands Boulevards.*

Pizza Rossi

$ | Pizza. This Italian joint may get less attention than some others in the neighborhood, such as Big Mamma's Popolare (where a wait is near guaranteed), but it's no reflection of the food. The pies here are light, authentic, and prepared with care by an alum of Naples's pizzaiolo school who puts tradition—and Italian ingredients—in the spotlight. **Known for:** Neapolitan pizza; tiramisu; eat-in and takeaway. *Average main: €10 ⊠ 24 rue Blondel, Sentier* ☏ *09–53–81–16–70* ☉ *Closed Sun.* Ⓜ *Strasbourg–St-Denis.*

Stohrer

$ | Bakery. Originally opened in 1730 by King Louis XV's celebrated pastry chef, Nicolas Stohrer, this is Paris's oldest pâtisserie. One can't leave without a proper sampling—even Queen Elizabeth II has come to try the lauded treats here. **Known for:** baba au rhum, a pastry invented by Stohrer; éclairs; the St-Honoré (an elaborate cake made of cream puffs). *Average main: €5 ⊠ 51 rue Montorgueil, Sentier* ☏ *01–42–33–38–20* ⊕ *stohrer.fr* Ⓜ *Étienne Marcel.*

Stoney Clove Bakery

$ | Bakery. Thanks to two nostalgic U.S. natives, you can grab authentic American-style desserts in the French capital. Opened in spring 2017, the bakery serves up an array of pies, cookies, and cakes (the real, multilayered, frosted deal you usually find across the pond, of course). **Known for:** warm service; chocolate chip cookies; apple pie. *Average main: €7 ⊠ 71 rue Greneta, Sentier* ☏ *09–51–96–89–85* ⊕ *www.stoneyclovebakery.com* ☉ *Closed Mon.* Ⓜ *Sentier.*

PARISIAN PASSAGEWAYS

You can't visit this neighborhood without seeing at least one 19th-century passage couvert or galerie, iron-and-glass-covered walkways. They date back to the 18th century, when construction (and the presence of private investors) were booming. Today, these gems house various boutiques, businesses, and restaurants.

Passage du Grand-Cerf. If you only see one passage in Paris, make it this one. Built in 1825, it boasts one of the highest glass ceilings of the Parisian passages and stunning wrought-iron details. To reach it, take the métro line 4 to Étienne Marcel. If hunger strikes during your visit, head to Le Pas Sage, a cute bistro (its name a play on words) that's housed inside the passage. Parallel to Rue Tiquetonne between Rue St-Denis and Place Goldoni.

Galerie Vivienne. Perhaps thanks to its proximity to Palais-Royal, this galerie doesn't lack in elegant design details. The space dates back to 1823 and is markedly well-preserved. To reach this galerie, take métro line 3 to Bourse. Get a taste of old-world charm at Bistrot Vivienne or Librairie Jousseaume bookshop, and don't forget to pick up a bottle of wine from Les Caves Legrand. Rue Vivienne between Boulevard Haussmann and Rue Réamur.

Passage des Panoramas. This passage is one of Paris's oldest, constructed in 1799. To reach it, take métro line 8 or 9 to Grands Boulevards. The passage is a strong pick for vintage stamp lovers as well as foodies, who will enjoy restaurants like Racines or Coinstot Vino, a must for natural-wine lovers. Between Boulevard Montmartre and Rue St-Marc.

🍴 Dining

A Noste

$$$$ | French. In Gascon, A Noste means "at home"—precisely the feeling former *Top Chef* contestant Julien Duboué aims to serve up at his restaurant, where the food is inspired by his home region of Gascony, in southwestern France. On the ground floor, a tapas restaurant serves drool-worthy small plates, such as charcuterie or corn *fougasse* (bread from Provence similar to focaccia) with sheep's cheese and smoked duck breast. **Known for:** sharing plates; €60 tasting menu; Sichuan-style pig ears with spaetzle. *Average main:* €60 ✉ 6 rue du 4 Septembre, Bourse ☎ 01-47-03-91-91 ⊕ www.a-noste. com Ⓜ Bourse.

Chez Ann

$ | Chinese. Just over the border into the 10e arrondissement, Chez Ann is *the* place to go for dim sum. The casual Chinese eatery places a premium on handmade food, with dumpling dough and fillings made daily. **Known for:** steamed dumplings; friendly service; vegan and gluten-free options. *Average main:* €15 ✉ 29 rue de l'Échiquier, Grands Boulevards ☎ 09-83-34-27-68 ⊕ echiquier.chezann.fr ⊙ Closed Sun. Ⓜ Bonne Nouvelle.

Daroco

$$ | **Italian.** Parisians are on a pizza kick, and Daroco is one of the most Instagram-worthy additions to the scene. The plant-filled oasis serves up a selection of aperitivi and antipasti to start—such as swordfish carpaccio with rhubarb and toasted almond—and a solid mix of pastas, pizzas, mains, and desserts. **Known for:** design-forward decor; former Jean Paul Gaultier atelier; Danico cocktail bar. *Average main: €18* ✉ *6 rue Vivienne, Sentier* ☎ *01–42–21–93–71* ⊕ *www.daroco.fr* Ⓜ *Bourse.*

Foodi Jia-Ba-Buay

$ | **Asian.** Taiwanese chef Virginia Chuang started sharing her native culinary traditions with the people of Paris in 2009 by offering regular Asian cooking classes at Foodi Jia-Ba-Buay. She has since opened a brick-and-mortar restaurant, ideal for those less interested in learning to make the bentos and dumplings, and more into eating them. **Known for:** authentic Taiwanese food; cooking classes; bento boxes. *Average main: €15* ✉ *2 rue du Nil, Sentier* ☎ *01–45–08–48–28* ⊕ *www.foodi-jia-ba-buay.fr* Ⓜ *Sentier.*

★ Frenchie

$$$$ | **Bistro.** A brick-and-stone-walled bistro on a pedestrian street near Rue Montorgueil, Frenchie has quickly became one of the most packed bistros in town, with tables booked months in advance, despite two seatings each evening. This success is due to the good-value, five-course dinner menu (prix fixe only); boldly flavored dishes such as calamari gazpacho with squash blossoms, and melt-in-the-mouth braised lamb with roasted eggplant and spinach are excellent options. **Known for:** casual laid-back atmosphere that belies the ultrasophisticated dishes; extensive and original wine list; graciously accommodating to vegetarians. *Average main: €34* ✉ *5 rue du Nil, 2e, Grands Boulevards* ☎ *01–40–39–96–19* ⊕ *www.frenchie-restaurant.com* ⊘ *Closed weekends, 2 wks in Aug., and 10 days at Christmas. No lunch Mon.–Wed.* Ⓜ *Sentier.*

La Bourse et La Vie

$$$$ | **Bistro.** Daniel Rose's bistro is his love letter to French culinary culture and tradition. While it may be pricey, the food here delivers: yes, you'll find classics like *entrecôte* and *pot au feu*, but the beef is 30-day matured Simmental and the pot au feu a succulent veal stew with a little added bonus—brains. **Known for:** attentive service; French classics; wine list. *Average main: €34* ✉ *12 rue Vivienne, Bourse* ☎ *01–42–60–08–83* ⊕ *www.labourselavie.com* ⊘ *Closed weekends* Ⓜ *Bourse.*

Liza

$$$$ | **Lebanese.** For an authentic taste of Lebanon without any kitsch, head to Liza. The restaurant is a Parisian version of the original location in Beirut, serving healthy, elevated renditions of Lebanese comfort food all done to perfection. **Known for:** mezze (Middle Eastern tapas); weekend brunch; beautiful, bright interior. *Average main: €38* ✉ *14 rue de la Banque, Bourse* ☎ *01–55–35–00–66* ⊕ *www.restaurant-liza.com* ⊘ *No dinner Sun.* Ⓜ *Bourse.*

Racines

$$$ | French Fusion. Located in the illustrious Passage des Panoramas, Racines has a storied history itself, with its kitchen formerly run by some of the greats. Today, celebrated Italian chef Simone Tondo brings his taste for fresh dishes to the "Bistrosteria," so named for its effortless blend of Italian and international cuisines. **Known for:** fresh pasta; intimate ambience; wine list. *Average main: €25 ⊠ 8 passage des Panoramas, Grands Boulevards ☎ 01-40-13-06-41 ⊕ www.racinesparis.com ☉ Closed weekends* Ⓜ *Grands Boulevards.*

★ Rrraw

$ | French. Just when Paris thought its already phenomenal chocolate scene couldn't get any better, chocolatier Frédéric Marr opened this chic chocolate factory and boutique. Now the words "healthy" and "chocolate" appear together in the organic, nondairy, vegan (and yes, tasty) chocolates made here from unheated raw beans in order to preserve all the nutrients, subtle flavors, and (minimal) natural sugars. **Known for:** amazing chocolate you can watch be made on the premises; vegan, gluten-free, organic, and low-sugar products; delicious hot chocolate. *Average main: €6 ⊠ 8 rue de Mulhouse , 2e, Grands Boulevards ☎ 01-45-08-84-04 ⊕ www.rrraw.fr ☉ Closed Sun. and Mon.* Ⓜ *Bonnes Nouvelle.*

★ Saturne

$$$$ | French Fusion. The minimal clay-color interior of this beloved neo-bistro, named for the Roman god of winemakers, says a lot about its ethos: quality, simplicity, and responsible agriculture. Come here to treat yourself to an elevated, modern French lunch or dinner with a Scandinavian twist. **Known for:** one Michelin star; tasting menu; sustainable sourcing. *Average main: €85 ⊠ 17 rue Notre-Dame des Victoires, Sentier ☎ 01-42-60-31-90 ⊕ www.saturne-paris.fr ☉ Closed weekends* Ⓜ *Bourse.*

🍸 Bars and Nightlife

Barramundi

The city's nouveau-riche chill to electro-lounge tunes and world music here, drinking in Barramundi's cool golden ambience as they sip cold tropical drinks at the long copper bar. *⊠ 3 rue Taitbout, 9e, Grands Boulevards ☎ 01-47-70-21-21 ⊕ www.barramundi.fr* Ⓜ *Richelieu–Drouot.*

Coinstot Vino

Natural wine lovers flock to the Passage des Panoramas for a sip from one of Coinstot Vino's bottles. There's no menu here. Simply put your trust in the knowledgeable staff and settle in. For those with an appetite, Bordier cheeses, Conquet charcuterie, knife-cut tartare, and a selection of desserts are also available. *⊠ 26 Passage des Panoramas, Grands Boulevards ☎ 01-44-82-08-54 ⊕ lecoinstotvino.com* Ⓜ *Grands Boulevards.*

★ Delaville Café

With its huge, heated sidewalk terrace, Belle Époque mosaic-tile bar, graffitied walls, and swishy lounge, Delaville Café boasts a funky ambience. Hot Paris DJs ignite the scene Thursday to Saturday, so arrive early on weekends if you want a seat. ⊠ *34 bd. Bonne Nouvelle, 10e, Grands Boulevards* ☎ *01–48–24–48–09* ⊕ *delavillecafe.com* Ⓜ *Bonne Nouvelle, Grands Boulevards.*

★ Experimental Cocktail Club

Fashioned as a speakeasy on a tiny brick-paved street, the Experimental Cocktail Club seems like it should be lighted by gas lamps. The show is all about the *alcool*; colorful, innovative cocktails like the Lemon Drop are mixed with aplomb by friendly (and attractive) bartenders. By 11 pm it's packed with a diverse mix of locals, professionals, and fashionistas, who occasionally dress up like characters from a Toulouse-Lautrec painting on special costume nights. ⊠ *37 rue Saint-Sauveur, 2e, Louvre* ☎ *01–45–08–88–09* Ⓜ *Réaumur–Sébastopol.*

Golden Promise

Grab one of the 20-something seats downstairs at this dimly lit whiskey speakeasy, get comfortable, and get to tasting. Scotches, Japanese whiskies, pure malts, and peaty cocktails curated by the experts at La Maison du Whisky make for an unforgettable experience from first to last sip. Head through the unmarked door to the left of the bar and check out their impressive tasting rooms.

Even farther back, personal lockers and private tastings are available to patrons who purchase a rare bottle. ⊠ *11 rue Tiquetonne, Sentier* ☎ *09–67–61–97–03* ⊕ *www.golden-promise.fr* Ⓜ *Étienne Marcel.*

★ Harry's New York Bar

No self-respecting cocktail connoisseur can leave Paris without paying a visit to Harry's New York Bar. Dating back more than a century, this jazzy cocktail haunt was opened by a New Yorker looking to escape the looming Prohibition period. Fortunately, Paris was primed for a place like Harry's. The bar has since been a haven for across-the-pond expats looking for a dose of home. The Bloody Mary was created here in 1920; Gershwin composed *An American in Paris* on the bar's piano; Hemingway and Coco Chanel were known to drop by. The drinks aren't cheap (cocktails start at €12), but it's a small price to share in this storied history. ⊠ *5 rue Daunou, Grands Boulevards* ☎ *01–42–61–71–14* Ⓜ *Opéra.*

Hero

This denlike restaurant and bar would as easily feel at home on a side street in Seoul as it does along the strip-club-lined Rue St-Denis. Old school French hip-hop and K-pop anthems stream through the two-story space, with the sultry ground floor serving as a cocktail bar. Don't leave without sampling a few of the Korean-influenced cocktails like the frozen Makolada (an Asian version of the classic piña colada made with *makgeolli*, a lightly sparkling rice wine), prepped with the know-how of the same team behind Paris institutions like Candelaria and Mary Céleste. ✉ 289 rue St-Denis, Sentier ☎ 01-42-33-38-01 ⊕ www.quixotic-projects.com/venue/hero Ⓜ Strasbourg-St-Denis.

Hoppy Corner

When in Sentier, beer fans should head to Hoppy Corner, evidence that something other than wine has started to claim its place on French tables. The selection of craft tap brews go for €5–€8, but the pub also has a vast selection of original bottled creations such as coffee-flavored Breakfast Stout by Siren Craft Brew and Brewdog Red Ale. ✉ 34 rue des Petits Carreaux, Sentier ☎ 09-83-06-90-39 Ⓜ Sentier.

Jefrey's

A custom-DJ'd music track, enticing love seats, and inventive cocktails make this an easy choice for an intimate evening in sophisticated surroundings. Need further incentive to return? Jefrey's lets you keep your bottle stored on the shelf, with your name on it, for next time. ✉ 14 rue Saint-Sauveur, 2e, Louvre ☎ 01-42-33-60-77 ⊕ www.jefreys.fr Ⓜ Étienne Marcel.

Le Rex

Open Wednesday through Sunday, this temple of techno and house is popular with students. One of France's most famous DJs, Laurent Garnier, is sometimes at the turntables. ✉ 5 bd. Poissonnière, 2e, Grands Boulevards ☎ 01-42-36-10-96 ⊕ rexclub.com Ⓜ Grands Boulevards.

Mabel

Rum and grilled cheese: that's the surprising yet winning combination you'll find at this bar. And yes, after a lively sampling from the impressive list of more than 150 tasting rums and innovative craft cocktails, the just-like-mom-makes sandwiches are every bit as appetizing as you'd imagine. ✉ 58 rue d'Aboukir, Sentier ☎ 01-42-33-24-33 ⊕ www.mabelparis.com Ⓜ Sentier.

Silencio

David Lynch named his nightclub after a reference in his Oscar-nominated hit, *Mulholland Drive*. Silencio, which hosts concerts, films, and other performances, is open only to members and their guests until midnight; after that everyone is allowed. Guest DJs spin until 4 am Tuesday through Thursday, and until 6 am on Friday and Saturday. ✉ 142 rue Montmartre, 2e, Grands Boulevards ☎ 01-40-13-12-33 ⊕ www.silencio-club.com Ⓜ Bourse.

🎫 Performing Arts

★ Le Grand Rex

Since it opened in 1932, the Grand Rex—a designated historic landmark—has been Europe's largest cinema, with 2,800 seats in its main auditorium and Paris's largest screen. The cinema's history is almost as colorful as its superb Art Deco architecture, considered some of the finest in the city. The Rex shows a large roster of international films, many in English, screened in either the original language

or subtitled or dubbed in French.
✉ *1 bd. Poissonnière, 2e, Grands Boulevards* ☎ *01–45–08–93–89* ⊕ *www.legrandrex.com* Ⓜ *Bonne Nouvelle, Grands Boulevards.*

★ L'Olympia

Paris's legendary music hall hosts an eclectic roster of performances that cover such far-flung genres as gospel, jazz, French *chanson*, and rock. Edith Piaf rose to fame after a series of Olympia concerts and Jeff Buckley's famous *Live at the Olympia* was recorded here. Now everyone from Leonard Cohen to Lady Gaga has been in on the action. ✉ *28 bd. des Capucines, 9e, Grands Boulevards* ☎ *08–92–68– 33–68 €0.34 per min* ⊕ *en.olympia- hall.com* Ⓜ *Madeleine, Opéra.*

★ Opéra Garnier

The magnificent, magical former haunt of the Phantom of the Opera, painter Edgar Degas, and any number of legendary opera stars still hosts performances of the Opéra de Paris, along with a fuller calendar of dance performances (the theater is the official home of the Ballet de l'Opéra National de Paris). The grandest opera productions are usually mounted at the Opéra Bastille, whereas the Garnier now presents smaller- scale works such as Mozart's *La Clemenza di Tito* and *Così Fan Tutte.* Tickets generally go on sale at the box office a month before any given show, earlier by phone and online; you must appear in person to buy the cheapest tickets. Last- minute returned or unsold tickets, if available, are offered an hour prior to a performance. The box office is open Monday to Saturday 11:30–6:30 and one hour before curtain; however, you should get in line up to two hours in advance. You can also check the website at noon on certain Wednesdays for flash sales of sold-out shows. Venue visits (€12) and guided tours in English (€15.50) are available and can be reserved online; check the website for details. ✉ *Pl. de l'Opéra, 9e, Grands Boulevards* ☎ *08–92–89–90–90 €0.34 per min, 01–71–25–24–23 from outside France* ⊕ *www.operadeparis.fr* Ⓜ *Opéra.*

GO FOR

Art Galleries
and Museums

Great
Restaurants

Boutiques

LES
PUCES

ÉPINETTES   CLIGNAN-
COURT   LA   LA VILLETTE
LES   CHAPELLE
BATIGNOLLES   MONTMARTRE

TERNES   MONCEAU   PIGALLE
LES GRANDS   CANAL   BELLEVILLE
BOULEVARDS   SENTIER   ST-MARTIN
CHAILLOT   CHAMPS-
ÉLYSÉES
PASSY   TROCADÉRO   PALAIS-   LES   OBERKAMPF   MÉNILMONTANT
ROYAL   HALLES   PÈRE-
BOIS DE   LES   LE   LACHAISE
BOULOGNE   INVALIDES   MARAIS
LES ÎLES
ST-GERMAIN-   BASTILLE   CHARONNE
VAUGIRARD   DES-PRÉS
QUARTIER   BEL-AIR
JAVEL   MONTPARNASSE   LATIN   BERCY
ST-LAMBERT   BUTTE-AUX-   BOIS DE
CAILLES   AUSTERLITZ   VINCENNES
MONTROUGE   MAISON
BLANCHE

Nestled alongside the Right Bank of the Seine in the 3e and 4e arrondissements, the Marais neighborhood has experienced a meteoric rise in popularity over the past few years. The neighborhood's name translates literally to "the swamp" (referring to its marshy appearance when the city was founded), but if that name still fits, the Marais is the most architecturally and culturally rich swamp out there. With its slender cobblestone streets and picturesque courtyards, it's no surprise the traditionally Jewish and gay quartier has become prime real estate for both locals and visitors. It has also become a haven for the city's creative and culinary sets, with myriad independent galleries, a growing number of trendy eateries, and some of the more interesting cocktail options in Paris. You could spend days covering the whole neighborhood, so give yourself ample time to explore the effortlessly hip art exhibitions, bars, and boutiques that line its streets.—*by Erin Dahl*

◉ Sights

★ Centre Pompidou

Love it or hate it, the Pompidou is certainly a unique-looking building. Most Parisians have warmed to the industrial, Lego-like exterior that caused a scandal when it opened in 1977. Named after French president Georges Pompidou (1911–74), it was designed by then-unknowns Renzo Piano and Richard Rogers. The architects' claim to fame was putting the building's guts on the outside and color-coding them: water pipes are green, air ducts are blue, electrics are yellow, and things like elevators and escalators are red. Art from the 20th century to the present day is what you can find inside.

The Musée National d'Art Moderne (Modern Art Museum, entrance on Level 4) occupies the top two levels. Level 5 is devoted to modern art from 1905 to 1960, including major works by Matisse, Modigliani, Marcel Duchamp, and Picasso; Level 4 is dedicated to contemporary art from the '60s on, including video installations. The Galerie d'Enfants (Children's Gallery) on the mezzanine level has interactive exhibits designed to keep the kids busy. Outside, next to the museum's sloping plaza—where throngs of teenagers hang out (and where there's free Wi-Fi)—is the Atelier Brancusi. This small, airy museum contains four rooms reconstituting Brancusi's Montparnasse studios with works from all periods of his career. On the opposite side, in Place Igor-Stravinsky, is the Stravinsky fountain, which has

16 gyrating mechanical figures in primary colors, including a giant pair of ruby red lips. On the opposite side of Rue Rambuteau, on the wall at the corner of Rue Clairvaux and Passage Brantôme, is the appealingly bizarre mechanical brass-and-steel clock, *Le Défenseur du Temps*.

The Pompidou's permanent collection takes up a relatively small amount of the space when you consider this massive building's other features: temporary exhibition galleries, with a special wing for design and architecture; a highly regarded free reference library (there's often a queue of university students on Rue Renard waiting to get in); and the basement, which includes two cinemas, a theater, a dance space, and a small, free exhibition space.

On your way up the escalator, you'll have spectacular views of Paris, ranging from Tour Montparnasse, to the left, around to the hilltop Sacré-Coeur on the right. The rooftop restaurant, Georges, is a romantic spot for dinner. Be sure to reserve a table near the window. ⊠ *Pl. Georges-Pompidou, Marais Quarter* ☎ *01–44–78–12–33* ⊕ *www.centre-pompidou.fr* 🎟 *Center access free, Atelier Brancusi free, museum and exhibits €14 (free 1st Sun. of month)* 🕓 *Closed Tues.* Ⓜ *Rambuteau.*

Galerie Thaddaeus Ropac

Works from 60 contemporary, international artists are on display at this art gallery. Ropac's primary space is located in the Marais, but the network extends further, with locations in Pantin (just outside of Paris), Salzburg, and London. ⊠ *7 rue Debelleyme, Marais Quarter* ☎ *01–42–72–99–00* ⊕ *ropac.net* Ⓜ *St-Sébastien–Froissart.*

Hôtel de Ville

Overlooking the Seine, City Hall contains the residence and offices of the mayor. Reconstructed in 1873 after an attack by rioting crowds, it is one of Paris's most stunning buildings, made all the more dramatic by elaborate nighttime lighting. The adjoining public library stages frequent free exhibits celebrating famous photographers like Doisneau or Atget and their notable subjects, often the city herself (the entrance is on the side across from the department store BHV). Alas, the impressive interior of the main administrative building, with its lavish reception halls and staircases, is only open for independent visits during Patrimony Weekend in September. If your French is good, however, free guided tours are given biweekly in summer, weekly in other seasons: call two months ahead for further information and reservations. The grand public square out front is always lively, playing host to events and temporary exhibitions. There's a carousel and a beach volleyball court (or similar) in summer, and an ice-skating rink (with skate rental available) in winter. ⊠ *Pl. de l'Hôtel-de-Ville, Marais Quarter* ☎ *01–42–76–43–43 for tours* ⊕ *www. paris.fr* 🎟 *Free* 🕓 *Closed weekends* ☞ *Access for visits at 29 rue de Rivoli* Ⓜ *Hôtel de Ville.*

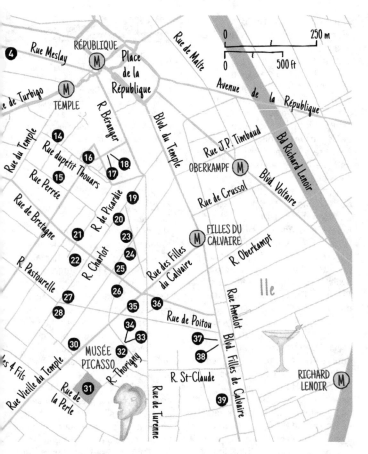

Kitchen	12	Carbon	28	Les Bains	5
Loustic	11	Elmer	3	Little Red Door	20
Partisan Café	7	Mr.T.	25	Max y Jeremy	18
Season	16	**BARS & NIGHTLIFE**		Tango	13
DINING		Andy Wahloo	8	**PERFORMING ARTS**	
The Beast	4	Candelaria	24	La Gaîté Lyrique	1
Biglove Caffé	26	Grazie	39		
Breizh Café	30	Le Barav	17		
CAM	9	Le Mary Celeste	36		

Maison de Victor Hugo

France's most famous scribe lived in this house on the southeast corner of Place des Vosges between 1832 and 1848. It's now a museum dedicated to the multitalented author. In Hugo's apartment on the second floor, you can see the tall desk, next to the short bed, where he began writing his masterwork *Les Misérables* (as always, standing up). There are manuscripts and early editions of the novel on display, as well as others such as *Notre-Dame de Paris,* known to English readers as *The Hunchback of Notre-Dame.* You can see illustrations of Hugo's writings, including Bayard's rendering of the impish Cosette holding her giant broom (which has graced countless *Les Miz* T-shirts). The collection includes many of Hugo's own, sometimes macabre, ink drawings (he was a fine artist) and furniture from several of his homes. Particularly impressive is the room of carved and painted Chinese-style wooden panels that Hugo designed for the house of his mistress, Juliet Drouet, on the island of Guernsey, when he was exiled there for agitating against Napoléon III. Try to spot the intertwined Vs and Js (hint: look for the angel's trumpet in the left corner). The first floor is dedicated to temporary exhibitions that often have modern ties to Hugo's work. ⊠ *6 pl. des Vosges, Marais Quarter* ☎ *01–42–72–10–16* ⊕ *www.maisons-victorhugo.paris.fr* ⊠ *Free; from €5 for temporary exhibitions* ☉ *Closed Mon.* Ⓜ *St-Paul, Bastille.*

GETTING HERE

The neighborhood is very walkable. Start by visiting the Centre Pompidou (off Rambuteau on métro line 11) and walk along Rue Rambuteau until it becomes Rue des Francs-Bourgeois, which will take you all the way to Place des Vosges. Another option is to start centrally; take line 1, which runs along the southern border of the Marais, to St-Paul or to Hôtel de Ville.

★ Maison Européenne de la Photographie *(Center for European Photography)*

Much of the credit for the city's ascendancy as a hub of international photography goes to Maison Européenne de la Photographie (MEP) and its former director, Jean-Luc Monterosso, who also founded Paris's hugely successful Mois de la Photo festival (a biennial event held in April of odd-numbered years). MEP hosts up to four simultaneous exhibitions, changing about every three months. Shows feature an international crop of photographers and video artists. Works by superstar Annie Leibovitz or designer-photographer Karl Lagerfeld may overlap with a collection of self-portraits by an up-and-coming artist. MEP often stages retrospectives of the classics (by Doisneau, Cartier-Bresson, Man Ray, and others) from its vast private collection. Programs are available in English, and English-language tours are sometimes given; check the website for details. ⊠ *5/7 rue de Fourcy, Marais Quarter* ☎ *01–44–*

*78–75–00 ⊕ www.mep-fr.org ⛟ €9
⊘ Closed Mon. and Tues., between
exhibitions Ⓜ St-Paul.*

Marché des Enfants Rouges

This historic covered market is the
oldest in Paris, taking its name from
a nearby orphanage where children
wore red as a symbol of Christian
charity. With food from around
the globe—Creole stuffed crab,
Japanese bento, Lebanese mezzes,
Moroccan tajine, you name it—it's
the perfect stop for an on-the-go
bite in the Marais. ⊠ *39 rue de
Bretagne, Marais Quarter ⊘ Closed
Mon. Ⓜ Filles du Calvaire.*

Mémorial de la Shoah *(Memorial to the Holocaust)*

The first installation in this compelling memorial and museum is the
deeply moving Wall of Names, tall
plinths honoring the 76,000 French
Jews deported from France to Nazi
concentration camps, of whom only
2,500 survived. Opened in 2005, the
center has an archive on the victims,
a library, and a gallery hosting
temporary exhibitions. The permanent collection includes riveting
artifacts and photographs from the
camps, along with video testimony
from survivors. The children's
memorial is particularly poignant
and not for the faint of heart—
scores of back-lighted photographs
show the faces of many of the
11,000 murdered French children.
The crypt, a giant black marble Star
of David, contains ashes recovered
from the camps and the Warsaw
ghetto. You can see the orderly
drawers containing small files on
Jews kept by the French police.

(France only officially acknowledged
the Vichy government's role in
1995.) The history of anti-Semitic
persecution in the world is revisited
as well as the rebounding state of
Jewry today. There is a free guided
tour in English the second Sunday of
every month at 3. ⊠ *17 rue Geoffroy
l'Asnier, Marais Quarter ☎ 01-42-77-
44-72 ⊕ www.memorialdelashoah.org
⛟ Free ⊘ Closed Sat. Ⓜ Pont Marie,
St-Paul.*

Musée d'Art et d'Histoire du Judaïsme

This excellent museum traces the
tempestuous history of French
and European Jews through art
and history. Housed in the refined
17th-century Hôtel St-Aignan,
exhibits have good explanatory
texts in English, but the free
English audioguide adds another
layer of insight; guided tours
in English are also available on
request (€4 extra). Highlights
include 13th-century tombstones
excavated in Paris; a wooden model
of a destroyed Eastern European
synagogue; a roomful of early
paintings by Marc Chagall; and
Christian Boltanski's stark, two-
part tribute to Shoah (Holocaust)
victims in the form of plaques on
an outer wall naming the (mainly
Jewish) inhabitants of the Hôtel
St-Aignan in 1939, and canvas
hangings with the personal data
of the 13 residents who were
deported and died in concentration
camps. The rear-facing windows
offer a view of the Jardin Anne
Frank. To visit it, use the entrance
on Impasse Berthaud, off Rue

Beaubourg, just north of Rue Rambuteau. ✉ *71 rue du Temple, Marais Quarter* ☎ *01-53-01-86-60* ⊕ *www.mahj.org* 🖅 *€10 with temporary exhibitions* ⊘ *Closed Mon.* Ⓜ *Rambuteau, Hôtel de Ville.*

Musée de la Chasse et de la Nature

Mark this down as one of Paris's most bizarre—and fascinating— collections. The museum, housed in the gorgeous 17th-century Hôtel de Guénégaud, features lavishly appointed rooms stocked with animal- and hunt-themed art by the likes of Rubens and Gentileschi, as well as antique weaponry and taxidermy animals. In a tribute to Art Nouveau, the decor incorporates chandeliers and railings curled like antlers. Older kids will appreciate the jaw-dropping Trophy Room's impressive menagerie of beasts, not to mention the huge polar bear stationed outside. There is a lovely multimedia exhibit on the myth of the unicorn, as well as an interactive display of bird calls. Temporary exhibits and silent auctions take place on the first floor. ✉ *62 rue des Archives, Marais Quarter* ☎ *01-53-01-92-40* ⊕ *www.chassenature.org* 🖅 *€8* ⊘ *Closed Mon.* Ⓜ *Rambuteau.*

Musée des Arts et Métiers

Science buffs should not miss this cavernous museum, Europe's oldest dedicated to invention and technology. It's a treasure trove of wonkiness with 80,000 instruments, machines, and gadgets— including 16th-century astrolabes, Pascal's first mechanical calculator, and film-camera prototypes by the Frères Lumière. You can watch video simulations of ground-breaking architectural achievements, like the cast-iron dome, or see how Jacquard's mechanical loom revolutionized clothmaking. Kids will love the flying machines (among them the first plane to cross the English Channel), and the impressive display of old automobiles in the high-ceilinged chapel of St-Martin-des-Champs. Also in the chapel is a copy of Foucault's Pendulum, which proved to the world in 1851 that the Earth rotated (demonstrations are staged daily at noon and 5). The building, erected between the 11th and 13th centuries, was a church and priory. It was confiscated during the Revolution, and, after incarnations as a school and a weapons factory, became a museum in 1799. Most displays have information in English, but renting an English audioguide (€5) helps. If you're taking the subway here, check out the platform of métro Line 11 in the Arts and Métiers station—one of the city's most elaborate—made to look like the inside of a Jules Verne–style machine, complete with copper-color metal walls, giant bolts, and faux gears. ✉ *60 rue Réaumur, Marais Quarter* ☎ *01-53-01-82-75* ⊕ *www.arts-et-metiers.net* 🖅 *From €8* ⊘ *Closed Mon.* Ⓜ *Arts et Métiers.*

★ Musée National Picasso-Paris

This immensely popular museum rose phoenixlike in late 2014, when it finally reopened after an ambitious (and often controversial) five-year makeover that cost an estimated €52 million. Home to the world's largest public collection of Picasso's inimitable oeuvre, it now covers almost 54,000 square feet in two buildings: the regal 17th-century Hôtel Salé and a sprawling new structure in the back garden that's dedicated to temporary exhibitions. Diego Giacometti's exclusively designed furnishings in the former are an added bonus.

The collection of 200,000-plus paintings, sculptures, drawings, documents, and other archival materials (much of it previously in storage for lack of space) spans the artist's entire career; and while it doesn't include his most recognizable works, it does contain many of the pieces treasured most by Picasso himself. The renovated museum (which now has more than double the dedicated public space) is split into three distinct areas. The first two floors cover Picasso's work from 1895 to 1972. The top floor illustrates his relationship to his favorite artists; landscapes, nudes, portraits, and still lifes taken from his private collection detail his "artistic dialogue" with Cézanne, Gauguin, Degas, Rousseau, Matisse, Braque, Renoir, Modigliani, Miró, and others. The basement centers around Picasso's workshops, with photographs and engravings, paintings, and sculptures that document or evoke key pieces created at the Bateau Lavoir, Château de Boisgeloup, Grands-Augustins, the Villa La Californie, and his farmhouse, Notre-Dame-

de-Vie, in Mougins. With plenty of multimedia components and special activities that cater to kids, this is ideal for both children and adult art lovers alike.

■TIP→ It's worth paying the extra €1 to buy tickets online well in advance of your planned visit. Also, try to avoid visiting on weekends, when the crowds are thickest. ✉ *5 rue de Thorigny, Marais Quarter* ☎ *01–85–56–00–36* ⊕ *www.museepicassoparis.fr* ✆ *From €13* ⊙ *Closed Mon.* Ⓜ *St-Sébastien–Froissart.*

Nicolas Flamel's Home

Built in 1407 and reputed to be the oldest house in Paris (though other buildings also claim that title), this abode has a mystical history. Harry Potter fans should take note: this was the real-life residence of Nicolas Flamel, the alchemist whose sorcerer's stone is the source of immortality in the popular book series. A wealthy scribe, merchant, and dabbler in the mystical arts, Flamel willed his home to the city as a dormitory for the poor—on the condition that boarders pray daily for his soul. Today, the building contains apartments and a restaurant. ✉ *51 rue Montmorency, Marais Quarter* Ⓜ *Rambuteau.*

★ Place des Vosges

The oldest square in Paris and—dare we say it?—the most beautiful, Place des Vosges represents an early stab at urban planning. The precise proportions offer a placid symmetry, but things weren't always so calm here. Four centuries ago this was the site of the Palais des

Tournelles, home to King Henry II and Queen Catherine de Medici. The couple staged regular jousting tournaments, and Henry was fatally lanced in the eye during one of them in 1559. Catherine fled to the Louvre, abandoning her palace and ordering it destroyed. In 1612 the square became Place Royale on the occasion of Louis XIII's engagement to Anne of Austria. Napoléon renamed it Place des Vosges to honor the northeast region of Vosges, the first in the country to pony up taxes to the Revolutionary government. At the base of the 36 redbrick-and-stone houses—nine on each side of the square—is an arcaded, covered walkway lined with art galleries, shops, and cafés. There's also an elementary school, a synagogue (whose barrel roof was designed by Gustav Eiffel), and several chic hotels. The formal, gated garden's perimeter is lined with chestnut trees; inside are a children's play area and a fountain. Aside from hanging out in the park, people come here to see the house of the man who once lived at No. 6—Victor Hugo, the author of *Les Misérables* and *Notre-Dame de Paris* (aka *The Hunchback of Notre-Dame*).

■TIP→ One of the best things about this park is that you're actually allowed to sit—or snooze or snack—on the grass during spring and summer. There is no better spot in the Marais for a picnic: you can pick up fixings at the nearby street market on Thursday and Sunday mornings (it's on Boulevard Richard Lenoir between Rues Amelot and

St-Sabin). The most likely approach to Place des Vosges is from Rue de Francs-Bourgeois, the main shopping street. However, for a grander entrance walk along Rue St-Antoine until you get to Rue de Birague, which leads directly into the square. ⊠ *Off Rue des Francs-Bourgeois, near Rue de Turenne, Marais Quarter* Ⓜ *Bastille, St-Paul.*

🛍 Shopping

The Broken Arm
Like the ready-made Duchamp "artwork" for which it is named, The Broken Arm projects a minimalist cool that puts the concept back in concept store. A hypercurated

selection of A-list brands for men and women includes vivid separates from the likes of Phillip Lim, Raf Simons, and the sublime Christophe Lemaire. A choice selection of objects and accessories (books, hats, shoes, jewelry, vases, leather goods) elevates the everyday to art. ✉ *12 rue Perrée, 3e, Marais Quarter* ☎ *01-44-61-53-60* ⊕ *www. the-broken-arm.com* Ⓜ *Temple.*

Buly 1803

Founded more than two centuries ago by a perfumer who inspired a Balzac character, the apothecary remains one of the more intriguing beauty brands in Paris today. Mosey into the Marais outpost and stay awhile, testing the vast range of products, from Mexican tuberose dry oil to orange-ginger-clove dental floss. ✉ *45 rue de Saintonge, Marais Quarter* ☎ *01-42-72-28-92* ⊕ *www.buly1803.com/en* ◷ *Closed Mon.* Ⓜ *Filles du Calvaire.*

Castor Fleuriste

Calling Castor Fleuriste a flower shop doesn't quite do it justice—it's more like an exhibition space where the artist's preferred medium is flowers. And this artist, who left his job as an art dealer to open this hidden shop in the Marais, has quite the eye for form and construction. All flowers are sourced from Rungis, the world's largest fresh produce market located just 8 km (5 miles) south of Paris, and the Île-de-France region. ✉ *14 rue Debelleyme, Marais Quarter* ☎ *01-40-56-34-68* ⊕ *www.castor- fleuriste.com* ◷ *Closed Sun. and Mon.* Ⓜ *St-Sébastien–Froissart.*

Empreintes

A new concept store that's making waves in the Marais and rivaling the more widely known Merci brand, Empreintes sells everything from tableware and sculpture to jewelry and paper goods. Browse more than 1,000 creations in the exhibition- like space, all crafted by hand in France. ✉ *5 rue de Picardie, Marais Quarter* ☎ *01-40-09-53-80* ⊕ *www. empreintes-paris.com* ◷ *Closed Sun.* Ⓜ *Temple.*

Études Studio

Études is a fashion brand, yes, but it's also a collaborative study of all things visual. The Marais showroom sells clothing, acces- sories, and books, and as a former art gallery, it's an ode to the founders' aesthetic: minimal, raw, experimental, and, of course, ever-evolving. ✉ *14 rue Debelleyme, Marais Quarter* ☎ *01-49-96-56-62* ⊕ *www.etudes-studio.com* ◷ *Closed Sun.* Ⓜ *St-Sébastien–Froissart.*

Free 'P' Star

Don't let the chaos at Free 'P' Star discourage you—there's gold in them there bins. Determined seekers on a budget can reap heady rewards, at least according to the young hipsters who flock here for anything from a floor-sweeping peasant skirt to a cropped chinchilla cape. A second Marais branch—at 61 rue de la Verrerie—is equally stuffed to the gills. Happy hunting! ✉ *52 rue de la Verrerie, 4e, Marais Quarter* ☎ *01-42-76-03-72* ⊕ *www. freepstar.com* Ⓜ *Hôtel de Ville.*

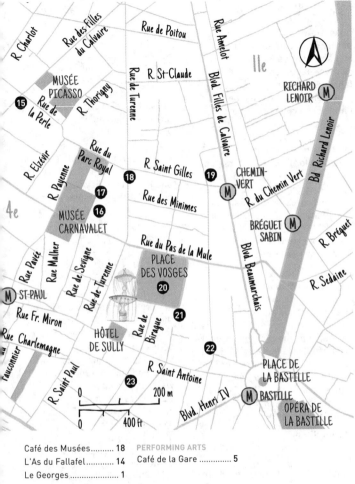

FrenchTrotters

The flagship store features an understated collection of contemporary French-made clothes and accessories for men and women that emphasize quality fabrics, classic style, and cut over trendiness. You'll also find a handpicked collection of exclusive collaborations with cutting-edge French brands (like sleek leather-and-suede booties by Avril Gau for FrenchTrotters), as well as FrenchTrotters' namesake label and a limited selection of housewares for chic Parisian apartments. ⊠ *128 rue Vieille du Temple, Marais Quarter* ☎ *01–44–61–00–14* ⊕ *www.frenchtrotters.fr* Ⓜ *St-Sébastien–Froissart.*

Jacques Genin

Genin offers the essence of great chocolate: not too sweet, with hand-picked seasonal ingredients for the velvety ganaches. The tea salon is a great spot to sample one of Genin's masterful takes on classic French pastries and a voluptuous *chocolat chaud.* ⊠ *133 rue de Turenne, 3e, Marais Quarter* ☎ *01–45–77–29–01* ⊕ *www.jacquesgenin.fr* Ⓜ *Filles du Calvaire, Oberkampf.*

★ Kilo Shop

"Choisissez, Pesez, Emportez" (Choose, Weigh, Take Away) is the motto of this vintage shop, where all items, from worn-in denim jackets to funky patterned blouses, are sold by weight, varying from €20–€60 per kilo. Unlike other vintage shops dotting the Marais, this address makes an effort to remain on-trend and budget-

friendly. ⊠ *65 rue de la Verrerie, Marais Quarter* ☎ *01–42–74–10–07* ⊕ *kilo-shop.com/fr* Ⓜ *Hôtel de Ville.*

L'Eclaireur

This Rue de Sevigné boutique is Paris's touchstone for edgy, up-to-the-second styles. L'Eclaireur's knack for uncovering new talent and championing established visionaries is legendary—no surprise after 30 years in the business. Hard-to-find geniuses, like leather wizard Isaac Sellam and British prodigy Paul Harnden, cohabit with luxe labels such as Ann Demeulemeester, Haider Ackermann, and Gucci. ⊠ *40 rue de Sevigné, 3e, Marais Quarter* ☎ *01–48–87–10–22* ⊕ *www.leclaireur. com* Ⓜ *St-Paul.*

L'Habibliothèque

A playful take on *bibliothèque* (library), L'Habibliothèque isn't in the business of loaning books, but rather women's clothes and accessories (much like the American site Rent the Runway). Sign up online and pick up your ephemeral wares in person. Stepping into the Beaubourg showroom is much like stopping by your chic Parisienne friend's apartment to have a gander at her fabulous closet. The pieces are so well curated, the space so stunning, and the concept so compelling, you'll be convinced: buying is so passé. ⊠ *35 rue Beaubourg, Marais Quarter* ☎ *07–82–86–53–81* ⊕ *www.lhabibliotheque.com* ⊙ *Closed Sun.* Ⓜ *Rambuteau.*

L'Habilleur

L'Habilleur is a favorite with the fashion press and anyone looking for a deal. For women there's a great selection from designers like Harley of Scotland, Roberto Collina, and Natural Selection. Men can find elegant suits from Paul Smith at slashed prices. ⊠ *44 rue de Poitou, 3e, Marais Quarter* ☎ *01–48–87–77–12* Ⓜ *St-Sébastien–Froissart.*

★ Merci

Paris's favorite concept store assembles fashions for men and women, home furnishings (including those irresistible French bed and bath linens) vintage, jewelry, and housewares plucked straight from top-tier French, European, and American designers. Every two months the store features a new design concept in the main entrance, with themes that range from Merci en Rose (featuring all things pink) to American Surf & Skate. The store's three cafés make lingering among Paris's fashion elite a pleasure. ⊠ *111 bd. Beaumarchais, 3e, Marais Quarter* ☎ *01–42–77–00–33* ⊕ *www.merci-merci.com* Ⓜ *St-Sebastien–Froissart.*

No42 Paris

French fashion has historically been more couture than street, but that's changing. Just look to No42 Paris, a shop that's bringing chic sportswear to the masses. The Marais address, like other locations in Berlin and London, is an elevated Adidas showroom where you'll find Y-3, Originals, and Performance lines, as well as pieces from collaborations with designers such as Stella McCartney and Jeremy Scott. ⊠ *42 rue de Sévigné, Marais Quarter* ☎ *01–44–61–78–11* ⊕ *www.no42-paris.com* ⊘ *Closed Sun. and Mon.* Ⓜ *Chemin Vert.*

☕ Coffee and Quick Bites

Cantine Merci

$ | Modern French. On the lower garden level of a chic concept store resides the perfect spot for a quick and healthy lunch between bouts of shopping. Highlights include a small soup menu, a risotto of the day, and hearty vegetarian salads. **Known for:** quick lunchtime spot; fresh juices and mint iced tea; rosé by the glass. *Average main: €17* ⊠ *111 bd. Beaumarchais, 3e, Marais Quarter* ☎ *01–42–77–79–28* ⊕ *www.merci-merci.com* ⊘ *Closed Sun. No dinner* Ⓜ *St-Sébastien–Froissart.*

Fondation Café

$ | Café. When in the Marais, Fondation is a must. Opened by Australian Chris Nielson (of Ten Belles in Canal St-Martin), this pint-size shop serves Cuillier coffee and a selection of specialty cakes, croissant sandwiches, and other treats. **Known for:** excellent lattes; cool crowd; minimalist decor. *Average main: €5* ⊠ *16 rue Dupetit-Thouars, Marais Quarter* Ⓜ *Temple.*

Fragments

$ | Café. Come to this popular café with exposed brick walls for breakfast, especially if you're a fan of good coffee and avocado toast. The space is small but cozy; the menu is short but sweet. **Known**

for: avocado toast; iced lattes; scrambled eggs. *Average main: €13 ⊠ 76 rue des Tournelles, Marais Quarter* Ⓜ *Chemin Vert*.

Kitchen

$ | Vegetarian. Kitchen is a wonderful breakfast option for vegetarians, or anyone looking for a healthy bite after one too many visits to the boulangerie. "Pimped" toasts (think avocado, hummus, feta, and egg toppings) and açaí bowls are morning options of choice, but if calories be damned, go for the pancakes (classic or vegan and gluten-free batter; with bananas or blueberries). Kitchen also serves vegan and gluten-free *futomaki* (fat sushi rolls), plus a selection of Lomi coffee drinks, teas, juices, kombucha, and more. **Known for:** "pimped" avocado toast; gluten-free pancakes; vegan futomaki. *Average main: €12 ⊠ 74 rue des Gravilliers, Marais Quarter* ☎ 09-52-55-11-66 ⊕ *kitchenparis. com* Ⓜ *Arts et Métiers*.

⭐ La Caféothèque

$ | Café. This was Paris's first coffee bar, founded by former Guatemalan ambassador to France-turned coffee ambassador Gloria Montenegro. With three spacious rooms, any coffee preparation under the sun, and a daily special brew chosen from among dozens of varieties of meticulously sourced beans from plantations around the globe, this place is a Paris institution. **Known for:** rigorously sourced, hard-to-find beans; excellent coffee of the day; all roasting done in-house. *Average*

main: €4 ⊠ 52 rue de l'Hotel de Ville, 4e, Marais Quarter* ☎ 01-53-01-83-84 ⊕ www.lacafeotheque.com Ⓜ *Pont Marie, St-Paul*.

Le Ruisseau Burger Joint

$ | Burger. For a Frenchified version of the American standby, head to Le Ruisseau, where burgers are made with high-quality Limousine beef and the buns are a pillowy brioche. While there are classic options, we recommend a creative take, such as the tartare burger (ever-so-slightly seared beef, cow's milk tomme cheese washed in cider, and iceberg lettuce). **Known for:** BBQ cheddar burger; tartare burger; chickpea veggie burger. *Average main: €11 ⊠ 22 rue Rambuteau, Marais Quarter* ☎ 01-43-70-02-21 ⊕ www.leburger-joint.com Ⓜ *Rambuteau*.

⭐ Loustic

$ | Café. Opened in 2013 at the start of Paris's artisanal coffee movement, Loustic has become an institution. Coffee enthusiasts will be impressed by the equipment and varieties (which change regularly), but everyone will enjoy the convivial, neighborhood mood. **Known for:** single-origin espresso; chai latte; cozy vibes. *Average main: €5 ⊠ 40 rue Chapon, Marais Quarter* ☎ 09-80-31-07-06 ⊕ www.cafeloustic.com Ⓜ *Arts et Métiers*.

Partisan Café

$ | Café. Floor-to-ceiling windows allow sunlight to pour into this new-age coffee shop, a large space by Paris standards. The house roasts their own coffee and serves up a selection of sweet bites by

local cafés, such as Muscovado.
Known for: knowledgeable baristas; photogenic lattes; lots of seating. *Average main: €5 ⊠ 36 rue de Turbigo, Marais Quarter* 🕾 *06-08-25-88-32* ⊕ *www.parispartisancafe.com* 🕙 *Closed Mon. and Tues.* Ⓜ *Arts et Métiers.*

Season

$$ | Café. A cross between a coffee shop, juice bar, and *néobistrot*, Season is the Marais's go-to for those on a healthy kick. Inspired by the popular toasts and bowls typical of LA or New York, Season offers a rotating menu that can be enjoyed in their cozy restaurant or taken to go. **Known for:** healthy options; pancakes for brunch; quinoa salad. *Average main: €17 ⊠ 1 rue Charles-François Dupuis, Marais Quarter* 🕾 *09-67-17-52-97* ⊕ *www.season-paris.com* Ⓜ *Temple.*

🍴 Dining

Au Bourguignon du Marais

$$ | Bistro. The handsome, contemporary look of this Marais bistro and wine bar is the perfect backdrop for traditional fare and excellent Burgundies served by the glass and bottle. Unusual for Paris, food is served nonstop from noon to 11 pm, and you can drop by just for a glass of wine in the afternoon. **Known for:** traditional bistro atmosphere; hearty Burgundian cuisine; sidewalk dining with nice views of the Marais. *Average main: €22 ⊠ 52 rue François-Miron, 3e, Marais Quarter* 🕾 *01-48-87-15-40* Ⓜ *St-Paul.*

The Beast

$$ | Barbecue. Paris and smokehouse aren't two words that typically go together, but barbecue at this bustling eatery is as authentic as it is in Texas. Frenchman Thomas Abramowicz honed his barbecue skills working with pit masters across the Lone Star State before returning to Paris and opening up the city's first smokehouse, importing everything from the beef to the Texan smoker. **Known for:** bourbon selection; Southern-style sides; smoked brisket. *Average main: €18 ⊠ 27 rue Meslay, Marais Quarter* 🕾 *07-81-02-99-77* ⊕ *www.thebeast.fr* 🕙 *Closed Mon. and Tues.* Ⓜ *République.*

Biglove Caffé

$ | Italian. This cozy, grocery-styled brunch spot is one of the impeccably designed Italian restaurants in the mini empire from Parisian institution Big Mamma Group. They do two things particularly well: brunch classics and gluten-free pizza. **Known for:** pain perdu (French toast); ricotta pancakes; gluten-free pizza. *Average main: €14 ⊠ 30 rue Debelleyme, Marais Quarter* 🕾 *01-42-71-43-62* ⊕ *www.bigmammagroup.com/fr/trattorias/biglove-caffe* 🚫 *No credit cards* Ⓜ *Filles du Calvaire.*

⭐ Breizh Café

$ | French. Eating a crêpe in Paris might seem a bit clichéd, until you venture into this modern offshoot of a Breton crêperie. The plain, pale-wood decor is refreshing, but what really makes the difference are the ingredients—farmers' eggs, unpasteurized Gruyère, shiitake mushrooms, Valrhona chocolate, homemade caramel, and extraordinary butter from a Breton dairy farmer. **Known for:** some of the best crêpes in Paris; adventurous ingredients; Cancale oysters also on the menu. *Average main: €12* ⊠ *109 rue Vieille du Temple, 3e, Marais Quarter* 🕾 *01–42–72–13–77* ⊕ *www.breizhcafe.com* 🕓 *Closed Mon., Tues., and Aug.* Ⓜ *St-Sébastien–Froissart.*

Bubar

$ | Wine Bar. In summer look for the crowd spilling out the front of this signless wine bar in the Marais named for Jean-Louis, the bartender (*bubar* or *barbu* is French slang for "bearded"). The wine menu—with many selections available by the glass—features French wines and small-batch vintages from South Africa, Chile, and Argentina. **Known for:** low-lit, almost clandestine atmosphere; wines to discover, guided by a knowledgeable and generous owner; bring your own snacks policy. *Average main: €12* ⊠ *3 rue des Tournelles, 4e, Marais Quarter* 🕾 *01–40–29–97–72* 🕓 *No lunch* Ⓜ *Bastille.*

Café des Musées

$ | Bistro. A true neighborhood haunt, this bustling little bistro near the Musée Picasso offers a convivial slice of Parisian life at a good value. Here traditional French bistro fare is adapted to a modern audience, and the best choices are the old tried-and-trues: hand-cut *tartare de boeuf*; rare entrecôte served with a side of golden-crisp frites and homemade béarnaise; and the classic parmentier with pheasant instead of the usual ground beef. **Known for:** reliable bistro fare; warm and friendly service; proximity to Marais museums. *Average main: €17* ⊠ *49 rue de Turenne, 3e, Marais Quarter* 🕾 *01–42–72–96–17* ⊕ *www. lecafedesmusees.fr* Ⓜ *St-Paul.*

CAM

$$$ | Asian Fusion. With no website, official phone number, or reservations, this restaurant—once a boutique selling mini Eiffel Towers—is now *the* quintessentially cool Paris resto. The aesthetic is minimal and unfussy, save a few plants, a Sid Vicious poster, and a bookshelf lined with photography books and independent magazines, and the cuisine is fresh Asian-influenced dishes. **Known for:** lamb dumplings; steak tartare with gochujang XO sauce; wine list. *Average main: €26* ⊠ *55 rue au Maire, Marais Quarter* 🕓 *Closed Mon. and Tues.* ▭ *No credit cards* Ⓜ *Arts et Métiers.*

Carbón

$$$ | French. This neo-bistro has a secret weapon: a wood-burning fire. Whether drawn by the perfectly charred meat-forward dishes, the plant-filled rustic-chic space, or the intimate speakeasy on the lower level, tastemakers and foodies flock to the trendy Marais address. **Known for:** sharing plates; rib-eye steak for two; hay-smoked burrata. *Average main: €25* ⊠ *14 rue Charlot, Marais Quarter* 🕾 *01–42–72–49–12* ⊕ *www.carbonparis.com* 🕓 *Closed Mon. No dinner Sun.* ▭ *No credit cards* Ⓜ *St-Sébastien–Froissart.*

Elmer

$$$$ | French. Elements of world travels from hot spots like Melbourne work their way into the menu at this modern French eatery by Chef Simon Horwitz. Heavy on metallic accents and raw wood, the decor, along with dishes, tell stories of travel, with plates crafted by a ceramist in Peru and ingredients sourced from small producers across France. **Known for:** modern French fare; rotisserie; well-curated wine selection. *Average main: €50 ⊠ 30 rue Notre Dame de Nazareth, Marais Quarter ☎ 01-43-56-22-95 ⊕ www.elmer-restaurant.fr ⊙ Closed Sun. and Mon. No lunch Sat.* Ⓜ *République.*

★ L'As du Fallafel

$ | Middle Eastern. If you're looking for one of the cheapest and tastiest meals in Paris, look no further than the fantastic falafel stands on the pedestrian Rue de Rosiers. L'As (the Ace) is widely considered the best of the bunch, which accounts for the lunchtime line that extends down the street. **Known for:** the best, freshest, and most heaping falafel sandwich in town; fast take-out or seated service at lunch; shawarma sandwiches. *Average main: €10 ⊠ 34 rue des Rosiers, 4e, Marais Quarter ☎ 01-48-87-63-60 ⊙ Closed Sat. No dinner Fri.* Ⓜ *St-Paul.*

Le Georges

$$$ | Modern French. One of those rooftop show-stopping venues so popular in Paris, Le Georges preens atop the Centre Georges Pompidou. Part of the Costes brothers' empire, the establishment trots out fashionable dishes such as sesame-crusted tuna and coriander-spiced beef fillet flambéed with cognac. **Known for:** stunning views of central Paris and beyond; cocktails on the terrace; hit-or-miss food except for the decadent desserts. *Average main: €32 ⊠ Centre Pompidou, 6th fl., 19 rue Beaubourg, 4e, Louvre ☎ 01-44-78-47-99 ⊕ www.restaurantgeorgesparis.com ⊙ Closed Tues.* Ⓜ *Rambuteau.*

★ Mr.T

$$ | Fusion. A minimal Mr.T neon sign lights the facade of this 3e arrondissement restaurant—which, by the way, has little in common with the mohawk-wearing, gold-chain-clad wrestler. It refers instead to Japanese chef Tsuyoshi Miyazaki, who dazzles with playfully inventive small plates such as his kebab, appropriately served in a classic peach-colored Styrofoam box, like the street food favorite. **Known for:** Mr.T Bulldog Burger; calamari tacos; fois gras Oreo. *Average main: €18 ⊠ 38 rue de Saintonge, Marais Quarter ☎ 01-42-71-15-34 ⊙ Closed Mon. ▭ No credit cards* Ⓜ *Filles du Calvaire.*

🍸 Bars and Nightlife

Andy Wahloo

With a hip crowd and an Andy Warhol–meets-*Casablanca* decor, here you can relax on oversize paint-can stools beneath high-kitsch silk-screened Moroccan coffee ads, and listen to funky Arabic Raï remixes. Dancing to DJs starts later in the night. ⊠ *69 rue*

des Gravilliers, 3e, Marais Quarter
☎ *01–42–71–20–38* ⊕ *andywahloo-bar.com* Ⓜ *Arts et Métiers.*

★ Candelaria

Steamy Candelaria is a taquería by day and a cocktail lounge by night. The tang of tequila hangs in the air at this hip hideaway, where deftly crafted drinks are poured for a contented crowd. ⊠ *52 rue de Saintonge, 3e, Marais Quarter* ☎ *01–42–74–41–28* ⊕ *www.candelari-aparis.com* Ⓜ *Filles du Calvaire.*

Grazie

Equal parts cocktail bar and gourmet pizzeria, this stylish offspring of the übercool concept store Merci promises top-quality libations and stone-oven-baked pizza. The decor is industrial-rustic, with pressed-tin ceilings and a corrugated-iron bar, all enhanced by mood lighting. It's jam-packed with neighborhood hipsters, so reservations are a must. ⊠ *91 bd. Beaumarchais, 3e, Marais Quarter* ☎ *01–42–78–11–96* ⊕ *www.graziegrazie.fr* Ⓜ *Saint-Sébastien–Froissart.*

La Belle Hortense

This spot is heaven for anyone who ever wished they had a book in a bar (or a drink in a bookstore). The *bar litteraire* is the infamous spot where gal-about-town Catherine M. launched her *vie sexuelle* that became a bawdy bestseller. ⊠ *31 rue Vielle-du-Temple, 4e, Marais Quarter* ☎ *01–48–04–74–60* Ⓜ *St-Paul.*

La Perle

Buzzy neighborhood staple La Perle is perpetually populated, but no one's entirely sure why. Gourmands needn't try to figure it out; this is a spot for casual drinks with friends and a place to see and be seen. After all, John Galliano's infamous tirade during Paris Fashion Week did go down here. ⊠ *78 rue Vieille du Temple, Marais Quarter* ☎ *01–42–72–69–93* ⊕ *cafelaperle.com* Ⓜ *Chemin Vert.*

★ Le Barav

This friendly wine bar might be in the middle of the bustling Haut Marais, but it still manages to feel like a small neighborhood address. Crowds seeking a convivial yet casual ambience flock to the indoor tables and sidewalk terrace to nibble on charcuterie, cheese, and other small bites while enjoying a €5 glass. You can also opt for a bottle from the *cave* next door and pay the reasonable €6 corkage fee. ⊠ *6 rue Charles-François Dupuis, Marais Quarter* ☎ *01–48–04–57–59* ⊕ *www.lebarav.fr* Ⓜ *République.*

★ Le Mary Celeste

Half-price oysters at happy hour (6–7 pm) aren't the only reason this refreshingly unpretentious cocktail bar is wildly popular. One of a trilogy of superhip watering holes (including Candelaria and Glass) opened by a trio of expat restau-rateurs, its craft cocktails, micro-brews, natural wines, and standout tapas menu deliver the goods and then some. If you're planning to dine, reserve ahead online. ⊠ *1 rue Commines, Marais Quarter* ⊕ *www.*

quixotic-projects.com/venue/mary-celeste Ⓜ *St-Sébastien–Froissart.*

Les Bains

Les Bains is mythic. Founded in 1885 as a bathhouse, it drew artists like Manet, Renoir, and Zola to its pool and saunas. Almost 100 years later it became one of Paris's most infamous nightclubs, attracting the likes of David Bowie, Andy Warhol, and Naomi Campbell. Fast-forward to Les Bains of today: the legend lives on as a five-star hotel, restaurant, bar, and nightclub with a swimming pool. If you try your luck getting into the club, don't forget your bathing suit. ✉ *7 rue du Bourg l'Abbé, Marais Quarter* ☎ *01-42-77-07-07* ⊕ *www.lesbains-paris.com* Ⓜ *Arts et Métiers.*

Little Red Door

Behind the red door, you'll discover a dark, cozy lounge that has style, sophistication, and atmosphere without the attitude. Creative cocktails—supplemented by artisanal beers and well-chosen wines by the glass (the last of which aren't always easy to come by in a cocktail bar)—can be enjoyed from a cushy velour barstool or cubbyhole alcove. ✉ *60 rue Charlot, 3e, Marais Quarter* ☎ *01-42-71-19-32* ⊕ *www.lrdparis.com* Ⓜ *Filles du Calvert.*

Max y Jeremy

An almost-too-cool crew can be found in Max y Jeremy's red ember-like interior, drinking cocktails and eating the sultry bite-size *pintxos* of Basque country. There's a distinct party atmosphere here, which can spill into the street, especially in

summer. ✉ *6 rue Dupuis, 3e, Marais Quarter* ☎ *01-42-78-00-68* ⊕ *www.maxyjeremy.com* Ⓜ *Temple.*

★ Sherry Butt

On a quiet street close to the Bastille, Sherry Butt's relaxed loftlike atmosphere, imaginative drinks, whiskey flights, and tasty bar menu draw a lively crowd that appreciates meticulously crafted cocktails. A DJ spins on weekends. ✉ *20 rue Beautreillis,*

4e, Marais Quarter ☎ 09–83–38–47–80 ⊕ *www.sherrybuttparis.com* Ⓜ *Bastille, Sully-Morland.*

Tango

Carefully safeguarding its dance-hall origins, Tango lures a friendly mixed crowd of gays, lesbians, and "open-minded" heteros. Late-night music is mostly French and American pop, but the DJ plays classic *chansons* (French torch songs) before midnight—so arrive early to waltz and swing. ✉ *13 rue au Maire, 3e, Marais Quarter* ☎ 01–42–72–17–78 ⊕ *www.boite-a-frissons.fr* Ⓜ *Arts et Métiers.*

🎟 Performing Arts

Café de la Gare

This spot offers a fun opportunity to experience a particularly Parisian form of entertainment, the *café-théâtre*—part satire, part variety revue, jazzed up with slapstick humor and performed in a café salon. You'll need a good grasp of French slang and current events to keep up with the jokes. There's no reserved seating; doors open 15 minutes before showtime. ✉ *41 rue du Temple, 4e, Marais Quarter* ☎ 01–42–78–52–51 ⊕ *www.cdlg.org* Ⓜ *Hôtel de Ville.*

La Gaîté Lyrique

Back in its theater days in the 1800s, La Gaîté Lyrique was a hit; the likes of the Russian ballet and l'Orchestre de Paris graced its stage. Today, the space hosts exhibitions, screenings, and workshops exploring digital technologies and their impact on society. The real draw comes at night, when you can catch some of the hippest indie bands around, including Albert Hammond Jr., Clara Luciani, and Kiddy Smile. ✉ *3 bis rue Papin, Marais Quarter* ☎ 01–53–01–52–00 ⊕ *gaite-lyrique.net* Ⓜ *Réaumur–Sébastopol.*

LES PUCES

CLIGNAN-COURT

ÉPINETTES

LA CHAPELLE

LA VILLETTE

LES BATIGNOLLES

MONTMARTRE

TERNES

MONCEAU

PIGALLE

LES GRANDS BOULEVARDS

CANAL ST-MARTIN

BELLEVILLE

CHAILLOT

CHAMPS-ÉLYSÉES

SENTIER

TROCADÉRO

PALAIS-ROYAL

LES HALLES

LE MARAIS

OBERKAMPF

MÉNILMONTANT

PÈRE-LACHAISE

BOIS DE BOULOGNE

PASSY

LES INVALIDES

LES ÎLES

AUTEUIL

VAUGIRARD

ST-GERMAIN-DES-PRÉS

QUARTIER LATIN

BASTILLE

CHARONNE

BERCY

BEL-AIR

JAVEL

MONTPARNASSE

BUTTE-AUX-CAILLES

SEINE

BOIS DE VINCENNES

ST-LAMBERT

MONTROUGE

MAISON BLANCHE

AUSTERLITZ

As the illustrious home of the Sorbonne University, the Panthéon, and the Notre-Dame, the Quartier Latin and the nearby island, Île de la Cité, form one of the most historically enticing neighborhoods in Paris. But this area by no means lives in the past. Echoes of the intelligentsia who once made the Latin Quarter their home, including Ernest Hemingway and Jean-Paul Sartre, reverberate to this day, and students and writers still comingle at bookshops, bars, and cafés. The area around central Place de la Contrescarpe is redolent with life and activity every night of the week, and many spend entire evenings dancing in hidden bars, stepping out only in the morning hours for a gyro or a crêpe. Even though the sunlit terraces where Hemingway and his ilk once sat to write now come with a hefty bill and have lost much of their allure, visitors to the Latin Quarter can still easily avoid the tourist traps and partake in some truly exquisite experiences.—*by Emily Monaco*

◉ Sights

★ Arènes de Lutèce

Beyond an unassuming doorway on Rue Monge sits one of the most impressive remains of Paris's Gallo-Roman era: a Roman amphitheater. Once the site of gladiatorial combat in an arena that sat more than 15,000 people, the amphitheater was presumed lost to history until the late 19th century, when it was discovered during the construction of a major thoroughfare. Today, the amphitheater is a park where locals come to picnic and play *pétanque* (a lawn-bowling game). ⊠ *49 rue Monge, Latin Quarter* Ⓜ *Place Monge.*

Grande Galerie de l'Évolution
(Great Hall of Evolution)

With a parade of taxidermied animals ranging from the tiniest dung beetle to the tallest giraffe, this four-story natural history museum in the Jardin des Plantes will perk up otherwise museum-weary kids. The flagship of three natural history museums in the garden, this restored 1889 building has a ceiling that changes color to suggest storms, twilight, or the hot savanna sun. Other must-sees are the gigantic skeleton of a blue whale and the stuffed royal rhino (he came from the menagerie at Versailles, where he was a pet of Louis XV). Kids ages 6 to 12 will enjoy La Galerie d'Enfants (The Children's Gallery): opened in 2010, it has bilingual interactive exhibits about the natural world. A lab stocked with microscopes often offers free workshops, and most of the staff speaks some English. Hang on to your ticket—it will get you a discount at the other museums within the Jardin des Plantes. ✉ *36 rue Geoffroy-St-Hilaire, Latin Quarter* ☎ *01-40-79-54-79* ⊕ *www.grandegaleriedelevolution.fr* ✉ *From €10* ⊘ *Closed Tues.* Ⓜ *Place Monge, Censier–Daubenton.*

Institut du Monde Arabe

This eye-catching metal-and-glass tower by architect Jean Nouvel cleverly uses metal diaphragms in the shape of square Arabic-style screens to work like a camera lens, opening and closing to control the flow of sunlight. The vast cultural center's layout is a reinterpretation of the traditional enclosed Arab courtyard. Inside, there are various spaces, among them a museum that explores the culture and religion of the 22 Arab League member nations. With the addition of elements from the Louvre's holdings and private donors, the museum's impressive collection includes four floors of Islamic art, artifacts, ceramics, and textiles. There is also a performance space, a sound-and-image center, a library, and a bookstore. Temporary exhibitions usually have information and an audioguide in English. Glass elevators whisk you to the ninth floor, where you can sip mint tea in the rooftop restaurant, Le Zyriab, while feasting on one of the best views in Paris. ✉ *1 rue des Fossés-St-Bernard, Latin Quarter* ☎ *01-40-51-38-38* ⊕ *www.imarabe.org* ✉ *€8* ⊘ *Closed Mon.* Ⓜ *Jussieu.*

★ Jardin des Plantes *(Botanical Gardens)*

Opened in 1640 and once known as the Jardin du Roi (King's Garden), this sprawling patch of greenery is a neighborhood gem. It's home to several gardens and various museums, all housed in 19th-century buildings that blend glass with ornate ironwork. The botanical and rose gardens are impressive, and plant lovers won't want to miss the towering greenhouses (*serre* in French)—they are filled with one of the world's most extensive collections of tropical and desert flora. If you have kids, take them to the excellent Grande Galerie de l'Évolution or one of the other natural history museums here: the Galerie de Paléontologie, replete with dinosaur and other skeletons, and the recently renovated Galerie de Minéralogie. If the kids prefer fauna, visit the Ménagerie, a small zoo founded in 1794 whose animals once fed Parisians during the 1870 Prussian siege. The star attractions are Nénette, the grande-dame orang-utan from Borneo, and her swinging friends in the monkey and ape house. ▰TIP→ If you need a break, there are three kiosk cafés in the Jardin. ✉ *Entrances on Rue Geoffroy-St-Hilaire, Rue Cuvier, Rue de Buffon, and Quai St-Bernard, Latin Quarter* ☎ *01-40-79-56-01* ⊕ *www.jardindes-plantes.net* ✉ *Museums from €7, zoo €13, greenhouses €7, gardens free* ⊘ *Museums and greenhouses closed Tues.* Ⓜ *Gare d'Austerlitz, Jussieu; Place Monge, Censier–Daubenton for Grande Galerie de l'Évolution.*

★ La Grande Mosquée de Paris

One of France's largest mosques rises more than 100 feet over the Latin Quarter, its blue-and-white tiled mosaics and sculpted horseshoe archways evocative of the Hispano-Moorish style. Explore the vast courtyard with its immense marble fountain and then enjoy a glass of sweet mint tea and a pastry (or a more filling North African couscous) on the mosque's outdoor terrace, surrounded by lush foliage. ✉ *2 bis pl. du Puits de l'Ermite, Latin Quarter* ☎ *01-45-35-97-33* ⊕ *www.mosqueede-paris.net* 🎟 *€3* ⊗ *Closed Fri. and Muslim holidays* Ⓜ *Place Monge.*

La Sorbonne

The 13th-century Sorbonne building was once home to Paris's public university, now divided among several campuses around the city and referred to by number. Students of University of Paris I, Paris III, and Paris IV still have classes within these illustrious halls, and visitors can gain access to the building (and its historic chapel) by reserving a slot on one of the regular Wednesday or Saturday tours. While commentary is only given in French, it's worth it to get a glimpse of this monument to higher education and to see the tomb of Cardinal Richelieu, the alumnus and former headmaster who founded the Académie française in 1635. The Académie is tasked to this day with the publication of the official dictionary of French. ✉ *47 rue des Ecoles, Latin Quarter* ☎ *01-40-46-23-39* ⊕ *www.sorbonne.fr* 🎟 *€15* Ⓜ *Cluny–La Sorbonne.*

GETTING HERE

Stop at St-Michel on métro line 4 to start your exploration of the neighborhood near Shakespeare and Company, with the Notre-Dame Cathedral nearby. Métro lines 7 and 10, as well as suburban rail line RER B, will also take you here; stop at Cardinal Lemoine (métro line 10) or Les Gobelins (métro line 7) to explore the vibrant area around Place de la Contrescarpe.

Musée de Cluny *(Musée National du Moyen Âge)*

An exceptional and rare example of medieval civic architecture, the Hôtel de Cluny is home to France's national medieval museum. The jewel of the collection is the *Lady and the Unicorn* tapestry, but there are quite a few other gems on display, including the original heads of Notre-Dame Cathedral's Gallery of Kings (beheaded by overexuberant Revolutionaries who believed these statues of Old Testament monarchs were actually representing kings of France). Also of note are the 3rd-century Gallo-Roman baths upon which the original Hôtel de Cluny was built. Known as the Thermes de Cluny, these remnants are some of the only Roman ruins remaining in Paris. The museum is undergoing massive renovations as of 2018, and a portion of the complex will remain closed until 2020. During this time, a selection of 70 treasures—including the famous medieval tapestry and ancient Roman frigidarium—will remain accessible to the public.

✉ *28 rue du Sommerard, Latin Quarter* ☎ *01-53-73-78-00* ⊕ *www. musee-moyenage.fr* 🎫 *€5* ⊗ *Closed Tues.* Ⓜ *Cluny–La Sorbonne.*

⭐ Notre-Dame

Looming above Place du Parvis, this Gothic sanctuary is the symbolic heart of Paris and, for many, of France itself. Napoléon was crowned here, and kings and queens exchanged marriage vows before its altar. Begun in 1163, completed in 1345, badly damaged during the Revolution, and restored in the 19th century by Eugène Viollet-le-Duc, Notre-Dame may not be the country's oldest or largest cathedral, but in beauty and architectural harmony it has few peers—as you can see by studying the front facade. Its ornate doors seem like hands joined in prayer, the sculpted kings above them form a noble procession, and the west rose window gleams with what seems like divine light.

The front facade has three main entrances: the Portal of the Virgin (left); the Portal of the Last Judgment (center); and the Portal of St. Anne (right). As you enter the nave, the faith of the early builders permeates the interior: the soft glow of the windows contrasts with the exterior's triumphant glory. At the entrance are the massive 12th-century columns supporting the towers. Look down the nave to the transepts—the arms of the church—where, at the south entrance to the choir, you'll glimpse the haunting 12th-century statue of Notre-Dame de Paris, *Our Lady of Paris*, for whom the cathedral is

named. On the choir's south side is the Treasury, with its small collection of religious artifacts. On the north side is the north rose window, one of the cathedral's original stained-glass panels; at the center is an image of Mary holding a young Jesus. Biblical scenes on the choir's north and south screens depict the life of Christ and apparitions of him after the Resurrection. Behind the choir is the Pietà, representing the Virgin Mary mourning over the dead body of Christ.

The best time to visit is early morning, when the cathedral is brightest and least crowded. Audioguides are available at the entrance (€5); free guided tours in English run Monday, Tuesday, and Saturday at 2:30, and Wednesday,Thursday, and Friday at 2. A separate entrance, to the left of the front facade, provides access to the towers via 387 stone steps. These wind up to the bell tolled by the fictional Quasimodo in Victor Hugo's 1831 *Notre-Dame de Paris*. The famed gargoyles (technically chimeras since they lack functioning waterspouts) were 19th-century additions. Reserving a tower visit online is now obligatory; lines to climb the tower are shortest on weekday mornings. Down the stairs in front of the cathedral is the Crypte Archéologique, an archaeological museum offering a fascinating subterranean view of this area from the 1st century, when Paris was a Roman city called Lutetia, through medieval times. Note that Notre-Dame was one of the first buildings to make use of flying buttresses—exterior supports that spread the weight of the building and roof. People first thought they looked like scaffolding that hadn't been removed. By day, the most tranquil place to appreciate these and other architectural elements is Square Jean-XXIII, the lovely garden behind the cathedral. By night, Seine boat rides

promise stellar views. ⊠ *6 parvis Notre-Dame–Place Jean-Paul II, Ile de la Cité* ☎ *01–42–34–56–10* ⊕ *www. notredamedeparis.fr* ☞ *Cathedral free; towers €10; crypt €8; treasury €4* ۞ *Crypt closed Mon.* Ⓜ *Cité.*

★ Panthéon
Originally built as a church in the 18th century, the Panthéon soon became a mausoleum for the great men of France, quite literally: today's Panthéon is the final resting place of 73 Frenchmen and only five Frenchwomen, including Marie Curie. Other illustrious honorees include Victor Hugo and Swiss philosopher Jean-Jacques Rousseau. After paying tribute to the deceased and taking in the Foucault pendulum, an 1851 device demonstrating the Earth's rotation, climb to the top of the building to enjoy the view. ⊠ *Pl. du Panthéon, Latin Quarter* ☎ *01–44–32–18–00* ⊕ *www.paris-pantheon.fr* ☞ *€9* Ⓜ *Cardinal Lemoine.*

Place de la Contrescarpe
At the top of the charmingly cobbled Rue Mouffetard sits Place de la Contrescarpe, a historic square overlooked by Ernest Hemingway's first Parisian apartment. Today, the square is bordered by two cafés with quaint sidewalk terraces and frequently plays host to live music in the summer months. ⊠ *Pl. de la Contrescarpe, Latin Quarter* Ⓜ *Place Monge.*

St-Étienne-du-Mont
This jewel box of a church has been visited by several popes paying tribute to Ste-Geneviève (the patron

FAMOUS LOCALS: ERNEST HEMINGWAY

The Latin Quarter has long been a hot spot for literary minds, but American expat writer Ernest Hemingway had a particular penchant for this neighborhood, detailing his experience here in his memoir *A Moveable Feast*. During his time in Paris, Hemingway lived and worked at the effervescent Place de la Contrescarpe; his first apartment can be found at 74 rue du Cardinal Lemoine, while his first office is just around the corner at 39 rue Descartes, in the same building where French poet Paul Verlaine once lived.

Hemingway would often venture across the Luxembourg Gardens to visit Gertrude Stein in her apartment on Rue de Fleurus or down to Rue de l'Odéon to comb through Sylvia Beach's shelves at Shakespeare and Company. It was Hemingway who coined the term "Odeonia" to represent the hub between the Rue and the Carrefour de l'Odéon, with all the allure and familiarity of a small village.

saint of Paris), who was buried here before Revolutionaries burned her remains. Built on the ruins of a 6th-century abbey founded by Clovis, the first king of the Franks, it has a unique combination of Gothic, Renaissance, and early Baroque elements, which adds a certain warmth that is lacking in other Parisian churches of pure Gothic style. Here you'll find the only rood screen left in the city—an ornate 16th-century masterwork of carved wood spanning the nave like a bridge, with a spiral staircase on either side. Observe the organ (dating from 1631, it is the city's oldest) and the marker in the floor near the entrance that commemorates an archbishop of Paris who was stabbed to death here by a defrocked priest in 1857. Guided tours are free, but a small offering is appreciated; call for times. ⊠ *Pl. Ste-Geneviève, 30 rue Descartes, Latin Quarter* ☎ *01–43–54–11–79* ⊕ *www.saintetiennedumont.fr* Ⓜ *Cardinal Lemoine*.

St-Julien-le-Pauvre

This tiny shrine in the shadow of Notre-Dame is one of the three oldest churches in Paris. Founded in 1045, it became a meeting place for university students in the 12th century and was Dante's church of choice when he was in town writing his *Divine Comedy*. Today's structure dates mostly from the 1600s, but keep an eye out for older pillars, which crawl with carvings of demons. You can maximize your time inside by attending one of the classical or gospel concerts held here. Alternately, go outside and simply perch on a bench in the garden to relish the view of Notre-Dame. ⊠ *1 rue St-Julien-le-Pauvre, Latin Quarter* ☎ *01–43–54–52–16* ⊕ *www.sjlpmelkites.fr* Ⓜ *St-Michel*.

★ Sainte-Chapelle

The medieval Ste-Chapelle chapel was built by St-Louis (King Louis IX) to house the relics of the Passion he acquired from the Byzantines in the 13th century: the Crown of Thorns and, later, pieces of the True Cross and the Holy Lance. While these relics were later moved to Notre-Dame, the chapel is well worth a visit for its series of 15 stained glass windows, which can be seen in the royal portion of the chapel on the second story. Of particular note is one window on the south side of the chapel depicting St-Louis himself, dressed as a penitent as he carries the relics on the final leg of their journey from Venice. ⊠ *8 bd. du Palais, Ile de la Cité* ☎ *01–53–40–60–80* ⊕ *www.sainte-chapelle.fr* ⊠ *€15* Ⓜ *Cité.*

🛍 Shopping

★ Fromagerie Laurent Dubois

Charles de Gaulle once famously quipped that it was impossible to govern a country with 246 varieties of cheese, but perhaps Laurent Dubois would have changed his mind. This master *fromager's* (cheesemaker's) shop is a wonderland for any turophile, with only the best varieties of France's favorite cheeses. His shop on Boulevard St-Germain often has free samples on offer to help visitors narrow down their choices. His Comté, a pressed cheese from the Jura region, is one of the best in Paris. ⊠ *47 ter bd. St-Germain, Latin Quarter* ☎ *01–43–54–50–93* ⊕ *www.fromageslaurentdubois.fr* ⊙ *Closed Mon.* Ⓜ *Maubert–Mutualité.*

Marché Monge

Paris is home to nearly 100 weekly street markets; the one on Place Monge has taken place since 1921. Around 40 different vendors convene to sell food, clothing, flowers, and more each Wednesday and Friday from 7 am to 2:30 pm and every Sunday from 7 am to 3 pm. Monge hosts several organic vendors (dubbed *bio* in French). Come just before closing for the best deals. ⊠ *Pl. Monge, Latin Quarter* Ⓜ *Monge.*

★ Mococha

Paris has no shortage of specialty chocolatiers, but Mococha merits a detour. This small shop on the pedestrian Rue Mouffetard shows off specialty chocolates from three master chocolatiers as though they were prized jewels, with beautiful displays and gorgeous packaging. In winter, Mococha's hot chocolate bar offers the perfect way to warm up from the chill. ⊠ *89 rue Mouffetard, Latin Quarter* ☎ *01–47–07–13–66* ⊕ *www.chocolatsmococha.com* ⊙ *Closed Mon.* Ⓜ *Censier-Daubenton.*

Parapluies Simon

Super-specialized shops such as this more-than-100-year-old boutique devoted entirely to umbrellas lend Paris a lot of her charm. Step in to peruse all variety of umbrellas and parasols, from expensive designer models to brightly colored, compact varieties—all great for shielding you from the notorious drizzle of northern France. ⊠ *56 bd. St-Michel, Latin Quarter* ☎ *01–43–54–12–04* ⊕ *www.parapluies-simon.com* ⊙ *Closed Sun.* Ⓜ *Cluny-La-Sorbonne.*

★ Rue Mouffetard

The pedestrian Rue Mouffetard is one of the oldest in Paris, with origins dating back to the Neolithic age. Today, it's a vibrant market street dotted with cheesemongers, butchers, charcutiers, winesellers, and fruit and vegetable vendors. Fans of the film *Julie and Julia* will recognize the old-fashioned cobblestones and streetside displays from Meryl Streep's shopping excursion as famed American cook Julia Child. Moving up the street (toward the Panthéon), you'll stumble upon inexpensive crêpe stalls and bars, favorites of students at the Sorbonne just a few blocks away. ⊠ *Rue Mouffetard, Latin Quarter* ⊙ *Closed Mon.* Ⓜ *Censier–Daubenton.*

★ Shakespeare and Company

Shakespeare and Company is an Anglophone institution, its history connecting it to both Lost Generation and Beat Generation writers who lived and wrote in Paris. Today, the bookshop is divided in two, with contemporary volumes on one side and antiquarian books on the other. Titles with a link to the shop's former illustrious visitors or Parisian life and history are given a special priority on the crowded shelves. Be sure to climb the steps to the second story, where a reading room allows visitors to immerse themselves in the unique atmosphere of the shop. ⊠ *37 rue de la Bûcherie, Latin Quarter* ☎ *01–43–25–40–93* ⊕ *www.shakespeareandcompany.com* ⊙ *Antiquarian shop closed Sun. and Mon.* Ⓜ *St-Michel.*

BACK IN THE DAY

The famous Shakespeare and Company bookshop overlooks Notre-Dame Cathedral, but it hasn't always. The first iteration of the shop, opened by Sylvia Beach in 1919, lived briefly on Rue Dupuytren before relocating to Rue de l'Odéon. A hub for American Lost Generation writers, this shop closed definitively in the '40s. The current shop, opened by George Whitman in 1951, shares the legendary store's name with Beach's blessing, and thanks to current owner Sylvia Whitman (George's daughter, named after Beach), it remains an essential Anglophone haunt.

🍵 Coffee and Quick Bites

Boulangerie la Parisienne

$ | **Bakery.** Every year the city of Paris holds a competition to determine who makes the best baguette in the capital, and in 2016, the honor went to La Parisienne. The St-Germain storefront is a great place to sample it or grab a quick lunch to go. **Known for:** award-winning "La Parisienne" baguette; pain de seigle (rye bread); sandwiches to go. *Average main: €6* ⊠ *52 bd. Saint Germain, Latin Quarter* ☎ *01–43–54–48–72* ⊕ *www.boulangerielaparisienne.com* ⊙ *Closed Sun.* Ⓜ *Maubert–Mutualité.*

★ Carl Marletti

$ | **French.** Carl Marletti is an innovative pastry master who creates individually portioned desserts as breathtaking as some of the fancier, larger cakes you'll find in other pastry shops. His pastries are *almost* too beautiful to eat. **Known for:** rose religieuse, a stacked cream puff; the Censier, chocolate cream on a Pop-Rocks pastry base; homemade marshmallows. *Average main: €7* ⊠ *51 rue Censier, Latin Quarter* ☎ *01–43–31–68–12* ⊕ *www. carlmarletti.com* ⊗ *Closed Mon.* Ⓜ *Censier–Daubenton.*

Dose Café *(Dose - Dealer de Café)*
$ | **Café.** Quality coffee used to be hard to come by in Paris, but a trend toward great coffee bars has brought places like Dose to the table. This café, which plays on the "need" for caffeine by dubbing its baristas coffee "dealers," highlights quality, organic ingredients at every turn. **Known for:** artisanal coffee, brewed to order; fresh-pressed organic juices; bread baked daily. *Average main: €13* ⊠ *73 rue Mouffetard, Latin Quarter* ☎ *01–43–36–65–03* ⊕ *www.dosedealerdecafe.fr* ⊗ *Closed Mon.* Ⓜ *Place Monge.*

★ **Gelati d'Alberto**
$ | **Italian.** Too many visitors to Paris opt for chain ice cream shops, which is a shame when there's handmade gelato to be had at Gelati d'Alberto. This neighborhood fave is the brainchild of a third-generation gelato maker, and it's open until midnight— perfect for a late-night snack. **Known for:** unique flavors like poppy, mojito, and Mont Blanc; flower-shaped scoops; light, unctuous whipped cream. *Average main: €4* ⊠ *45 rue Mouffetard, Latin Quarter* ☎ *01–77–11–44–55* Ⓜ *Place Monge.*

L'Enclos de Ninon
$ | **Café.** This sweet coffeeshop just steps from the Panthéon offers a backdrop of exposed stone walls and a spacious outdoor terrace. It's also managed by one of the foremost American-style wedding cake makers in the city, so the cakes are out of sight. **Known for:** loose-leaf teas, brewed to order; house-made quiches; Paris's best red velvet cake. *Average main: €15* ⊠ *68 rue du Cardinal Lemoine, Latin Quarter* ☎ *01–46–34–07–43* ⊕ *www. lenclosdeninon.fr* ⊗ *Closed Mon.* Ⓜ *Cardinal Lemoine.*

L'Ourcine
$$$$ | **French.** "Cook's food, wine-maker's wine," is the slogan at this authentic French bistro slightly off the beaten path. On any given night, L'Ourcine is mostly filled with locals, who come for seasonal flavors with the occasional international spin. **Known for:** prix-fixe menu; game meats like pigeon and wild boar; a great wine list featuring Languedoc. *Average main: €38* ⊠ *92 rue Broca, Les Gobelins* ☎ *01–47–07–13–65* ⊕ *www. restaurant-lourcine.fr* ⊗ *Closed Sun. and Mon.* Ⓜ *Les Gobelins.*

Odette
$ | **French.** Odette does one thing and does it right. The only thing on the menu here are cream puffs in flavors like coffee, chocolate, and vanilla—and they're some of the best you'll ever have. **Known for:** berry-flavored puffs; pièces montées (cream puff towers); occasionally running out before the end of the day. *Average main: €2* ⊠ *77 rue Galande,*

Latin Quarter ☎ *01–43–26–13–06.*
⊕ *www.odette-paris.com* Ⓜ *St-Michel.*

Shakespeare and Company Café

$ | **Café.** It was a dream of Shakespeare and Company bookshop founder George Whitman to have an adjoining café, and in 2015, it finally happened. The café serves up a blend of American- and French-style baked goods and loads of vegan lunch options with a view of Notre-Dame. **Known for:** coffee from Parisian favorite Café Lomi; scones from Bob's Bake Shop; lemon pie. *Average main: €9* ⊠ *37 rue de la Bûcherie, Latin Quarter* ☎ *01–43–25–40–93* ⊕ *www.shakespeareandcompany.com* Ⓜ *St-Michel.*

🍴 Dining

Bonjour Vietnam

$ | **Vietnamese.** No need to trek all the way to the 13e arrondissement (Paris's Chinatown) for quality, well-priced Vietnamese food. The lunchtime prix fixe at this cozy spot is a steal—if a bit diminutive, portion-wise—and the flavors will keep you coming back for more. **Known for:** filling bo buns; rich and flavorful pho; crisp banana beignet. *Average main: €12* ⊠ *6 rue Thouin, Latin Quarter* ☎ *01–43–54–78–04* ⊙ *Closed Tues.* 🚫 *No credit cards* Ⓜ *Cardinal Lemoine.*

★ Café de la Nouvelle Mairie

$ | **French.** Café de la Nouvelle Mairie is a prime example of the neo-bistro movement happening in Paris right now. The unassuming dining room and simple black-board menu do little to convey the quality of the cuisine here, a perfect blend between classic French and modern, seasonal fare. **Known for:** natural, no-sulfur-added wines; eggs with house-made mayo; above-average coffee from l'Arbre à Café. *Average main: €17* ⊠ *19–21 rue des Fossés St-Jacques, Latin Quarter* ☎ *01–44–07–04–41* ⊙ *Closed weekends* Ⓜ *Cardinal Lemoine.*

★ Hugo & Co

$$ | **Modern French.** Hugo & Co has quickly become a true neighborhood joint, with exquisite shared plates and a convivial open kitchen serving up regional French specialties and international dishes. Owner Tomy Gousset's menu is made up of only the best seasonal, organic products, prepared simply. **Known for:** French cheeses, cured meats, and olives; bao buns, gomasio (a sesame seed condiment), and chimichurri; hot madeleines. *Average main: €19* ⊠ *48 rue Monge, Latin Quarter* ☎ *09–53–92–62–77* ⊕ *www.tomygousset.com/hugo-and-co* ⊙ *Closed weekends* Ⓜ *Cardinal Lemoine.*

★ La Tour d'Argent

$$$$ | **Modern French.** You can't deny the splendor of this legendary Michelin-starred restaurant's setting overlooking the Seine; if you don't want to splurge on dinner, treat yourself to the three-course lunch menu for €85. This entitles you to succulent slices of one of the restaurant's numbered ducks (the great duck slaughter began in 1919 and is now well past the millionth mallard, as your certificate will attest). **Known**

for: duck in all its glorious forms; one of the city's best wine lists; fabulous Seine-side setting with glorious views. *Average main: €105* ⊠ *15–17 quai de la Tournelle, 5e, Latin Quarter* ☎ *01–43–54–23–31* ⊕ *www.latourdargent.com* ⊗ *Closed Sun., Mon., and Aug.* 🎩 *Jacket and tie* Ⓜ *Cardinal Lemoine.*

★ **Le Buisson Ardent**

$$$ | **Bistro.** This charming Quartier Latin bistro with woodwork and murals dating from 1925 is always packed and boisterous. A glance at the €39.90 set menu—a bargain €28 at lunch for three courses—makes it easy to understand why. **Known for:** authentic Parisian bistro atmosphere; excellent value daily prix-fixe menu; fresh twist on French classics. *Average main: €26* ⊠ *25 rue Jussieu, 5e, Latin Quarter* ☎ *01–43–54–93–02* Ⓜ *Jussieu.*

Le Refuge du Passé

$$ | **French.** You'll feel as if you've stepped into the past at this country-style French restaurant, decorated with vintage street signs, posters, and knickknacks galore. Manager Nicolas even sources some of the vegetables that grace the menu, full of classics of southwestern France, from his own permaculture garden. **Known for:** roasted whole Camembert with honey; duck confit; warm, friendly service. *Average main: €22* ⊠ *32 rue du Fer à Moulin, Les Gobelins* ☎ *01–47–07–29–91* ⊗ *Closed Mon. and Tues.* Ⓜ *Les Gobelins.*

★ **Les Papilles** *(Le Bistroy... Les Papilles)*

$$ | **French.** When Bertrand Bluy opened Les Papilles in 2003, he sought to highlight the neo-bistro fare that was popping up all over the capital while retaining the friendly ambience of a classic bistro. He has absolutely succeeded with this wine-bar-cum-restaurant, where nearly everyone opts for the €38, seasonal, four-course prix fixe—and nearly everyone is blown away. **Known for:** seasonal soups; well-priced wine; cheese course paired with stewed or roasted fruit. *Average main: €18* ⊠ *30 rue Gay-Lussac, Latin Quarter* ☎ *01–43–25–20–79* ⊕ *www.lespapillesparis. fr* ⊗ *Closed Sun. and Mon., July 20–Aug.* Ⓜ *Cluny–La Sorbonne.*

★ **Sola**

$$$$ | **Eclectic.** This foodie sanctuary is where dishes like miso-lacquered foie gras or sake-glazed suckling pig—perfectly crisp on the outside and melting inside—pair traditional Japanese and French ingredients to wondrous effect. The three-course set weekday lunch menu offers a choice of fish or meat and finishes with some stunning confections, and the four-course dinner menu (with an option to add a pairing of four glasses of wine or sake) is an excellent value for what you're getting. **Known for:** beautiful atmosphere in a 17th-century building; contemporary French-Japanese cooking at its finest; traditional Japanese dining downstairs. *Average main: €35* ⊠ *12 rue de l'Hôtel Colbert, 5e, Latin*

Quarter ☎ 01-43-29-59-04 ⊕ *www. restaurant-sola.com* ⊘ *Closed Sun. and Mon.* Ⓜ *Maubert–Mutualité.*

🍸 Bars and Nightlife

Académie de la Bière

Belgian beer lovers need look no further: this spot has served up Belgian (and international) brews in Paris since the '60s, with 12 on draft and about 150 by the bottle at any given time. A classic *moules-frites* is the perfect accompaniment if you're a bit peckish; the mussels are delivered to the restaurant fresh daily. ✉ *88 bis bd. du Port-Royal, Latin Quarter* ☎ 01-43-54-66-65 ⊕ *www. academie-biere.com* Ⓜ *Vavin.*

★ Brewberry

Craft beer fans will fall head over heels for the 24 draft brews and 400 beers by the bottle here. With two storefronts on the charming Rue du Pot-de-Fer, Brewberry allows you to choose the establishment to fit your mood: either the bar or the *cave* (more like a tasting room). The two have slightly different atmospheres, menus, and opening hours (the bar stays open later). ✉ *11 rue du Pot-de-Fer, Latin Quarter* ☎ 01-45-31-12-28 ⊕ *www.brewberry. fr* Ⓜ *Place Monge.*

Corcoran's Irish Pub

This Irish pub is technically part of a mini-chain you'll find throughout Paris, but step inside the Saint-Michel location and it feels like home. Friendly Anglophone barmen serve up inexpensive beers, and the bar's playlist is super nostalgic.

It's also a top spot to watch Anglo teams playing rugby or soccer. ✉ *28 rue St-André des Arts, Latin Quarter* ☎ 01-43-64-25-33 Ⓜ *St-Michel.*

Fifth Bar

This bar and club catering mainly to the neighborhood's students is the perfect spot for late-night dancing. Inexpensive drinks in a publike atmosphere can be found upstairs, while downstairs you can dance until the wee hours of the morning. The pub even has beer pong tables, if you're in the mood for friendly competition with fellow night owls. ✉ *62 rue Mouffetard, Latin Quarter* ☎ 01-43-37-09-09 Ⓜ *Place Monge.*

Le Crocodile

It might take you a moment or two to choose a cocktail from the encyclopedic list of more than 100, each of which comes with a gummy crocodile, the house signature. Drinks are quite strong and only €6 during happy hour (6 pm–11 pm on weeknights or until 10 pm on the weekend)—all the better to lubricate the encounters you're sure to have at the ultrafriendly spot. ✉ *6 rue Royer-Collard, Latin Quarter* ☎ 06-50-07-91-00 ⊕ *lecrocodile. business.site* Ⓜ *Cardinal Lemoine.*

Polly Maggoo

This convivial hangout is legendary as the student rioters' unofficial HQ during the May '68 uprising and is named after the satirical French art-house movie about a supermodel. Weekends are wild, with drinks at the wacky tile bar and live Latin music that keeps the party thumping until morning. ✉ *3-5* rue du Petit Pont, 5e, Latin Quarter ☎ 01-46-33-33-64 Ⓜ St-Michel.

Vin et Whisky

Partake in the French tradition of *apéro*, a shared drink before dinner, at this wine and whiskey shop. Devoted, knowledgeable staff are at the ready to pour one of 24 wines or 80 whiskies served by the glass. A simple cheese or charcuterie plate is the perfect pairing. ✉ 62 rue Monge, Latin Quarter ☎ 01-45-87-17-95 ⊕ www.vinetwhisky-claudel.com Ⓜ Cardinal Lemoine.

🎭 Performing Arts

★ Caveau de la Huchette

If you've seen *La La Land*, you're already familiar with this legendary underground jazz club, which first opened in 1946. Jazz and swing are alive at the Caveau, where regular concerts and events encourage even the uninitiated to try their hand (and feet) at a Lindy Hop or Modern Jive. ✉ 5 rue de la Huchette, Latin Quarter ☎ 01-43-26-65-05 ⊕ www.cave-audelahuchette.fr 🎟 €13 Sun.–Thurs., €15 Fri. and Sat. Ⓜ St-Michel.

Filmothèque du Quartier Latin

Cinematic legends grace the big screen at this movie theater, known for its eclectic, classics-packed schedule. Regular film festivals highlight everything from Stanley Kubrick to American musicals. All English-language films are shown in VOST (English with French subtitles) unless otherwise specified. ✉ 9 rue Champollion, Latin Quarter ☎ 01-43-26-70-38 ⊕ www.lafilmo-theque.fr Ⓜ Cluny–La Sorbonne.

Irish Cultural Center (Centre Culturel Irlandais)

Film showings, literary evenings, and live concerts all occasionally grace the halls of this historic building, once a college for Irish priests in Paris. The center hosts an outdoor concert in its stone courtyard every year in honor of Fête de la Musique, a nationwide music festival held on June 21. ✉ 5 rue des Irlandais, Latin Quarter ☎ 01-58-52-10-30 ⊕ www.centrecultureirlandais.com Ⓜ Cardinal Lemoine.

★ Le Champo (Le Champo–Espace Jacques Tati)

A Latin Quarter staple since 1938, this arthouse cinema was a favorite of French filmmakers such as François Truffaut and Jean-Luc Godard. Today, the cinema is known for its Art Deco facade and regular retrospective festivals honoring directors from around the world. ✉ 51 rue des Écoles, Latin Quarter ☎ 01-43-54-51-60 ⊕ www.cinema-lechampo.com 🎟 €9 Ⓜ St-Michel.

Saint-André des Arts

One of a number of popular cinemas near the Sorbonne, Saint-André des Arts is also one of the best cinemas in Paris. It hosts an annual festival devoted to a single director (like Bergman or Tarkovski) and shows indie films every day at 1 pm. Some of the latter are part of "Les Découvertes de Saint-André" series, which focuses on the work of young filmmakers; these screenings are followed by a discussion. ✉ 30 rue St-André des Arts, 6e, Latin Quarter ☎ 01-43-26-48-18 ⊕ cinesaintandre.fr Ⓜ St-Michel.

St-Germain-des-Prés and Les Invalides

LES PUCES

ÉPINETTES

CLIGNAN-COURT

LA CHAPELLE

LA VILLETTE

LES BATIGNOLLES

MONTMARTRE

TERNES

MONCEAU

PIGALLE

LES GRANDS BOULEVARDS

CANAL ST-MARTIN

BELLEVILLE

CHAILLOT

CHAMPS-ÉLYSÉES

SENTIER

MÉNILMONTANT

BOIS DE BOULOGNE

PASSY

TROCADÉRO

PALAIS-ROYAL

LES HALLES

LE MARAIS

OBERKAMPF

PÈRE-LACHAISE

LES INVALIDES

ST-GERMAIN-DES-PRÉS

LES ÎLES

BASTILLE

CHARONNE

AUTEUIL

VAUGIRARD

QUARTIER LATIN

BERCY

BEL-AIR

JAVEL

MONTPARNASSE

BUTTE-AUX-CAILLES

SEINE

BOIS DE VINCENNES

ST-LAMBERT

MONTROUGE

MAISON BLANCHE

AUSTERLITZ

Occupying a vast swath of the Left Bank from the Eiffel Tower to St-Germain-des-Prés, the 6e and 7e arrondissements are home to legendary cafés, picturesque narrow streets, ultrachic boutiques, stupendous museums, and peaceful parks that embody quintessential Paris. While St-Germain's early- to mid-20th-century coolness—fostered by writers, artists, jazz musicians, and existentialist philosophers—has gradually tempered, the posh area still draws locals and visitors hungry for a bygone era or a heavy dose of beauty. Indeed, one of the best things to do in the neighborhood is simply flâner, a French term that means to stroll aimlessly, something Hemingway could be found doing a hundred years ago in his favorite park, the Jardin du Luxembourg. Today you can try it at the area's newest park, Les Berges, an area running along the Seine that's wildly popular among young, hip locals. You'll still find them camped out on the district's café terraces, perhaps with a craft beer in hand rather than un verre de vin (glass of wine). Although the area is staunchly classical, contemporary Paris is gradually drifting over from the Right Bank and is appearing in the form of exceptional new restaurants, modern wine bars, and fantastic shopping, which make it an exciting place to see both old and new Paris.—*by Lily Heise*

. . . .

👁 Sights

Champ de Mars

Flanked by tree-lined paths, this long expanse of grass lies between the Eiffel Tower and École Militaire. It was previously used as a parade ground and was the site of the world exhibitions in 1867, 1889 (when the tower was built), and 1900. Landscaped at the start of the 20th century, the park today is a great spot for temporary art exhibits, picnics, pickup soccer games, and outdoor concerts. You can also just sprawl on the center span of grass, which is unusual for Paris. There's a playground where kids can let off steam, too. Visiting during Bastille Day? If you can brave the crowds, arrive early to get a premier viewing position for the spectacular July 14 fireworks display, with the Eiffel Tower as a backdrop. Be vigilant at night. ⊠ *Eiffel Tower* Ⓜ *École Militaire; RER: Champ de Mars–Tour Eiffel.*

Cour du Commerce St-André

Few places in Paris reveal as many layers of the city's history as this charming passageway. Built in the

1730s, it runs along a section of the massive wall constructed by King Philippe-Auguste in the late 12th century; you can still spot one of its surviving watchtowers through the window of Un Dimanche à Paris, a tea salon and pastry shop at No. 4 Boulevard St-Germain. Across the lane is Le Procope, the oldest café in the city, dating back to 1686. It was frequented by the likes of Voltaire, Benjamin Franklin, and French Revolutionaries Robespierre and Danton. The lane's Revolutionary fervor extends to No. 9, where a certain Joseph Ignace Guillotin perfected his head-chopping device—on sheep. ⊠ *130 bd. St-Germain, St-Germain-des-Prés* Ⓜ *Odéon.*

★ **Eiffel Tower** *(Tour Eiffel)*
The Eiffel Tower is to Paris what the Statue of Liberty is to New York and what Big Ben is to London: the ultimate civic emblem. French engineer Gustave Eiffel—already famous for building viaducts and bridges—spent two years working to erect this iconic monument for the World Exhibition of 1889.

Because its colossal bulk exudes such a feeling of permanence, you may have trouble believing that the tower nearly became 7,000 tons of scrap (it contains 12,000 pieces of metal and 2,500,000 rivets) when the concession expired in 1909. Only its potential use as a radio antenna saved the day; and it still bristles with a forest of radio and television transmitters. Given La Tour's landmark status, it is equally hard to believe that so many Parisians—

including arbiters of taste like Guy de Maupassant and Alexandre Dumas—initially derided the 1,063-foot structure. (De Maupassant reputedly had lunch in the tower's restaurant every day because it was the only place in Paris from which the tower wasn't visible.)

Gradually, though, the Tour Eiffel became part of the city's topography, entering the hearts and souls of residents and visitors alike. Today it is most breathtaking at night, when every girder is highlighted in a sparkling display originally conceived to celebrate the turn of the millennium. The glittering light show was so popular that the 20,000 lights were reinstalled for permanent use in 2003. The tower does its electric dance for five minutes every hour on the hour until 1 am.

More recent enhancements are also noteworthy. A two-year, €30-million renovation of the first level, completed in 2014, added a vertigo-inducing "transparent" floor 187 feet above the esplanade, plus a pair of glass-facade pavilions, which hug the side of the tower and house interactive educational areas. A new miniturbine plant, four vertical-turbine windmills, and eco-friendly solar panels will minimize the tower's carbon footprint over time, too.

You can stride up 704 steps as far as the second level,

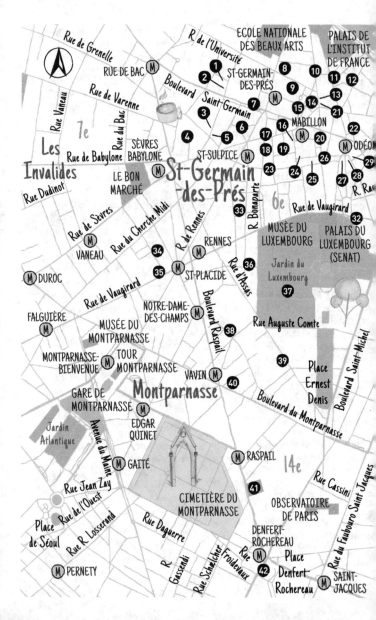

but if you want to go to the top you'll have to take the elevator. (Be sure to look closely at the fantastic ironwork.) Although the view of the flat sweep of Paris at 1,000 feet may not beat the one from the Tour Montparnasse skyscraper, the setting makes it considerably more romantic—especially if you come in the late evening, after the crowds have dispersed. Beat the crushing lines by reserving your ticket online; you can also book a skip-the-line guided tour from one of many local companies (from €34). ⊠ *Quai Branly, Eiffel Tower* ☎ *08–92–70–12–39 €0.35 per min* ⊕ *www.toureiffel.paris* 🖅 *By elevator: from €16. By stairs: from €10* 🕑 *Closed last 2 wks in Jan. for annual maintenance* ☞ *Stairs close at 6 pm in off-season (Oct.–June)* Ⓜ *Trocadéro, Bir-Hakeim, École Militaire; RER: Champ de Mars–Tour Eiffel.*

Fondation Cartier Pour L'art Contemporain

There's no shortage of museums in Paris, but this eye-catching gallery may be the city's premier place to view cutting-edge art. Funded by luxury giant Cartier, the foundation is at once an architectural landmark, a corporate collection, and an exhibition space. Architect Jean Nouvel's 1993 building is a glass house of cards layered seamlessly between the boulevard and the garden. The foundation regularly hosts *Soirées Nomades* (Nomadic Nights) featuring lectures, dance, music, film, or fashion on various evenings. Some are in English. Family tours and creative workshops

GETTING HERE

St-Germain-des-Prés and Les Invalides are easily walkable. A good starting point is the Jardin du Luxembourg, which you can reach via the Luxembourg stop on RER B or the Odéon stop on métro lines 10 and 4. Alternatively, take the RER C to the Musée d'Orsay stop to start at the famous museum, or to the Champ de Mars–Eiffel Tower stop. Most other sites of interest in the area are along métro lines 4, 12, or 13.

for children ages 9 to 13 are available. There are free guided tours of exhibits at 6 pm Tuesday through Friday, depending on space. ⊠ *261 bd. Raspail, Montparnasse* ☎ *01–42–18–56–50* ⊕ *www.fondationcartier.com* 🖅 *€11: €1 fee to purchase online* 🕑 *Closed Mon.* Ⓜ *Raspail.*

★ Hôtel des Invalides

The Baroque complex known as Les Invalides (pronounced "lehz-ahn-vah- leed") is the eternal home of Napoléon Bonaparte (1769–1821) or, more precisely, the little dictator's remains, which lie entombed under the towering golden dome.

Louis XIV ordered the facility built in 1670 to house disabled soldiers (hence the name), and at one time 4,000 military men lived here. Today, a portion of it still serves as a veterans' residence and hospital. The Musée de l'Armée, containing an exhaustive collection of military artifacts from antique armor to weapons, is also here.

If you see only a single sight, make it the Église du Dome (one of Les Invalides' two churches) at the back of the complex. Napoléon's tomb was moved here in 1840 from the island of Saint Helena, where he died in forced exile. The emperor's body is protected by a series of no fewer than six coffins—one set inside the next, sort of like a Russian nesting doll—which are then encased in a sarcophagus of red quartzite. The bombastic tribute is ringed by statues symbolizing Napoléon's campaigns of conquest. To see more Napoléoniana, check out the collection in the Musée de l'Armée featuring his trademark gray frock coat and huge bicorne hat. Look for the figurines reenacting the famous coronation scene when Napoléon crowns his empress, Josephine. You can see a grander version of this scene by the painter David hanging in the Louvre.

The Esplanade des Invalides, the great lawns in front of the building, are favorite spots for pickup soccer, Frisbee games, sunbathing, and dog walking—despite signs asking you to stay off the grass. ■TIP→ The best entrance to use is at the southern end, on Place Vauban (Avenue de Tourville); the ticket office is here, as is Napoléon's Tomb. There are automatic ticket machines at the main entrance on Place des Invalides. ⊠ Pl. des Invalides, Eiffel Tower ☎ 01-44-42-38-77 ⊕ www.musee-armee.fr ⊠ €12 with temporary exhibitions; €10 after 5 pm Apr.–Oct. and after 4 pm Nov.–Mar. ☞ Last

admission 30 min before closing Ⓜ La Tour–Maubourg, Varenne.

Jardin Catherine-Labouré
Camouflaged by a large stone wall next to Le Bon Marché department store, this little-known park is a delight. The green space was once the private garden and vegetable patch of the 17th-century Filles de la Charité convent, whose remaining buildings stand at the southern edge of the park. The garden's manicured lawns, complete with a vine-laden pergola and fruit trees, were designed in the shape of a cross. ⊠ 29 rue de Babylone, St-Germain-des-Prés Ⓜ Sèvres–Babylone, Vaneau.

★ Jardin du Luxembourg
Everything that is charming, unique, and befuddling about Parisian parks can be found in the Luxembourg Gardens: cookie-cutter trees, ironed-and-pressed walkways, sculpted flower beds, and immaculate emerald lawns meant for admiring, not necessarily for lounging. The tree- and bench-lined paths are a marvelous reprieve from the bustle of the two neighborhoods it borders: the Quartier Latin and St-Germain-des-Prés. Beautifully austere during the winter months, the garden grows intoxicating as spring brings blooming beds of daffodils, tulips, and hyacinths, and the circular pool teems with wooden sailboats nudged along by children. The park's northern boundary is dominated by the Palais du Luxembourg, which houses the Sénat (Senate), one of

two chambers that make up the Parliament. The original inspiration for the gardens came from Marie de Medici, nostalgic for the Boboli Gardens of her native Florence; she is commemorated by the Fontaine de Medicis.

Les Marionettes du Théâtre du Luxembourg is a timeless attraction, where, on weekends at 11 and 3:15 and Wednesday at 3:15 (hours may vary), you can catch classic *guignols* (marionette shows) for €6.40. The wide-eyed kids might be the real attraction—their expressions of utter surprise, despair, and glee have fascinated the likes of Henri Cartier-Bresson and François Truffaut. The park also has a merry-go-round, swings, and pony rides; the bandstand hosts free concerts on summer afternoons.

As you stroll the paths, you might be surprised by a familiar sight: one of the original (miniature) casts of the Statue of Liberty was installed in the gardens in 1906. Check out the rotating photography exhibits hanging on the perimeter fence near the entrance on Boulevard St-Michel and Rue de Vaugirard. If you want to burn off that breakfast *pain au chocolat,* there's a well-maintained trail around the perimeter that is frequented by gentrified joggers. Gendarmes regularly walk the grounds to ensure park rules are enforced; follow guidelines posted on entry gates. ⊠ *Bordered by Bd. St-Michel and Rues de Vaugirard, de Medicis, Guynemer, Auguste-Comte, and*

d'Assas, St-Germain-des-Prés ⊕ *www.senat.fr/visite/jardin* ✆ *Free* ☾ *Closed dusk–dawn* Ⓜ *Odéon; RER: B Luxembourg.*

★ Les Catacombes

This is just the thing for anyone with morbid interests: a descent through dark, clammy passages brings you to Paris's principal ossuary, which also once served as a hideout maze for the French Resistance. Bones from the defunct Cimetière des Innocents were the first to arrive in 1786, when decomposing bodies started seeping into the cellars of the market at Les Halles, drawing swarms of ravenous rats. The legions of bones dumped here are stacked not by owner but by type—rows of skulls, packs of tibias, and piles of spinal disks, often rather artfully arranged. Among the nameless 6 million or so are the bones of Madame de Pompadour (1721–64), laid to rest with the riffraff after a lifetime spent as the mistress of Louis XV. Unfortunately, one of the most interesting aspects of the catacombs is one you probably won't see: *cataphiles,* mostly art students, have found alternate entrances into its 300 km (186 miles) of tunnels and here they make art, party, and purportedly raise hell. Arrive early as the line can get long and only 200 people can descend at a time. Audioguides are available for €5. Not recommended for claustrophobes or young children. ⊠ *1 av. du Colonel Henri Roi-Tanguy, Montparnasse* ☎ *01–43–22–47–63* ⊕ *www.catacombes.paris.fr* ✆ *€13*

⊘ *Closed Mon.* Ⓜ *Métro or RER: Denfert-Rochereau.*

★ Musée d'Orsay

Opened in 1986, this gorgeously renovated Belle Époque train station displays a world-famous collection of Impressionist and Postimpressionist paintings on three floors. To visit the exhibits in a roughly chronological manner, start on the first floor, take the escalators to the top, and end on the second. If you came to see the biggest names here, head straight for the top floor and work your way down. English audioguides and free color-coded museum maps (both available just past the ticket booths) will help you plot your route.

Galleries off the main alley feature early works by Manet and Cézanne in addition to pieces by masters such as Delacroix and Ingres. The Pavillon Amont has Courbet's masterpieces *L'Enterrement à Ornans* and *Un Atelier du Peintre.* Hanging in Salle 14 is Édouard Manet's *Olympia,* a painting that pokes fun at the fashion for all things Greek and Roman (his nubile subject is a 19th-century courtesan, not a classical goddess). Impressionism gets going on the top floor, with iconic works by Degas, Pissarro, Sisley, and Renoir. Don't miss Monet's series on the cathedral at Rouen and, of course, samples of his water lilies. Other selections by these artists are housed in galleries on the ground floor. On the second floor, you'll find an exquisite collection of sculpture

as well as Art Nouveau furniture and decorative objects. There are rare surviving works by Hector Guimard (designer of the swooping green Paris métro entrances), plus Lalique and Tiffany glassware. Postimpressionist galleries include work by van Gogh and Gauguin, while Neo-impressionist galleries highlight Seurat and Signac.

■TIP→ To avoid the lines here, which are among the worst in Paris, book ahead online or buy a Museum Pass, then go directly to Entrance C. Otherwise, go early. Thursday evening the museum is open until 9:45 pm and less crowded. Don't miss the views of Sacré-Coeur from the balcony—this is the Paris that inspired the Impressionists. The Musée d'Orsay is closed Monday, unlike the Pompidou and the Louvre, which are closed Tuesday. ⊠ *1 rue de la Légion d'Honneur, St-Germain-des-Prés* ☎ *01-40-49-48-14* ⊕ *www. musee-orsay.fr* 🎫 *€12; €9 after 4:30, except Thurs. after 6 (free 1st Sun. of month)* ⊘ *Closed Mon.* Ⓜ *Solférino; RER: Musée d'Orsay.*

Musée du Quai Branly

This eye-catching museum overlooking the Seine was built by star architect Jean Nouvel to house the state-owned collection of "non-Western" art, culled from the Musée National des Arts d'Afrique et d'Océanie and the Musée de l'Homme. Exhibits mix artifacts from antiquity to the modern age, such as funeral masks from Melanesia, Siberian shaman drums, Indonesian textiles, and African statuary. A corkscrew ramp leads from the lobby to a cavernous exhibition space, which is color coded to designate sections from Asia, Africa, and Oceania. The lighting is dim—sometimes too dim to read the information panels (which makes investing in the €5 audioguide a good idea).

Renowned for his bold modern designs, Nouvel has said he wanted the museum to follow no rules; however, many critics gave his vision a thumbs-down when it was unveiled in 2006. The exterior resembles a massive, rust-color rectangle suspended on stilts, with geometric shapes cantilevered to the facade facing the Seine and louvered panels on the opposite side. The colors (dark reds, oranges, and yellows) are meant to evoke the tribal art within. A "living wall" composed of some 150 species of exotic plants grows on the exterior, which is surrounded by a wild jungle garden with swampy patches—an impressive sight after dark when scores of cylindrical colored lights are illuminated. The trendy Les Ombres restaurant on the museum's fifth floor (separate entrance) has prime views of the Tour Eiffel—and prices to match. The budget-conscious can enjoy the garden at Le Café Branly on the ground floor. ✉ 37 quai Branly, Eiffel Tower ☎ 01-56-61-70-00 ⊕ www.quaibranly.fr 🎫 From €10 (free 1st Sun. of month) ⊙ Closed Mon. ☞ Ticket office closes 1 hr before museum Ⓜ Alma-Marceau.

WORTH A TRIP

One of the prettiest buildings in Paris is tucked away on a residential street a few blocks from the Eiffel Tower. Designed by Jules Aimé Lavirotte in 1901, the stunning Art Nouveau building at **29 avenue Rapp** was an expression of the architect's love of his wife. Down the street at **3 Square Rapp** is another gorgeous building by the same architect—turn around and you'll have a surprising view of the Eiffel Tower.

★ Musée Rodin

Auguste Rodin (1840–1917) briefly made his home and studio in the Hôtel Biron, a grand 18th-century mansion that now houses a museum dedicated to his work. He died rich and famous, but many of the sculptures that earned him a place in art history were originally greeted with contempt by the general public, which was unprepared for his powerful brand of sexuality and raw physicality. The reaction to this museum's new look was markedly different when it finally emerged from a three-year, tip-to-toe renovation in 2015. Everything from the building and grounds to Rodin's sculptures themselves was restored and re-presented. The reputed cost was €16 million; the overall effect remains nothing short of dazzling.

Most of Rodin's best-known sculptures are in the gardens. The front one is dominated by The Gates of Hell (circa 1880). Inspired by the monumental bronze doors of Italian

Renaissance churches, Rodin set out to illustrate stories from Dante's *Divine Comedy*. He worked on the sculpture for more than 30 years, and it served as a "sketch pad" for many of his later works. Look carefully and you can see miniature versions of *The Kiss* (bottom right), *The Thinker* (top center), and *The Three Shades* (top center). Inside, look for *The Bronze Age*, which was inspired by the sculptures of Michelangelo: this piece was so realistic that critics accused Rodin of having cast a real body in plaster. In addition, the museum now showcases long-neglected models, plasters, and paintings, which offer insight into Rodin's creative process. Pieces by other artists, gleaned from his personal collection, are on display as well—including paintings by van Gogh, Renoir, and Monet. Antiquities Rodin collected (and was inspired by) have been removed from storage and given their own room. There's also a room devoted to works by Camille Claudel (1864–1943), his student and longtime mistress, who was a remarkable sculptor in her own right. Her torturous relationship with Rodin eventually drove her out of his studio—and out of her mind. In 1913 she was packed off to an asylum, where she remained until her death. An English audioguide (€6) is available for the permanent collection and for temporary exhibitions. Tickets can be purchased online for priority access (€1 service fee). If you wish to linger, the lovely Café du Musée Rodin serves meals and snacks in the shade of the garden's linden trees. ⊠ *77 rue de Varenne, Eiffel Tower* ☏ *01-44-18-61-10* ⊕ *www.musee-rodin.fr* ⊠ *From €10; €4 gardens only (free 1st Sun. of month)* ⊘ *Closed Mon.* Ⓜ *Varenne.*

Musée Zadkine

The hub of Paris's early-20th-century art scene, the area was once speckled with art studios; this is one of the rare few that still exist. The site, home and studio of Russian-born artist Ossip Zadkine from 1928 to 1967, was converted into a museum in his honor in 1982. You can admire the talented Cubist's sculptures or enjoy a moment of calm in his beautiful private garden. ⊠ *100 rue d'Assas, Montparnasse* ☏ *01-55-42-77-20* ⊕ *www.zadkine.paris. fr* ⊠ *Free* ⊘ *Closed Mon.* Ⓜ *Vavin, Notre-Dame-des-Champs.*

Passage Dauphine

Constructed during the the passageway-building trend of the early 1800s, Passage Dauphine is one of the few built on the Left Bank. Unlike those built on the Right Bank, this passage doesn't have a glass rooftop and instead opens into a wide courtyard. It's here you'll find L'Heure Gourmande, a lovely tea salon where you can further absorb the passageway's charm over a drink or light meal. ⊠ *30 rue Dauphine, St-Germain-des-Prés* Ⓜ *Odéon.*

★ Place St-Sulpice

While the Place St-Germain-des-Prés usually steals the limelight, this attractive square located a block south has a more beguiling charm. The spacious plaza is surrounded by elegant shops and is flanked on the east end by the regal Église St-Sulpice, a 17th-century Baroque church made famous by Dan Brown's best-selling novel *The Da Vinci Code*. It also houses awe-inspiring frescos by Delacroix, located in the chapel to the right of the entrance. The square is crowned by one of the city's loveliest fountains, depicting four French religious figures of the 17th century. Pass through at dusk or at night when the square is particularly magical. ⊠ *Pl. St-Sulpice, St-Germain-des-Prés* Ⓜ *St-Sulpice.*

★ Promenade des Berges de la Seine

Hugely popular with pedestrians, Les Berges has become one of the best places to hang out on the Left Bank. A former expressway along the Seine, the promenade extends 2 1/3 km (1½ miles) from the Musée d'Orsay to the Pont de l'Alma. All ages come to the diverse public space; it features sports facilities, playgrounds, floating gardens, and a number of bustling cafés (see Nightlife section). ⊠ *Promenade des Berges de la Seine , from Quai Anatole France to Quai d'Orsay, Invalides* Ⓜ *Invalides, Solferino.*

★ Rue de Furstemburg

Hidden within St-Germain's dense maze of narrow streets behind the defunct St-Germain Abbey is one of Paris's prettiest squares. It bears the name of Cardinal Guillaume-Egon de Fürstenberg, who had the lane built as a private access to his stately palace. Reigned over by large Paulownia trees, classic Parisian lamp posts, and alluring boutiques, the square is home to the former studio (now a museum) of Romantic-era painter Eugène Délacroix. ⊠ *6 rue Furstemburg, St-Germain-des-Prés* Ⓜ *St-Germain-des-Prés.*

Square Roger Stéphane

Tucked away at the end of the pedestrian Rue Récamier is a small park that feels oh-so-secret, with meandering paths, a gurgling waterfall, and secluded nooks with romantic benches. It was originally called Square Récamier, in honor of a stunning early-19th-century socialite, and was renamed in 2008 after journalist Roger Stéphane. ⊠ *7 rue Récamier, St-Germain-des-Prés* Ⓜ *Sèvres–Babylone.*

🛍 Shopping

A.P.C.

The A.P.C. brand may be antiflash and minimal, but a knowing eye can always pick out its jeans in a crowd. The clothes here are rigorously well made and worth the investment in lasting style. Prime wardrobe pieces include dark indigo and black denim, zip-up cardigans, peacoats, and streamlined ankle boots. ⊠ *38 rue Madame, 6e, St-Germain-des-Prés* ☎ *01-42-22-12-77* ⊕ *www.apc. fr* ☾ *Closed Sun.* Ⓜ *St-Sulpice.*

★ Avril Gau

After designing a dozen collections for Chanel, Gau struck out on her own, opening her neo-Baroque boutique on the charming Rue des Quatre Vents. Gau takes her inspiration from glamorous French movie icons, dreaming up styles that are elegant and sexy without being trashy. Sleek pumps, wedge booties, ballerina flats, and riding boots (all in the finest quality calf, reptile, and lambskin) are as classy as they come. Bags share the spotlight, with updated riffs on the classics. ⊠ *17 rue des Quatre Vents, 6e, St-Germain-des-Prés* ☎ *01-43-29-49-04* ⊕ *www. avrilgau.com* ⊗ *Closed Sun.* Ⓜ *Odéon.*

City Pharma

At this unassuming drug store, the only discount "para-pharmacy" in Paris, you can stock up on favorite beauty products at exceptional prices. Make room in your suitcase for bargain bottles of Avène, La Roche-Posay, and Nuxe, as well as homeopathic and traditional medicines. ⊠ *26 rue du Four, St-Germain-des-Prés* ☎ *01-46-33-20-81* ⊕ *pharmacie-citypharma. fr* ⊗ *Closed Sun.* Ⓜ *Mabillon, St-Germain-des-Prés.*

★ Deyrolle

This fascinating 19th-century taxidermist has long been a stop for curiosity seekers. A 2008 fire destroyed what was left of the original shop, but it has been lavishly restored and remains a cabinet of curiosities par excellence. Create your own box of butterflies or metallic beetles from scores of bug-filled drawers or just enjoy the menagerie that includes stuffed zebras, monkeys, lions, bears, and more. Also in stock: collectible shells, corals, and crustaceans,

VIEWFINDER

You're in prime territory for a photo of the Eiffel Tower here. Snap a shot at Champ de Mars, especially with the springtime cherry blossoms, or capture it within a very Parisian setting on Rue de l'Université or Rue St-Dominique. For a backdrop of the river, try the Passerelle Debilly or the romantic Pont Alexandre III. Get up close over a meal at Les Ombres, the rooftop restaurant of nearby Musée du Quai Branly, or right at the tower, snap a whimsical pic with the old-fashioned carousel found at the tip of Pont d'Iéna.

Share your photo with us!
@FodorsTravel #FodorsOnTheGo

plus a generous library of books and posters that once graced every French schoolroom. There is a line of cool wallpaper murals, too. ⊠ *46 rue du Bac, 7e, St-Germain-des-Prés* ☎ *01-42-22-30-07* ⊕ *www.deyrolle. com* ⊗ *Closed Sun.* Ⓜ *Rue du Bac.*

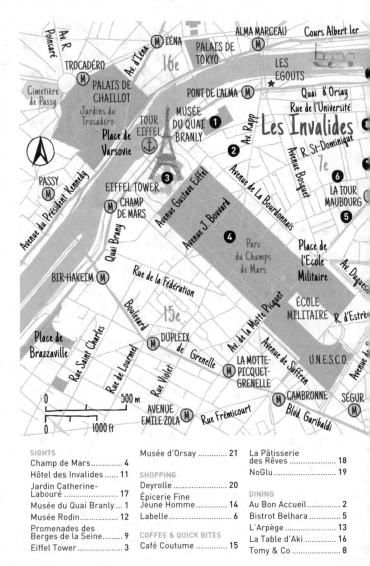

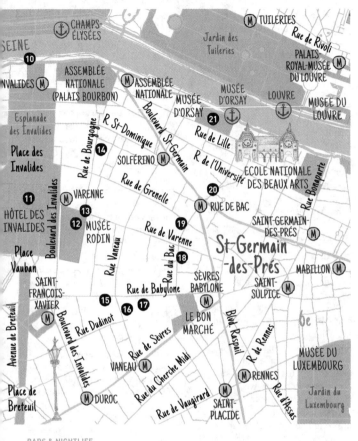

BARS & NIGHTLIFE

Épicerie Fine Jeune Homme
Stock up on supplies for a chic picnic on Les Berges at this refined food shop a few blocks south of the Seine. The *jeune homme* (young man) in question is young entrepreneur Nicolas Fortchantre, who's applied his experience working for the high-end culinary brand Lenôtre to carefully select his range of exquisite, and somewhat *cher* (pricey), artisanal products, from pâtés and wild onion spread to camembert popcorn and craft beer. ✉ *17 rue de Bourgogne, Eiffel Tower* ☏ *09–67–72–31–75* ⊕ *www.epiceriejeunehomme.fr* ⊗ *Closed Sun.* Ⓜ *Invalides.*

⭐ **Gab & Jo**
Forget about Eiffel Tower keychains; the coolest souvenirs to bring back from your trip are at this hip 100% made-in-France concept shop. Hand-picked by husband and wife team Alexis Leroy and Fanny de Parscau, the shop's eclectic collection features the likes of Charles de Gaulle–shape bottle openers, blue-white-and-red boxers, and quirky cell phone cases—a bona fide Ali Baba's cave of French delights. ✉ *28 rue Jacob, St-Germain-des-Prés* ☏ *09–84–53–58–43* ⊕ *www.gabjo.fr* ⊗ *Closed Sun.* Ⓜ *St-Germain-des-Prés.*

Labelle
Find the perfect Parisian accessory at this boutique in the 7e arrondissement showcasing the best in local Parisian designers. Founded by three young entrepreneurs and fashion lovers, the collection features limited-edition jewelry, irresistible handbags, and a regularly changing range of boho chic clothes, which are also available via their e-shop. ✉ *176 rue de Grenelle, Invalides* ☏ *09–84–05–09–22* ⊕ *www.lab-elle.com* ⊗ *Closed Sun.* Ⓜ *La Tour-Maubourg.*

⭐ **La Dernière Goutte**
This inviting *cave* (literally wine store or wine cellar) focuses on wines by small French producers. Each is handpicked by the owner, along with a choice selection of estate Champagnes, Armagnac, and the classic Vieille Prune (plum brandy). The friendly English-speaking staff makes browsing a pleasure. ■TIP➜ Don't miss the Saturday afternoon tastings with the winemakers. ✉ *6 rue de Bourbon le Château, 6e, St-Germain-des-Prés* ☏ *01–46–29–11–62* Ⓜ *Odéon.*

⭐ **MKT Studio**
While perusing the boutiques on the popular St-Germain shopping street Rue Bonaparte, pop into this local designer for some basics to complete your French Girl look. Elegance and modern edginess rub shoulders in their women's tops, jeans, skirts, dresses, and jackets inspired by late 20th-century style and icons like Kate Moss and Patti Smith. ✉ *55 rue Bonaparte, St-Germain-des-Prés* ☏ *01–42–33–88–39* ⊕ *mktstudio.com* ⊗ *Closed Sun., 3 wks in Aug.* Ⓜ *St-Germain-des-Prés, Mabillon.*

Patrick Roger
Paris's bad-boy chocolatier likes to shock with provocative shapes and wicked humor. Everything is sinfully

CAFÉ CULTURE

Is there anything more Parisian than leisurely sipping coffee at a café? Mais, non. And if you want to do as the locals do, you're in the right neighborhood. St-Germain is strongly associated with cafés—the city's first café, Le Procope, opened here in 1686. Although pausing at a café has traditionally been less about the quality of the brew than about the contemplating, people-watching, and lingering, there are now a growing number of spots to try good coffee in the neighborhood.

Traditional Picks

The heyday of the Left Bank's cafés crescendoed in the early 20th century when the likes of Hemingway, Picasso, Simone de Beauvoir, and Jean-Paul Sartre could be found debating around the tables of famous cafés such as Les Deux Magots, Café de Flore, and the Brasserie Lipp. Today these legendary establishments still draw a mix of locals and foreigners, leisurely reading over the same allongé (long espresso).

New Cafés on the Block

The arrival of Starbucks in 2004 caused some concern that the death of the Parisian café was imminent; nevertheless, the classic café still percolates strongly, alongside a growing number of contemporary coffee shops that have challenged regular cafés to up their game. As you're ambling around the district, stop to order an exceptional coffee at Café Coutume, one of the city's first new-wave coffee roasters, with lower prices than the famous cafés, or snatch a seat on the terrace of local hangouts La Palette and Le Bar du Marché. See Nightlife section.

good. The Boulevard St-Germain shop is one of seven citywide. ✉ 108 bd. St-Germain, 6e, St-Germain-des-Prés ☎ 01-43-29-38-42 ⊕ www.patrickroger.com Ⓜ Odéon.

Paul & Joe

Nonchalant Parisian chic is epitomized in every item hanging at the main boutique of this trendy French brand, a darling of French fashion media. Named after designer Sophie Albou's two sons, Paul & Joe features young, daring, and fun ready-to-wear clothes for women, men, and children as well as accessories and beauty products. ✉ 64 rue des Sts-Pères, St-Germain-des-Prés ☎ 01-42-22-47-01 ⊕

www.paulandjoe.com ⊗ Closed Sun. Ⓜ St-Germain-des-Prés.

★ Sabbia Rosa

You could easily walk straight past this discreet, boudoirlike boutique. It is, however, one of the world's finest lingerie stores and the place where actresses Catherine Deneuve and Isabelle Adjani (along with others who might not want to reveal their errand) buy superb French silks. ✉ 71–73 rue des Sts-Pères, 6e, St-Germain-des-Prés ☎ 01-45-48-88-37 Ⓜ St-Germain-des-Prés.

★ Verbreuil

The classic-contemporary handbags here are for women whose sense of style transcends any logo. Refined, discrete, and meticulously crafted down to the finest detail, each of the four styles—in calf, crocodile, and shagreen, with luxe variations for evening—will add infinite style and elegance to any outfit. ⊠ *4 rue de Fleurus, 6e, St-Germain-des-Prés* ☎ *01-45-49-22-69* ⊕ *www.verbreuil. com* Ⓜ *Vavin, St-Sulpice.*

☕ Coffee and Quick Bites

Café Coutume
$ | Café. A lofty space between the Musée Rodin and the Bon Marché makes this the perfect pit stop between museum-going and shopping. Look for healthy salads, sandwiches, snacks, desserts, and a delicious cup of any kind of coffee drink that takes your fancy. **Known for:** some of the finest coffee in town; healthy salads for lunch; prime location near major museums. *Average main: €8* ⊠ *47 rue de Babylone, 7e, Eiffel Tower* ☎ *01-45-51-50-47* ⊕ *www.coutume-cafe.com* ◷ *No dinner* Ⓜ *St-François-Xavier, Sèvres–Babylone.*

Café de Flore
$$ | Café. Picasso, Chagall, Sartre, and de Beauvoir, attracted by the luxury of a heated café, worked and wrote here in the early 20th century. Today you'll find more tourists than intellectuals, and prices are hardly aimed at struggling artists, but the outdoor terrace is great for people-watching and popular with Parisians. **Known for:** excellent people-watching; old-world atmosphere; legendary setting on a pretty square across

from Paris's oldest church. *Average main: €22* ⊠ *172 bd. St-Germain, 6e, St-Germain-des-Prés* ☎ *01-45-48-55-26* Ⓜ *St-Germain-des-Pres.*

Claus St-Germain-des-Prés
$$$ | Modern French. After the success of his original venue near Palais-Royal, Claus Estermann is wooing stylish Left Bankers with his sophisticated pastries and brunches. Opened in 2017, the luminous café is the perfect place for a classy coffee break or a gluten-free brownie to take window shopping in the heart of St-Germain. **Known for:** homemade baked goods; inventive recipes beyond French classics; farm-raised eggs and organic options. *Average main: €25* ⊠ *2 rue Clément, St-Germain-des-Prés* ☎ *01-55-26-95-10* ⊕ *www.clausparis. com* ◷ *No dinner* Ⓜ *Mabillon, Odéon.*

Colorova
$$$$ | French Fusion. A quiet side street in the 6e arrondissement conceals this popular breakfast and brunch spot, where the modern interior design is just as colorful as the tea salon's playful brunch. Menu options bear names like "swaggy" and "smiley" that will indeed leave you smiling—as long as you don't look at the prices. **Known for:** inventive takes on classic pastries; French toast; weekend crowds. *Average main: €35* ⊠ *47 rue de l'Abbé Grégoire, St-Germain-des-Prés* ☎ *01-45-44-67-56* Ⓜ *St-Placide.*

Eggs & Co.
$ | Bistro. With a cheerfully bright and tiny, wood-beamed dining room—there's more space in

the loftlike upstairs—this spot is devoted to the egg in all its forms. Whether you like yours baked with smoked salmon, whisked into an omelet with truffle shavings, or beaten into fluffy pancakes, there will be something for you on the blackboard menu. **Known for:** great breakfast and brunch spot; quick, healthy shopping break; cheerful, child-friendly atmosphere. *Average main: €12* ✉ *11 rue Bernard Palissy, 6e, St-Germain-des-Prés* ☎ *01–45–44–02–52* ⊕ *www.eggsandco.fr* Ⓜ *St-Germain-des-Prés.*

La Pâtisserie des Rêves

$ | French. All of your French pastry dreams will come true after a sensational snack at this jewel box of a pastry shop. Chef Philippe Conticini has refined and perfected the classic pastry, presenting culinary works of art under glass cases—your challenge will be choosing among these bijoux. **Known for:** cream-filled Paris-Brest; Grand Cru chocolate pastries; seasonal creations. *Average main: €6* ✉ *93 rue du Bac, St-Germain-des-Prés* ☎ *09–72–60–93–19* ⊕ *lapatisser-iedesreves.com* ⊘ *Closed Mon.* Ⓜ *Rue du Bac, Sèvres–Babylone.*

NoGlu

$ | Bakery. Left Bankers come here to enjoy the wheat-free, organic delicacies of one of Paris's first and foremost gluten-free restaurants. Dig into a decadent breakfast, healthy lunch, or teatime in their stylish dining room, or grab one of their phenomenal pastries and an almond milk latte at their takeaway counter. **Known for:** energy-boosting

granola with goji berries; good-value vegan and detox lunch menus; madeleines. *Average main: €12* ✉ *69 rue de Grenelle, St-Germain-des-Prés* ☎ *01–58–90–18–12* ⊕ *www.noglu.fr* Ⓜ *Rue du Bac.*

Saint Pearl

$ | Modern American. For a snack, fresh-pressed juice, or coffee to go in the 7e arrondissement, head to this tiny café on Rue des Sts-Pères. The friendly modern space, with exposed-stone walls and a perch facing the street for people-watching, also serves a range of light lunch items, including tasty vegan options. **Known for:** matcha cheesecake; young, hip crowd; soy and almond milk lattes. *Average main: €6* ✉ *38 rue des Sts-Pères, St-Germain-des-Prés* ☎ *01–71–50–16–73* ⊘ *Closed Sun., 3 wks in Aug.* Ⓜ *St-Germain-des-Près, Rue de Bac.*

★ Treize au Jardin

$$ | American. Southern-inspired lunch and brunch fare is served at this contemporary, American-run café, which opened in 2018 across from the Jardin du Luxembourg. The airy space, decked out in hanging plants, wildflowers, and eclectic furniture, reflects the spirit of 21st-century Parisian cafés and has boozy teatime to boot. **Known for:** incredible buttermilk biscuits; carrot cake; friendly welcome and relaxing ambience. *Average main: €15* ✉ *5 rue de Medicis, Île Saint-Louis* ⊕ *www.treizebakeryparis.com* Ⓜ *Luxembourg.*

🍴 Dining

Au Bon Accueil

$$$$ | Bistro. To see what well-heeled Parisians like to eat these days, book a table at this chic little bistro run by Jacques Lacipière as soon as you get to town. The contemporary dining room is unusually comfortable, and the sidewalk tables have an Eiffel Tower view, but it's the excellent, well-priced *cuisine du marché* that has made this spot a hit. **Known for:** good value, three-course dinner menu; excellent price-to-quality ratio; scintillating views of the Eiffel Tower from the charming sidewalk terrace. *Average main: €39* ⊠ *14 rue de Monttessuy, 7e, Eiffel Tower* ☎ *01–47–05–46–11* ⊕ *www.aubonaccueilparis.com* ⊗ *Closed weekends and 3 wks in Aug.* Ⓜ *Métro or RER: Pont de l'Alma.*

Avant Comptoir du Marché

$ | French. Star chef Yves Camdeborde focuses on traditional market products at his newest small-plate venue at the Marché St-Germain. The chalkboard tapas menu changes regularly, but expect to find the likes of slow-cooked pork shoulder, charcuterie made by the chef's brother, seasonal veggies, and a fine selection of mostly natural wines. **Known for:** acclaimed French chef; quality meats; buzzing ambience. *Average main: €12* ⊠ *14 rue Lobineau, St-Germain-des-Prés* ☎ *01–44–27–07–97* Ⓜ *Mabillon.*

Bistrot Belhara

$$ | French. The Basque country cuisine of this attractive bistro, named after a coastal village in the region, has made quite the splash in the Left Bank's culinary scene. The chef pays homage to his native region with sophisticated takes on its classic recipes, using ingredients from the Pyrenees and fresh seafood from the Atlantic. **Known for:** pintxos (Basque tapas); excellent value prix-fixe menus; simple, chic dining room. *Average main: €20* ⊠ *23 rue Duvivier, Invalides* ☎ *01–45–51–41–77* ⊕ *www.bistrotbelhara.com* ⊗ *Closed Sun. and Mon., 2 wks in Aug.* Ⓜ *École Militaire, La Tour-Maubourg.*

Breizh Café

$ | French. An outpost of the wildly popular Marais location, this crêperie is hard to beat on originality and quality. Their flavor-packed savory and sweet crêpes are made with organic stone-milled flour and top-notch ingredients shipped in from Brittany, the motherland of this French specialty. **Known for:** Paris's most inventive crêpes; 60 types of cider; sake (owner Bertrand Larcher also has a branch in Japan). *Average main: €13* ⊠ *1 rue de l'Odéon, St-Germain-des-Prés* ☎ *01–42–49–34–73* ⊕ *breizhcafe.com* Ⓜ *Odéon.*

★ Clover Green

$$$ | Contemporary. Michelin-starred chef Jean-François Piège puts aside traditional French gastronomy and goes decidedly green at this intimate restaurant, managed with his wife Elodie and tucked away on a St-Germain side street. Vegetables steal the spotlight, yet the menu leaves some laurels for exceptionally high-quality fish and meat dishes that are intensely flavorful and inventive. **Known for:** French celebrity chef and judge of Top Chef France; vegetarian tasting menu; wine list of independent producers. *Average main: €25 ⊠ 5 rue Perronet, St-Germain-des-Prés* ☎ *01–75–50–00–05* ⊕ *www.jeanfrancoispiege.com* ☉ *Closed Sun. and Mon., 2 wks in Aug.* Ⓜ *Rue du Bac, St-Germain-des-Prés.*

The Cod House

$$ | Japanese Fusion. The Odéon area got undeniably hipper when this innovative Japanese tapas and cocktail venue opened in late 2017. A modern-day izakaya bar with a Parisian twist, the restaurant is an airy loftlike space where you can sip on outstanding signature cocktails and nibble on an eclectic range of Japanese-French small plates, sashimi, and maki. **Known for:** patatas bravas (potatoes in spicy tomato sauce) de Tokyo; Nihon Cha Punch with matcha-infused cachaça; a cool French and international crowd. *Average main: €18 ⊠ 1 rue de Condé, St-Germain-des-Prés* ☎ *01–42–49–35–59* ⊕ *www.thecodhouse.fr* Ⓜ *Odéon.*

★ Fish La Boissonerie

$$ | Bistro. A perennial favorite, expats and locals prize this lively, unpretentious bistro for its friendly atmosphere, consistently good food, solid wine list, and English-speaking staff—a quartet sorely lacking in the neighborhood. Dishes like velvety black squid-ink risotto, roasted cod with tender braised fennel, and crispy pumpkin tempura always hit the spot, especially when followed by decadent molten chocolate cake, honey-roasted figs, or banana-bread pudding. **Known for:** convivial atmosphere; excellent selection of natural wines; good-value menu. *Average main: €22 ⊠ 69 rue de Seine, 6e, St-Germain-des-Prés* ☎ *01–43–54–34–69* Ⓜ *St-Germain-des-Prés, Odéon.*

★ L'Arpège

$$$$ | Modern French. Breton-born Alain Passard, one of the most respected chefs in Paris, famously shocked the French culinary world by declaring that he was bored with meat. Though his vegetarianism is more lofty than practical—L'Arpège still caters to fish and poultry eaters—he does cultivate his own vegetables outside Paris and his dishes elevate the humblest vegetables to sublime heights. **Known for:** legendary Paris chef; one of Paris's rare three-star restaurants; redefining what a cook can do with simple vegetables. *Average main: €100 ⊠ 84 rue de Varenne, 7e, Eiffel Tower* ☎ *01–47–05–09–06* ⊕ *www.alain-passard.com* ☉ *Closed weekends* Ⓜ *Varenne.*

★ La Table d'Aki

$$$$ | Modern French. Set in a quiet, aristocratic *quartier* near the Musée Rodin, La Table d'Akihiro might just be the most perfect little-gem restaurant in all of Paris. Its simple elegance highlights the thrilling cuisine centered on the sea. **Known for:** romantic ambience; perfectly prepared fish; open kitchen serving just 16 diners at a time. *Average main: €40 ⊠ 49 rue Vaneau, 7e, Eiffel Tower* ☎ *01–45–44–43–48* ☉ *Closed Sun., Mon., 2 wks in Feb., and Aug.* Ⓜ *Saint-François-Xavier.*

Marcello

$$ | Italian. This swanky venue, hidden away next to the Marché St-Germain, serves the best of Italy in Paris. Wake up with an espresso made of Brûlerie de Belleville coffee, have a light lunch of *tramezzini* sandwiches (crustless deli sandwiches) in the industrial-style dining room, or sip on a Marcello's Spritz on the gorgeous *terrazzo*. **Known for:** stylish clientele and prices to match; supersize ravioli; the Paris-Turin, an Italian version of the Paris-Brest dessert. *Average main: €20* ⊠ *8 rue Mabillon, St-Germain-des-Prés* ☎ *01–43–26–52–26* ⊕ *www.marcello-paris.com* Ⓜ *Mabillon.*

Niébe

$$ | Brazilian. Refined versions of Brazilian, African, and Creole specialties are at the forefront in this bright, artsy restaurant, whose name means "black-eyed pea." Considered a magical bean in many countries, the ingredient is prominent in the signature Brazilian bean and pork stew, *feijoada* , although chef Rosilène Vitorino works her own wizardry in all the beautifully presented soul food dishes. **Known for:** comprehensive vegan menu; feijoada; organic cachaça. *Average main: €22* ⊠ *16 rue de la Grande Chaumière, Montparnasse* ☎ *01–43–29–43–31* ⊕ *www.restaurantniebe.com* ⊗ *Closed Sun. and Mon., Aug.* Ⓜ *Vavin.*

★ Quinsou

$$$ | French. The serious, unpretentious, and mightily creative cuisine here has quickly catapulted Quinsou to culinary fame. An emphasis on first-rate growers and suppliers puts vegetables in the limelight, though fish, shellfish, and game make a welcome appearance in the few market-fresh dishes that grace the daily menu . **Known for:** highly original seasonal cuisine; warm and welcoming service; good value prix-fixe menus. *Average main: €32* ⊠ *33 rue de l'Abbé Grégoire, 6e, St-Germain-des-Prés* ☎ *01–42–22–66–09* ⊕ *quinsou.business.site* ⊗ *Closed Sun. and Mon. No lunch Tues.* Ⓜ *Rennes, Saint-Placide.*

★ Semilla

$$$ | Bistro. The duo behind the popular neighborhood bistro Fish and the excellent wineshop La Dernière Goutte have poured their significant expertise into this laid-back bistro in the heart of tony St-Germain-des-Prés. Its sophisticated cuisine, superb wines by the bottle or glass, and total lack of pretension have quickly made Semilla the toast of the town. **Known for:** convivial dining room with a lively, appreciative crowd; great options for vegetarians; open kitchen with plenty of bistro classics. *Average main: €25* ⊠ *54 rue de Seine, 6e, St-Germain-des-Prés* ☎ *01–43–54–34–50* ⊕ *www.semillaparis.com* Ⓜ *Odéon, St-Germain-des-Prés.*

★ Tomy & Co

$$$ | Modern French. The inventive cuisine at chef Tomy Gousset's restaurant proves there's great food to be had not far from the Eiffel Tower. Bottles and vegetables line the walls, and beautiful dishes are perfectly executed in a mouthwatering collision of flavors and textures. **Known for:** avant-garde takes on French classics like tête de veau (calf's head); excellent value lunch menu; vegetables from the chef's own garden. *Average main: €30* ⊠ *22 rue Surcourf, Invalides* ☎ *01–45–51–46–93* ⊕ *www.tomy-gousset.com* ⊙ *Closed weekends, Aug.* Ⓜ *Invalides, La Tour-Maubourg.*

▼ Bars and Nightlife

Bar du Marché
This is the most popular and atmospheric café on Rue de Buci, the street where locals go for an evening drink. Come early to snatch a seat on its highly coveted terrace, order a reasonably priced drink served by waiters in red overalls, and take in the nightly comings and goings of the lively street. ⊠ *75 rue de Seine, St-Germain-des-Prés* ☎ *01–43–26–55–15* Ⓜ *Mabillon, Odéon.*

★ Castor Club
The Left Bank's cocktail scene got much more exciting when this speakeasy opened in 2016 just off Boulevard St-Germain. Hard to find if you're not in the know, the bar is unmarked save for a menu and very small window outside. The wooden facade may convince you that you've ended up at a hunting lodge in Montana, but once you step inside it's hip and cozy with killer cocktails (try the spicy Turkish Delight). ⊠ *14 rue Hautefeuille, St-Germain-des-Prés* ☎ *09–50–64–99–38* ☞ *Closed Sun. and Mon.* Ⓜ *Odéon.*

Compagnie de Vins Surnaturels
Not just natural, but "supernatural" wines are championed at this swanky *bar à vin* by the partners behind hot spots like the Experimental Cocktail Club and the Ballroom du Beef Club. Low lighting, intimate seating, and refined snacks set the tone for a chic, romantic evening. ⊠ *7 rue Lobineau, St-Germain-des-Prés* ☎ *09–54–90–20–20* ⊕ *www.compagniedesvinssur-naturels.com* Ⓜ *Mabillon.*

Faust
The rival to neighboring hot spot Rosa Bonheur sur Seine, Faust is a stylish retro lounge with the advantage of being underneath Pont Alexandre III. Things heat up here on Friday and Saturday, when you can drink cocktails on leather chesterfields and plush armchairs or dance until dawn with the help of top guest DJs. ⊠ *Pont Alexandre III - Rive Gauche, Invalides* ☎ *06–60–58–45–15* ⊕ *www.faustparis.fr* Ⓜ *Invalides.*

Fitzgerald
In the cocktail desert of the 7e arrondissement, quench your thirst for a quality drink at the Prohibition-style bar hidden at the back of this posh restaurant. The Great Gatsby himself would approve of its seductive decor, grazing-flamingo wallpaper, and intimate candlelit tables, complemented by light bites and a comprehensive cocktail menu with clever nods to the Lost Generation era. ⊠ *54 bd. de la Tour Maubourg, Invalides* ☎ *01–45–50–38–63* ⊕ *fitzgerald.paris* ☞ *Closed Sun.* Ⓜ *La Tour-Maubourg.*

La Palette

Soak up the artsy ambience of St-Germain at this café, popular with art gallery owners, École des Beaux Arts students, and stylish residents since 1902. On the edge of gallery-packed Rue de Seine, the bar's overflowing terrace is the perfect place to rest your feet, savor *un petit café* (quick coffee), or rub shoulders with locals during *apéro* (predinnertime). ⊠ *43 rue de Seine, St-Germain-des-Prés* ☎ *01-43-26-68-15* ⊕ *www.cafelapaletteparis.com/en* Ⓜ *Mabillon, Odéon*.

La Robe & La Mousse

Opened in 2017, this Left Bank branch of the Right Bank favorite La Fine Mousse is evidence that Paris's craft beer scene is expanding. Slightly more chic than its Right Bank contemporary, the aesthetics suit this posh district, but the dedication to the best artisanal beer remains the same. Here, the focus is on French production, in addition to a small selection of natural or biodynamic wines and ciders. ⊠ *3 rue Monsieur le Prince, St-Germain-des-Prés* ⊕ *www.lafinemousse.fr/la-robe-et-la-mousse* Ⓜ *Odéon*.

Prescription Cocktail Club

This club is brought to you by the owners of popular cocktail bars in London, New York, and Paris, including the Ballroom du Beef Club and the Experimental Cocktail Club. So rest assured: the atmosphere will be stylish (think upholstered chairs, dim lighting, and vintage touches), the crowd will be hip, and the drinks will be tasty. Located in fashionable St-Germain-des-Prés, it's a good after-shopping apéro or dinner option. ⊠ *23 rue Mazarine, 6e, St-Germain-des-Prés* ☎ *09-50-35-72-87* ⊕ *www.prescriptioncocktailclub.com* Ⓜ *Odéon*.

★ Tiger

There might not be a bathtub, but there are 130 types of gin on hand at this cool cocktail bar, located on one of St-Germain's buzzing bar streets. Light wood paneling and hanging vines make the inside fresh and inviting, but the hip, local crowd still spills out onto the sidewalk on weekends, grooving to the DJ's electro beats. ⊠ *13 rue Princesse, St-Germain-des-Prés* ☎ *01-84-05-81-74* ⊕ *www.tiger-paris.com* ☞ *Closed Sun.* Ⓜ *Mabillon*.

🎭 Performing Arts

Le Lucernaire

Occupying an abandoned factory, Le Lucernaire wins a standing ovation as far as cultural centers are concerned. With three theaters staging a total of six performances per day, three movie screens, a bookstore, photography exhibitions, a lively restaurant-bar, and the equally lively surrounding neighborhood of Vavin, it caters to young intellectuals. ⊠ *53 rue Notre-Dame-des-Champs, 6e, Montparnasse* ☎ *01-45-44-57-34* ⊕ *www.lucernaire.fr* Ⓜ *Notre-Dame-des-Champs*.

Trocadéro and Champs-Élysées

GO FOR

Iconic
Landmarks

World-Class
Museums

Swanky Bars

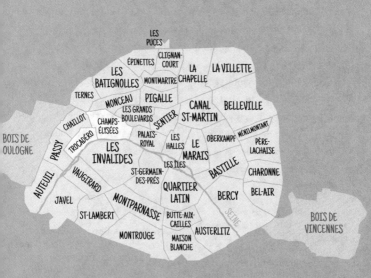

LES
PUCES

CLIGNAN-
COURT

ÉPINETTES

LA
CHAPELLE

LA VILLETTE

LES
BATIGNOLLES

MONTMARTRE

TERNES

MONCEAU

PIGALLE

LES GRANDS
BOULEVARDS

CANAL
ST-MARTIN

BELLEVILLE

CHAILLOT

CHAMPS-
ÉLYSÉES

SENTIER

BOIS DE
OULOGNE

TROCADÉRO

PALAIS-
ROYAL

LES
HALLES

LE
MARAIS

OBERKAMPF

MÉNILMONTANT

PÈRE-
LACHAISE

PASSY

LES
INVALIDES

LES ÎLES

AUTEUIL

VAUGIRARD

ST-GERMAIN-
DES-PRÉS

BASTILLE

CHARONNE

JAVEL

MONTPARNASSE

QUARTIER
LATIN

BERCY

BEL-AIR

ST-LAMBERT

BUTTE-AUX-
CAILLES

SEINE

BOIS DE
VINCENNES

MONTROUGE

AUSTERLITZ

MAISON
BLANCHE

The Seine snakes through the center of Paris, carving out two distinctly different sides of the city the same way the East River divides Brooklyn and Manhattan. La Rive Gauche, or Left Bank, considered the city's cultural soul, was the stomping grounds of Hemingway and philosopher Jean-Paul Sartre; la Rive Droite, or Right Bank, is more buttoned-up with its symmetrical squares, tulip-filled gardens, and grand boulevards, including the famous Champs-Élysées. Both banks, declared a UNESCO World Heritage site, are scenic enough for films (Woody Allen's Midnight in Paris is just one of many) and flâneurs, or people on a stroll. Eye the Eiffel Tower from the Jardins du Trocadéro before museum-hopping along the romantic riverbank to the Place de la Concorde and its 3,300-year-old Egyptian obelisk. The square marks the eastern end of the Champs-Élysées, the 2-km (1¼-mile) avenue stretching to the Arc de Triomphe. Designer-lined streets intersect the bustling boulevard, and ritzy hotels and cocktail bars are a given. But this landmark-rich neighborhood is undergoing a petit face-lift in the form of cutting-edge concept shops, revamped restaurants, and modernized monuments, such as the Grand Palais, slated for a €500 million sprucing up in 2020.—*by Lane Nieset*

◉ Sights

★ Arc de Triomphe
The Eiffel Tower isn't the only monument worth climbing in Paris. From the panoramic terrace on the top of the Arc de Triomphe, you'll have sweeping views across the city (and down the striking Champs-Élysées). If you're passing by in the evening, the flame of remembrance is relit every day at 6:30 pm to honor the Unknown Soldier, buried at the arch's base in 1921. ✉ *Pl. Charles-de-Gaulle, Champs-Élysées* ☎ *01-55-37-73-77* ⊕ *paris-arc-de-triomphe.fr* ⌖ *€12, free 3rd weekend* *of Sept. and 1st Sun. of month* Ⓜ *Charles de Gaulle–Etoile.*

Avenue des Champs-Élysées
Marcel Proust lovingly described the genteel elegance of the storied Champs-Élysées (pronounced "chahnz- *eleezay*," with an "n" sound instead of "m," and no "p") during its Belle Époque heyday, when its cobblestones resounded with the clatter of horses and carriages. Today, despite unrelenting traffic and the intrusion of chain stores and fast-food franchises, the avenue still sparkles. There's always something happening here: stores are open

late (and many are open on Sunday, a rarity in Paris); nightclubs remain top destinations; and cafés offer prime people-watching, though you'll pay for the privilege—after all, this is Europe's most expensive piece of real estate. Along the 2-km (1¼-mile) stretch, you can find marquee names in French luxury, like Cartier, Guerlain, and Louis Vuitton. Car manufacturers lure international visitors with space-age showrooms. Old stalwarts, meanwhile, are still going strong—including the Lido cabaret and Fouquet's, whose celebrity clientele extends back to James Joyce. The avenue is also the setting for the last leg of the Tour de France bicycle race (the third or fourth Sunday in July), as well as Bastille Day (July 14) and Armistice Day (November 11) ceremonies. The Champs-Élysées, which translates to "Elysian Fields" (the resting place of the blessed in Greek mythology), began life as a cow pasture and in 1666 was transformed into a park by the royal landscape architect André Le Nôtre. Traces of its green origins are visible toward the Concorde, where elegant 19th-century park pavilions house the historic restaurants Ledoyen and Laurent. ⊠ *Champs-Élysées* Ⓜ *Champs-Élysées–Clemenceau, Franklin-D.-Roosevelt, George V, Charles-de-Gaulle–Étoile.*

Brach Paris

When this sports club-style hotel moved into the 16e arrondissement in late 2018, it gave the neighborhood new life. The Philippe Starck-designed beauty is draped in African art and 1930s-era décor, resulting in a Studio 54-meets-safari look. The buzzy, open kitchen-style Mediterranean eatery is worth reserving well in advance on weekends; if you have to wait for a table, the craft cocktails—perfumed with herbs grown on the rooftop garden—will help the time fly. The real pièce de résistance, however, lies underground at the 1930s boxing club-inspired sports center, complete with a thermal pool and Himalayan salt sauna. ⊠ *1-7 rue Jean Richepin, Trocadéro* ☎ *01–44–30–10–00* ⊕ *brachparis. com* Ⓜ *Rue de la Pompe.*

Cité de l'Architecture et du Patrimoine

The Cité de l'Architecture et du Patrimoine highlights architectural styles from the 11th century to the present day, including sites that weren't ever constructed. Full-scale re-creations of projects like Jean Nouvel's unbuilt Tour Sans Fins, a building that would've ranked tallest concrete skyscraper in the world, sit alongside life-size creations of painted cupolas and cathedral doorways, offering a look into the past thousand years of French architecture. ▌**TIP**→ Take in views of the Eiffel Tower from the café terrace, one of the lesser visited (and less expensive) spots in tourist-heavy Trocadéro. ⊠ *1 pl. du Trocadéro et du 11 novembre, Trocadéro* ☎ *01–58–51–52–00* ⊕ *www.citechaillot.fr* 🎟 *€8* ⊙ *Closed Tues.* Ⓜ *Trocadéro.*

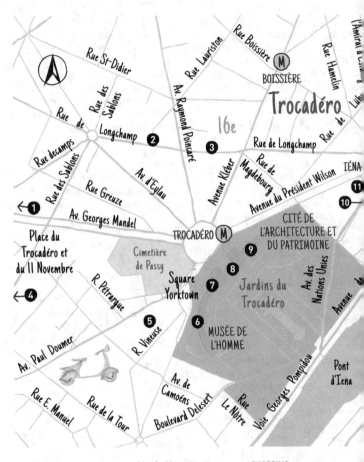

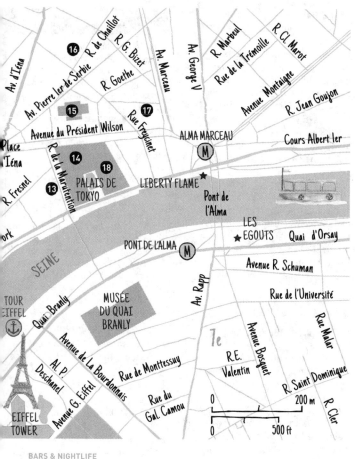

BARS & NIGHTLIFE

Grand Palais

The Grand Palais serves as the backdrop for some of Paris's most exclusive catwalks, concerts, and championships, morphing into anything from an equestrian center for Hermès to a stage for legends like Prince. From the Champs-Élysées, you can't miss the iconic landmark—its stone, steel, and glass dome stands out on the skyline, crowned by a French flag. Inside, you'll get a 3-in-1 site, consisting of the Nave (home to contemporary art fairs and equestrian events), the Palais de la Découverte science museum, and the National Galleries, which showcase exhibitions of master painters like Picasso. ✉ *3 av. du Général Eisenhower, Champs-Élysées* ☎ *01–44–13–17–17* ⊕ *www.grandpalais.fr* Ⓜ *Champs-Élysées–Clemenceau.*

Musée d'Art Moderne de la Ville de Paris

Cross off cultural sites one after another, popping into this modern art museum after a visit to the nearby Eiffel Tower. The Musée d'Art Moderne de la Ville de Paris (or MaM) sits in the east wing of the Palais de Tokyo, where its 13,000-piece collection highlights the best of 20th-century contemporary art (including masterpieces like the first two versions of Matisse's *La Danse*). Dive deeper into the collections with a guided tour (no reservations required) or take part in a well-being workshop centered on Qi-energy-based dance, Wu Tao. ✉ *11 av. du Président Wilson,*

GETTING HERE

The neighborhood, which encompasses the 8e and 16e arrondissements, is crowned by three main entry points: Place de la Concorde, Place du Trocadéro, and the Champs-Élysées. Start your stroll along the Champs from the top at the Arc de Triomphe, taking métro line 1, 2, or 6 (or RER A) to the Charles de Gaulle-Étoile station. You can also take métro line 1 to the Champs-Élysées–Clemenceau station if you'd rather start at the bottom (or visit landmarks like the Grand Palais). Lines 6 and 9 head to Trocadéro, home to Palais de Chaillot and Trocadéro Gardens, where you'll snag that iconic Eiffel Tower Instagram shot. To reach Place de la Concorde at the eastern tip of the Champs-Élysées, hop on line 1, 8, or 12 to the Concorde métro station.

Trocadéro ☎ *01–53–67–40–00* ⊕ *www.mam.paris.fr* ✉ *Free entry to permanent exhibitions* ⊗ *Closed Mon.* Ⓜ *Iéna.*

Musée de l'Homme

After a five-year renovation, the Musée de l'Homme reopened in 2015 in a wing of the Palais de Chaillot, constructed for the 1937 World's Fair. The revamped, 27,000-square-foot Galerie de l'Homme (the museum's permanent collection) traces human evolution through two floors of fossils and statuettes. Another product of the extensive restoration: the spruced-up glass-and-steel ceiling, a remnant of the palace's past life. ✉ *Palais de Chaillot, 17 pl. Trocadéro,*

Trocadéro ☎ 01–44–05–72–72 ⊕ www.museedelhomme.fr 🎟 €10 ⊗ Closed Tues. Ⓜ Trocadéro.

Musée du Vin Paris

Oenophiles with some spare time will enjoy this quirky museum housed in a 15th-century abbey, a reminder of Passy's roots as a pastoral village. Though hardly exhaustive and geared to beginners, the small collection contains old wine bottles, glassware, and ancient wine-related pottery excavated in Paris. Wine-making paraphernalia shares the grotto-like space with hokey figures retired from the city's wax museum, including Napoléon appraising a glass of Burgundy. But you can partake in a thoroughly nonhokey wine tasting, or bring home one of the 200-plus bottles for sale in the tiny gift shop. Check online for a calendar of wine tastings and classes offered in English. You can book ahead for a casual lunch, too (restaurant open Tuesday through Saturday, noon to 3, reservations required). ✉ Rue des Eaux/5 sq. Charles Dickens, Western Paris ☎ 01–45–25–63–26 ⊕ www.museeduvinparis.com 🎟 From €14 ⊗ Closed Sun. and Mon. Ⓜ Passy.

Musée Guimet

While traversing the globe in 1876, industrialist Emile Guimet collected objects in Japan, China, and India—the start to the museum's collection. The Musée Guimet debuted a little over a decade later in 1889 and now houses Asian art spanning 5,000 years, including Buddhas from Afghanistan and Samurai armor,

making it Europe's largest museum to feature such a collection. ✉ 6 pl. d'Iéna, Trocadéro ☎ 01–56–52–54–33 ⊕ www.guimet.fr 🎟 €12 ⊗ Closed Tues. Ⓜ Iéna.

★ Musée Marmottan Monet

This underrated museum boasts the largest collection of Monet's work anywhere. More than 100 pieces, donated by his son Michel, occupy a specially built basement gallery in an elegant 19th-century mansion, which was once the hunting lodge of the Duke de Valmy. Among them you can find such works as the Cathédrale de Rouen series (1892–96) and Impression: Soleil Levant (Impression: Sunrise, 1872), the painting that helped give the Impressionist movement its name. Other exhibits include letters exchanged by Impressionist painters Berthe Morisot and Mary Cassatt. Upstairs, the mansion still feels like a graciously decorated private home. Empire furnishings fill the salons overlooking the Jardin du Ranelagh on one side and the private yard on the other. There's also a captivating room of illuminated medieval manuscripts. To best understand the collection's context, pick up an English-language audioguide (€3) on your way in. ✉ 2 rue Louis-Boilly, Western Paris ☎ 01–44–96–50–33 ⊕ www.marmottan.fr 🎟 €11 ⊗ Closed Mon. Ⓜ La Muette.

★ Musée Yves Saint Laurent Paris

After a 15-year closure, French designer Yves Saint Laurent's haute couture house is back in action. The museum, housed in a Second Empire mansion, mimics the atelier's original atmosphere, chronicling nearly 30 years of the couturier's collections and housing more than 5,000 haute couture models. For priority access to the museum, book a timed ticket online. ⊠ 5 av. Marceau, Champs-Élysées ☎ 01-44-31-64-00 ⊕ www.museeysl-paris.com ☞ €10 ⊗ Closed Mon. Ⓜ Alma-Marceau.

Palais de Chaillot

This honey-color Art Deco cultural center on Place du Trocadéro was built in the 1930s to replace a Moorish-style building constructed for the 1878 World's Fair. Its esplanade is a top draw for camera-toting visitors intent on snapping the perfect shot of the Eiffel Tower. In the building to the left is the Cité de l'Architecture et du Patrimoine—billed as the largest architectural museum in the world—and the Théâtre National de Chaillot, which occasionally stages plays in English. Also here is the Institut Français d'Architecture, an organization and school. The twin building to the right contains the recently renovated Musée de l'Homme, a thoroughly modern anthropology museum. Sculptures and fountains adorn the garden leading to the Seine. ⊠ Pl. du Trocadéro, Champs-Élysées Ⓜ Trocadéro.

Palais de Tokyo

The go-to address for some of the city's funkiest exhibitions, the Palais de Tokyo is a stripped-down venue that spotlights provocative, ambitious contemporary art. There is no permanent collection: instead, cutting-edge temporary shows are staged in a cavernous space reminiscent of a light-filled industrial loft. The programming extends to performance art, concerts, readings, and fashion shows. Night owls will appreciate the midnight closing. The museum's new Les Grands Verres restaurant and cocktail bar—serving an avant-garde take on traditional French fare—is a haunt of hip locals, especially at lunch. Visit the offbeat gift shop for souvenirs that are as edgy and subversive as the exhibits. ⊠ 13 av. du Président Wilson, Champs-Élysées ☎ 01-81-97-35-88 ⊕ www.palaisdetokyo.com ☞ €12 ⊗ Closed Tues. Ⓜ Iéna.

Palais Galliera–Musée de la Mode

When the Palais Galliera reopens in December 2019, the redbrick-vaulted cellars will be transformed into exhibition galleries, doubling the fashion museum's size. The new rooms, dubbed Salles Gabrielle Chanel, will feature temporary exhibits and a portion of the 200,000-piece permanent collection, with haute couture gowns and royal chemises dating back to the 17th century. ⊠ 10 av. Pierre 1er de Serbie, Trocadéro ☎ 01-56-52-86-00 ⊕ www.palaisgal-liera.paris.fr ☞ €12 ⊗ Closed Mon. and public holidays Ⓜ Iéna.

Petit Palais–Musée des Beaux-Arts de la Ville de Paris

The Petit Palais's architecture is just as impressive as the art in the trapezium-shaped building, with Symbolist murals lining the two large galleries, plaster busts of famous artists like Delacroix, and stained-glass windows welcoming guests into the entrance rotunda. The collection, which consists of more than 1,300 works of art, ranges from ancient and medieval to pieces from 1900s Paris, with paintings by the likes of Cézanne and Renoir as well as 18th-century tableware and tapestries. ⊠ *Av. Winston Churchill, Champs-Élysées* ☎ *01-53-43-40-00* ⊕ *www.petitpalais.paris.fr* ⊗ *Closed Mon. and public holidays* Ⓜ *Champs-Élysées–Clemenceau.*

🛍 Shopping

★ 86Champs

When iconic French pastry chef Pierre Hermé partnered with another man just as legendary—L'Occitane founder Olivier Baussan—to create a beauty line, the result was instant success. Now the duo are riding that wave with the opening of their first concept shop, 86Champs, which blends the best of beauty and Parisian pastries. Shop-exclusive *macarons* sit on display in the jewel-color Pâtisserie Counter, while baked-to-order sweets are whipped up on the spot by chefs at the centerpiece Dessert Bar. ⊠ *86 av. des Champs-Élysées, Champs-Élysées* ☎ *01-70-38-77-38* ⊕ *www.86champs.com* Ⓜ *George V, Franklin-D.-Roosevelt.*

Ladurée

The Ladurée family may have launched their *salon de thé* (tearoom)—one of Paris's first—in the Madeleine more than 150 years

---

WORTH A TRIP:
FONDATION LOUIS VUITTON

Many of Paris's major museums are huddled around the city center, but one of the newcomers, the striking **Fondation Louis Vuitton**, is worth the mini day trip to the Bois de Boulogne, the Hyde Park–inspired gardens on the city's western edge. Hop on a shuttle from the Place Charles de Gaulle (near the Arc de Triomphe) and set off for the contemporary art museum. Frank Gehry designed the building's 12 ship-like sails (composed of 3,600 glass panels), while Michelin-starred chef Jean-Louis Nomicos curated signature restaurant Le Frank's haute cuisine.

---

ago, but it wasn't until the past decade that the empire started spreading around the globe. One of the more iconic locales? The Champs-Élysées, with an opulent glass wall and terrace opening up to the city's famous stretch. The boutique offers pretty boxes of *macarons* to go, but this is the kind of place where it's worth sitting and staying a while, indulging in the decadent namesake *petit déjeuner* (breakfast). ⊠ *75 av. des Champs-Élysées, Champs-Élysées* ☎ *01-40-75-08-75* ⊕ *www.laduree.fr* Ⓜ *George V, Franklin-D.-Roosevelt.*

La Maison du Whisky

Whiskey lovers will feel like kids in a candy shop when they step into this airy space near the Champs-Élysées. More than 1,300 different products line the dark-wood, library-like shelves, offering connoisseurs plenty to geek

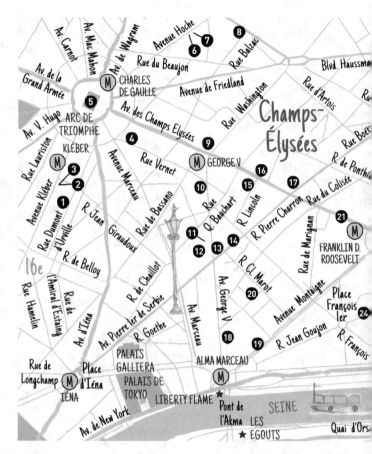

out over, including bottles from now-closed distilleries. Peruse a selection featuring everything from Scottish single cast malt to Breton whisky crafted from buckwheat. If you would rather drink than shop, head to the boutique's dedicated whiskey bar, Golden Promise, in the 2e arrondissement. ⊠ *20 rue d'Anjou, Madeleine* ☎ *01–42–65–03–16* ⊕ *www.whisky.fr* ☉ *Closed Sun.* Ⓜ *Madeleine, Concorde.*

Le66

Finding just the right totally chic, totally black anything is a breeze here. This up-to-the-second concept store, composed of three boutiques on two levels (including shoes, jewelry, accessories, and mens-wear), lines up all the top names that you know, along with those that you may not but should. Diffusion lines of the major labels mingle with Acne, Marni, Helmut Lang, Rimowa, Alexander Wang, Damir Doma, and nearly 200 others, all hand-picked to ensure fabulousness. If pressed for time, it's a good bet for all-around satisfaction. ⊠ *66 av. des Champs-Élysées, 8e, Champs-Élysées* ☎ *01–53–53–33–80* ⊕ *www.le66.fr* Ⓜ *Franklin-D.-Roosevelt.*

Le Tigre Chaillot

Walking into this tucked-away yoga club feels like stumbling into a secret garden. Yoga and Pilates rooms are scattered throughout the building, which is like a chic version of a holistic spa (think sleek wooden floors, Buddha statues, and crystals). Offering a full roster of fitness classes, plus meditation and relaxation therapies, the club's

studios look out on the plant-filled courtyard, and the cozy, rug-lined entry space, furnished with French flea market finds, features an outpost of superfood hot spot Wild & The Moon. ⊠ *19 rue de Chaillot, Champs-Élysées* ☎ *09–84–54–17–34* ⊕ *www.chaillot.tigre-yoga.com* Ⓜ *Iéna, Boissière.*

Les Suites

In an age of online shopping, Les Suites proves that brick-and-mortar boutiques still serve a purpose in Paris. The two-story historic monument, dominated by a grand staircase, is a throwback to the days of fittings with couturiers like Christian Dior. Personal stylists guide shoppers through high-end selections from top designers like Azzaro and Oscar de la Renta—as well as more obscure (but just as exclusive) brands—with three suite-style fitting rooms that feel just as glam as Paris's palace hotels. ⊠ *47 rue Pierre Charron, Triangle d'Or* ☎ *01–56–59–11–11* ⊕ *www.boutiquelessuites. com* ☉ *Closed Sun.* Ⓜ *George V, Franklin-D.-Roosevelt.*

★ The Peninsula Spa

Like French fashion, the Peninsula Spa prides itself on its mini-malist chic design. The largest luxury hotel spa in the city, the 19,000-square-foot spa has mastered the art of feng shui, with soothing lights illuminating the metal-and-wood treatment rooms, which have an instant calming effect the moment you step inside. Set on a side street off the Arc de Triomph, this subterranean, teahouse-inspired spot's Asian aesthetic is an interesting contrast to the more traditional French interior of the gilded rooms in the 19th-century hotel above it. ⊠ *The Peninsula Paris, 19 av. Kléber, Champs-Élysées* ☎ 01-58-12-66-82 ⊕ *www.peninsula.com* Ⓜ *Kléber.*

Pierre Hermé

Vogue called Pierre Hermé the "Picasso of Pastry," and it's not hard to see why when you step into his *macaron-* and chocolate-filled boutique on rue Cambon, an easy stop en route to landmarks like the Louvre. Take your time making your way around the long curved counter housing petits fours that are almost too pretty to eat and *macarons* in whimsical flavors like the rose-and quince-tinged Venus. ⊠ *4 rue Cambon, Concorde* ☎ 01-43-54-47-77 ⊕ *www.pierreherme.com* Ⓜ *Concorde.*

Sense, a Rosewood Spa

When the 18th-century Hôtel de Crillon reopened in 2017 after a four-year restoration, the landmark added one feature that it previously lacked: a spa. While couture legend Karl Lagerfeld took the reins redesigning two of the sumptuous suites overlooking Place de la Concorde, ceramist Peter Lane designed the gold-flecked murals lining the walls of the spa's pièce de résistance: a 46-foot skylit pool filled with 17,600 gold scale mosaic tiles. ⊠ *Hôtel de Crillon, a Rosewood Hotel, 10 pl. de la Concorde, Concorde* ☎ 01-44-71-15-45 ⊕ *www.rosewoodhotels.com* Ⓜ *Concorde.*

☕ Coffee and Quick Bites

★ Honor

$ | **Café.** Tucked behind the fashionable Rue du Faubourg St-Honoré, Paris's first alfresco craft coffee shop brings a sip of the city's specialty brew to this ritzier part of town. Launched by an English-Australian couple (who double as baristas), the kiosk café sits in a cobblestone courtyard next to the Trading Museum Comme des Garçons, offering a cozy shopping retreat—plus beans from one of Paris's top roasters, Coutume. **Known for:** coffee by guest European roasters; home-made quiche du jour; retail coffee bags. *Average main: €11* ⊠ *54 rue du Faubourg St-Honoré, Madeleine* ☎ 07-82-52-93-63 ⊕ *www.honor-cafe.com* ☉ *Closed Sun.* Ⓜ *Madeleine, Concorde.*

Le Petit Flottes

$ | **Deli.** The pretty pink épicerie is what every little girl dreams of: a real-life tea party where you can have your crêpes and cupcakes and eat them, too. The pastel-color shop is lined with grab-and-go goodies and cutesy knickknacks that will make your kitchen as dreamy as a dollhouse. **Known for:** bagel sandwiches; freshly prepped pasta; hand-crafted cannelés. *Average main: €7* ⊠ *2 rue Cambon, Concorde* ☎ 01-42-60-00-84 ⊕ *lepetitflottes.com* ☉ *Closed Sun.* Ⓜ *Concorde.*

Marxito

$ | **Fast Food.** Michelin-starred Thierry Marx's empire spans from Mandarin Oriental, Paris, all the way to the Charles de Gaulle airport, but the chef known best for his molecular gastronomy is taking things down a notch with the opening of Marxito near the Champs-Élysées. Partnering with French designer Ora Ïto, Marx is serving up fast food with a fashionable twist, offering organic, street-food-inspired fare dubbed Marxitos (sweet and savory buckwheat buns). **Known for:** ingredients from small French producers; puffed buckwheat buns inspired by Japanese Dorayaki pancakes; freshly baked fare to go, plus high-end groceries. *Average main: €6* ⊠ *1 rue Jean Mermoz, Champs-Élysées* ☎ *07-67-72-16-42* ⊕ *www.marxito. com* Ⓜ *Franklin-D.-Roosevelt.*

🍴 Dining

Bistrot Alexandre III
$$ | **French.** Housed on a barge and modeled after classic bistros with its zinc roof and tin counters, Bistrot Alexandre III is named after the bridge it sits under, which connects Invalides on the Left Bank to the Grand Palais and Petit Palais on the Right Bank. The views from the Seine are one reason to visit, but the terrace bar seating also serves up quintessential French fare that doesn't fall flat. **Known for:** seasonal menus; fantastic French wine; gourmet coffee and hot chocolate. *Average main: €19* ⊠ *Port des Invalides, Invalides* ☎ *01-47-53-07-07* ⊕ *www.bistrotalexandre3.fr* ☉ *Closed Mon. and Tues.* Ⓜ *Invalides.*

Ginger
$$$ | **Asian.** The chef's Thai heritage plays a large role in the spices sneaking their way into Ginger's Asian dishes, such as the bass tartare. The loungelike space is Paris-meets-Los-Angeles, with just the right amount of well-placed glitz. **Known for:** tasting menu; lunch bo buns; dim sum. *Average main: €29* ⊠ *11 rue de la Trémoille, Triangle d'Or* ☎ *01-47-23-37-32* ⊕ *www.ginger-paris.com* ☉ *No lunch Sun.* Ⓜ *Alma-Marceau, George V, Franklin-D.-Roosevelt.*

⭐ Hiramatsu
$$$$ | **French Fusion.** In this Art Deco dining room near Trocadéro, Takashi Nakagawa continues his variations on the subtly Japanese-inspired French cuisine of restaurant namesake Hiroyuki Hiramatsu, who still sometimes works the kitchen. Luxury ingredients feature prominently in dishes such as thin slices of lamb with onion jam and thyme-and-truffle-spiked jus, or an unusual pot-au-feu of oysters with foie gras and black truffle. **Known for:** €90 seven-course dinner menu, a steal for this quality; Scottish salmon marinated in fines herbs with caviar and leek mousse; staggering wine list. *Average main: €50* ⊠ *52 rue de Longchamp, 16e, Eiffel Tower* ☎ *01-56-81-08-80* ⊕ *www. hiramatsu.co.jp/fr* ☉ *No lunch. Closed weekends, 1 wk at Christmas, and Aug.* Ⓜ *Trocadéro.*

Il Carpaccio
$$$$ | **Italian.** The glass conservatory ceiling adds a garden party sensibility to this one-Michelin-star

eatery known for some of the city's most authentic Italian fare (risotto and ravioli are just the start). For something more low-key, take a seat on the terrace for a scene reminiscent of a restaurant on the Mediterranean, with seafood straight from Sicily and seashell-covered chandeliers adding to the coastal theme. **Known for:** Pierre Hermé desserts; extensive Italian wine list; decadent black truffle menu (with gluten-free pasta options). *Average main: €120 ⊠ Le Royal Monceau Raffles Paris, 37 av. Hoche, Champs-Élysées ☎ 01–42–99–88–12 ⊕ www.raffles.com ⊗ Closed Sun. and Mon., summer Ⓜ Ternes, George V.*

★ L'Abeille

$$$$ | Modern French. Everything here, from the dove-gray decor to the sparkling silver, speaks of quiet elegance—all the better to savor Christophe Moret's masterful cuisine. Choices include a "harlequin" of yellow, red, and white beets with a ginger-tinged yogurt and aloe vera emulsion; Breton langoustine in a cinnamon-perfumed gelée, with grapefruit pulp and a ginger-and-Tahitian-vanilla-infused mayonnaise; and lightly caramelized scallops in an ethereal cloud of white-chocolate foam. **Known for:** some of the best service in town (including a jar of honey as a parting gift); relaxed, intimate dining; elegant decor overlooking interior garden. *Average main: €100 ⊠ Paris Shangri-La Hotel, 10 av. d'Iéna, 16e, Eiffel Tower ☎ 01–53–67–19–90 ⊕ www.shangri-la.com ⊗ Closed Sun. and Mon. No lunch Sat.–Wed. Ⓜ Iéna.*

La Table Lauriston

$$$ | Bistro. This chic bistro near the Trocadéro has a winning formula: top-notch ingredients, simply prepared and generously served. The trademark dish, a gargantuan rib steak, is big enough to silence even the hungriest Texan. **Known for:** favorite with local diners; friendly service; famously delicious (and giant) baba au rhum for dessert. *Average main: €26 ⊠ 129 rue de Lauriston, 16e, Eiffel Tower ☎ 01–47–27–00–07 ⊕ www.restaurantlatablelauriston.com ⊗ Closed Sun. and 4 wks in Aug. No lunch Sat. Ⓜ Trocadéro.*

★ Le Drugstore

$$ | Brasserie. The more casual of the two restaurants housed in concept shop Publicis Drugstore, Le Drugstore is a throwback to the days of *Mad Men*. Mid-century French touches nod to the 1960s era of advertising, with a lounge inspired by a gentleman's study and a brass-accented marble bar where you can indulge in a cocktail or bite, in the form of fine fillets and classic cheeseburgers. **Known for:** mod decor; teatime with finger sandwiches; Japanese wagyu beef. *Average main: €24 ⊠ Publicis Drugstore, 133 av. des Champs-Élysées, Champs-Élysées ☎ 01–44–43–75–07 ⊕ www.publicisdrugstore.com Ⓜ Charles de Gaulle–Étoile, George V.*

Les Marches

$ | Bistro. Inspired by roadside French restaurants, Les Marches serves up family-style fare at affordable prices—plus, the terrace affords views of the Eiffel Tower. This is about as traditional as you can get, from the red-checked tablecloths to the hearty plates of classic staples like Béarnaise-slathered beef. **Known for:** fish of the day; pitchers of house wine; classic starters like hard-boiled eggs with mayonnaise. *Average main: €16 ⊠ 5 rue de la Manutention, Trocadéro* ☎ *01-47-23-52-80* ⊕ *www. lesmarches-restaurant.com* Ⓜ *léna, Alma–Marceau.*

LiLi

$$$$ | **Cantonese.** The operatically beautiful LiLi, in the Peninsula Hotel, places sophisticated Cantonese cuisine in its rightful place—the gastronomic center of the world. The menu features all the classics, raised to the status of haute cuisine: small plates of dim sum (seafood, vegetable, or pork dumplings) alongside more substantial fare like fried rice studded with market-fresh vegetables, succulent Sichuan shrimp, and barbecued suckling pig. **Known for:** authentic Peking duck; gourmet dim sum; cocktails at the Bar Kléber. *Average main: €36 ⊠ The Peninsula Paris, 19 rue Kléber, 16e, Eiffel Tower* ☎ *01-58-12-67-50* ⊕ *paris. peninsula.com* Ⓜ *Kléber, Charles de Gaulle–Étoile.*

Manko

$$$ | **Peruvian.** Ambassador of Peruvian cuisine Gastón Acurio brings his native notes to Paris at his first restaurant, which fits in perfectly alongside the flag-ship designer boutiques lining the Avenue Montaigne. The experience at the combination cabaret-eatery starts with passing around plates of Peruvian fare woven with Asian and African influences at the lower-level restaurant, and ends with making your way up the gilded staircase to the 1920s music hall. **Known for:** sharing plates; leche de tigre–marinated tiradito (raw fish in citrus); Peruvian cocktails. *Average main: €35 ⊠ 15 av. Montaigne, Triangle d'Or* ☎ *01-82-28-00-15* ⊕ *www.manko-paris.com* ⊘ *Closed Sun. No lunch Sat.* Ⓜ *Alma–Marceau.*

Matsuhisa Paris

$$$$ | **Japanese Fusion.** At celebrity chef Nobu Matsuhisa's first restaurant in France, you'll find hints of his signature Asian–Latin American fusion, plus a few newcomers tailored to the French crowd (seaweed tacos with black truffle and crispy oysters with caviar are two of the more decadent dishes). The minimalist room turns into a scene at night, with sushi chefs putting on a show at the counter in the back. **Known for:** seafood tacos; Nobu signatures like black cod with miso; traditional sushi. *Average main: €40 ⊠ Le Royal Monceau Raffles Paris, 37 av. Hoche, Champs-Élysées* ☎ *01-42-99-98-70* ⊕ *www. raffles.com* ⊘ *No lunch weekends or summer* Ⓜ *Ternes, George V.*

Mini Palais

$$$ | **Modern French.** Inside the Grand Palais, Mini Palais is among Paris's most stylish dining rooms, but the menu is the real draw. The burger *de magret et foie gras*, a flavorful mélange of tender duckling breast and duck foie gras drizzled with truffled jus on a buttery brioche bun, underscores what's best about this place: a thoroughly modern cuisine with an old-fashioned extravagance. **Known for:** soaring outdoor terrace with views of the Petit Palais and Pont Alexandre III; late-night snacks; decent prices, considering the neighborhood. *Average main: €25* ⊠ *3 av. Winston Churchill, 8e, Champs-Élysées* ☎ *01-42-56-42-42* ⊕ *www.minipalais. com* Ⓜ *Champs-Élysées–Clemenceau.*

Miss Kō

$$ | Sushi. Follow the crowd a few steps off the Champs-Élysées to the posh Miss Kō, a tucked-away Japanese joint designed to feel like a scene from a street food market, its interior a kaleidoscope of urban art, neon lights, and exposed brick. Even at midnight you'll be hard-pressed to snag a seat in the bustling restaurant, where the city's fashionable set nibble on nigiri under a cloud of upside-down Chinese umbrellas and colorful paper lanterns. **Known for:** Vietnamese bo buns; miso-marinated black cod; sushi bar. *Average main: €21* ⊠ *51 av. George V, Champs-Élysées* ☎ *01-53-67-84-60* ⊕ *www.miss-ko.com* Ⓜ *George V.*

Rosa Bonheur sur Seine

$ | Pizza. Come early if you want to board this floating bar along along the Seine; it's the hopping riverside branch of the popular Buttes-Chaumont venue. You'll sip reasonably priced wine, share Mediterranean-style tapas, and enjoy stunning views of the gilded Pont Alexandre III bridge. **Known**

for: wood-fired pizzas; wine list; dancing. *Average main: €10* ⊠ *Port des Invalides, Invalides* ☎ *01-47-53-66-92* ⊕ *www.rosabonheur.fr* Ⓜ *Invalides.*

🍸 Bars and Nightlife

Blind Bar

This slick cocktail bar is a favorite of the fashion set working in the designer-packed district. Dim lighting, dark wood, and a modern, built-in fireplace at the bar evoke a cigar lounge, while the terrace is a sliver of Miami in the bustling metropolis. Play the bar's namesake guessing game, Le Blind Cocktail, and try to guess the bottle—and ingredients—being shaken up by the bartender in your mystery drink. ⊠ *La Maison Champs-Élysées Hotel, 8 rue Jean Goujon, Triangle d'Or* ☎ *01-40-74-64-94* ⊕ *www. lamaisonchampselysees.com* Ⓜ *Champs-Élysées–Clemenceau.*

Buddha Bar

While it may be past its prime with Parisians, visitors can't get enough of the high-camp towering gold Buddha that presides over this bar's giant palm fronds, red satin walls, and colorful chinoiserie. A themed dining room serves pan-Asian fare. There's also an upscale speakeasy, Le Secret 8, which you access by answering a daily riddle on the bar's Facebook page and getting a password (only 25 are given out per day). ⊠ *8 rue Boissy d'Anglas, 8e, Champs-Élysées* ☎ *01-53-05-90-00* ⊕ *www. buddhabar.com* Ⓜ *Concorde.*

Café de l'Homme

Not everything near the Eiffel Tower is a tourist trap. Sitting along the Seine next to the Trocadéro gardens, Café de l'Homme is a hidden terrace in the heart of the city. The wine cellar is serious (200 bottles hail from top-notch wineries like Château Margaux) and so are the Eiffel Tower views, particularly from the intimate rooftop lounge. ⊠ *17 pl. du Trocadéro, Trocadéro* ☏ *01-44-05-30-15* ⊕ *www.cafedelhomme.com* Ⓜ *Trocadéro.*

⭐ Le Bar at Hotel George V

At this fashion week favorite in the Four Seasons, the wood-paneled lounge looks out across the glamorous Avenue George V. The aesthetic is regal enough for royalty (plush red velvet chairs, white tablecloths) without stuffy service. Prepare to splurge on the cocktails. ⊠ *Four Seasons Hotel George V, Paris, 31 av. George V, Champs-Élysées* ☏ *01-49-52-70-06* ⊕ *www.fourseasons.com* Ⓜ *George V.*

⭐ Le Bar Botaniste

The Shangri-La Hotel's opulent bar, inspired by eccentric botanist Prince Roland Bonapart (nephew to Napoleon), serves up a dazzling menu of imaginative cocktails spiked with plant and flower essences and fruit nectars. ⊠ *10 av. d'Iéna, 16e, Champs-Élysées* ☏ *01-53-67-19-98* ⊕ *www.shangri-la.com* Ⓜ *Iéna.*

Le Bar du Bristol

Le Bristol is known for its classic Parisian elegance (it *is* a palace, after all), but the bar isn't your average hotel watering hole. Sure, you'll find chandeliers and cigar-lounge-style leather chairs. But don't expect elevator music and martinis. DJs spin on weekends and the head barman is referred to as an "alchemist" for his gastronomical twist on classic cocktails. ⊠ *Hôtel Le Bristol Paris, 112 rue du Faubourg St-Honoré, Champs-Élysées* ☏ *01-53-43-42-41* ⊕ *www.oetkercollection.com* Ⓜ *Champs-Élysées–Clemenceau, Miromesnil.*

Le Rooftop at the Peninsula Paris

Before its extensive renovation and rebranding as the Peninsula Paris, the Belle Époque–era hotel led quite the life. What started as the home of Queen Isabella II of Spain soon became the site of the "dinner party of the century," bringing together creative glitterati like Marcel Proust and Picasso. The hotel is definitely a looker, but one of the best views is found six floors up at the secluded rooftop bar. Here, you can watch the sunset (or the twinkling Eiffel Tower) sans crowds, sipping cheekily named cocktails like "God Save the Queen." ⊠ *The Peninsula Paris, 19 av. Kléber, Champs-Élysées* ☏ *01-58-12-67-30* ⊕ *www.peninsula.com* Ⓜ *Kléber.*

⭐ Les Ambassadeurs

Snag a seat at the gorgeous U-shaped bar, the perfect perch for people-watching. This is the place to see and be seen, and Les Ambassadeurs (once a room in Duc de Crillon's private residence) is every bit as gilded as the glittering clientele walking through the door. Admire views of the only

Dîner en Blanc, a pop-up dinner party attended in flash-mob style, got its start in Paris more than 30 years ago before spreading to more than 80 cities on six continents, from Sydney to Seoul. Founder François Pasquier's garden was too small to host a soirée, so he invited his guests to Paris's Bois de Boulogne, following the concept "Bring a meal and bring a new friend." The only requirements: wear white (a twist on wearing a rose or red scarf to find a blind date) and bring your own meal. Now the annual event has grown to gatherings of more than 17,000, with waiting lists of up to 10 years. The only way to snag an invite: go with a member, or book an all-inclusive pass through a partner like Sofitel, the French brand behind superluxe Le Royal Monceau Raffles Paris. Those on the exclusive guest list are given a meeting point, but the locale remains under wraps until the very last moment, when anywhere from the Eiffel Tower to the Champs-Élysées transforms into a dinner party for thousands. Guests bring their entire setup, from tables to canopy tents, for a Great Gatsby–esque affair that, just like Cinderella, disappears before midnight.

neighbor—Place de la Concorde—while sipping one of more than 100 labels of champagne from a menu that spans multiple pages (and price points—some bottles soar more than $7,000). ✉ Hôtel de Crillon, a Rosewood Hotel, 10 pl. de la Concorde, Concorde ☎ 01-44-71-15-80 ⊕ www.rosewoodhotels.com Ⓜ Concorde.

Les Heures Bar

At Les Heures Bar, it's always "Midnight in Paris," and the bar is open all day long. The Art Deco beauty, featuring cascading chandeliers and barware as decadent as its drinks, takes a cue from the Roaring Twenties with an anything-goes atmosphere. Opt for a modernized twist on a classic cocktail (like the Tonka bean syrup Sazerac) and take your drink to an entirely different scene out on the peaceful, Mediterranean patio lined with mosaics. ✉ Prince de Galles Hotel, 33 av. George V, Triangle d'Or ☎ 01-53-23-77-77 ⊕ www.bar-les-heures.fr Ⓜ George V, Alma-Marceau.

Les 110 de Taillevent

Oak reigns throughout this wine bar, from the wood-paneled walls to the wines themselves. As the name suggests, 110 wines are available by the glass. Food and wine pairings are taken seriously here, with four wines (tiered according to price point) matched with each of the 30 seasonal dishes. ✉ 195 rue du Faubourg St-Honoré, Champs-Élysées ☎ 01-40-74-20-20 ⊕ www.les-110-taillevent-paris.com Ⓜ Ternes.

Renoma Café Gallery

When the grandson of Le Crazy Horse's owner took over the restaurant, he borrowed a line or two from the legendary cabaret. The decor takes on an industrial theme with exposed ceilings and art-covered brick, but the look instantly shifts when the venue transforms for one of its themed parties. From

Thursday through the weekend, the scene quickly becomes a spectacle as DJs, burlesque dancers, and magicians parade the floor. ⊠ *45 rue Pierre Charron, Triangle d'Or* ☎ *01–47–20–46–19* ⊕ *www.renoma-cafe-gallery.com* Ⓜ *George V.*

🎭 Performing Arts

★ Crazy Horse

This world-renowned cabaret has elevated the striptease to an art form. Founded in 1951, it's famous for gorgeous dancers and naughty routines characterized by lots of humor and very little clothing. What garments there are have been dazzlingly designed by the likes of Louboutin and Alaïa and shed by top divas (including Dita von Teese). Reserved seats for the show start at €85. ⊠ *12 av. George V, 8e, Champs-Élysées* ☎ *01–47–23–32–32* ⊕ *www.lecrazyhorseparis.com* Ⓜ *Alma–Marceau.*

Lido

The legendary Lido now adds a modern-day dose of awe-inspiring stage design to the cabaret's trademark style. The 100-minute productions—still featuring those beloved Bluebell Girls and 12 "Lido boys"—run at 9 pm and 11 pm, 365 days a year. Dinner for Two packages for the earlier show include the Soirée Etoile (€170), Soirée Champs-Élysées (€195), and the Soirée Triomphe (€300). If you're on a budget, €115 gets you a ticket plus half a bottle of bubbly. Yes, those prices are per person, but this is Paris nightlife as it's meant to be experienced. It's best to book your tickets in advance by phone, online, or on-site. ⊠ *116 bis, av. des Champs-Élysées, 8e, Champs-Élysées* ☎ *01–40–76–56–10* ⊕ *www. lido.fr* Ⓜ *George V.*

Les Batignolles and Les Puces

LES PUCES

CLIGNAN-COURT

ÉPINETTES

LA CHAPELLE

LA VILLETTE

LES BATIGNOLLES

MONTMARTRE

TERNES

MONCEAU

PIGALLE

CANAL ST-MARTIN

BELLEVILLE

LES GRANDS BOULEVARDS

SENTIER

CHAILLOT

CHAMPS-ÉLYSÉES

MÉNILMONTANT

BOIS DE BOULOGNE

PASSY

TROCADÉRO

PALAIS-ROYAL

LES HALLES

LE MARAIS

OBERKAMPF

PÈRE-LACHAISE

LES INVALIDES

LES ÎLES

ST-GERMAIN-DES-PRÉS

BASTILLE

CHARONNE

VAUGIRARD

BEL-AIR

AUTEUIL

JAVEL

MONTPARNASSE

QUARTIER LATIN

BERCY

ST-LAMBERT

BUTTE-AUX-CAILLES

SEINE

BOIS DE VINCENNES

MONTROUGE

AUSTERLITZ

MAISON BLANCHE

n the early 2000s no Parisian would have used the words "cool" and "Les Batignolles" in the same sentence. In the last 10 years, however, this former village in the northwest corner of the city has undergone a vibrant awakening thanks to an upswing in unpretentiously hip residents, or bobos. Once a hunting ground for royals, the area attracted a rising middle class after the French Revolution, when they came here to build small country homes known as bastilloles. Although the northern part of the 17e arrondissement became rather grimy, Les Batignolles were protected from this brashness. The fate of the area changed dramatically when refurbishing the derelict St-Lazare train yards became a key feature in the city's repeated—and finally successful—bid for the Summer Olympics, set for 2024. An exciting new park surrounded by avant-garde architecture and the ongoing extension of métro line 14 have helped fuel this change, which has trickled through the streets of Les Batignolles, now dotted with innovative restaurants, lively bars, and funky boutiques. The neighborhood's newly acquired cool factor has remained off the radar of mass tourism, making it an excellent place to experience a taste of today's Paris. A trip to les puces (flea markets) nearby in St-Ouen, virtually stuck back in the Belle Époque era, will grant you a window into the city's past.—*by Lily Heise*

◉ Sights

La Cité des Fleurs
This beguiling residential street takes you back to the village days of Les Batignolles. Of the many attractive two- and three-story houses lining the pedestrian lane, there are two you'll want to seek out: the house at No. 25 hosted a Resistance unit during World War II, and No. 27 was the home of Impressionist painter Alfred Sisley. The lane was also once home to

a clinic where famous French actresses Catherine Deneuve and Françoise Dorléac were born. ⊠ *154 av. de Clichy, Les Batgnolles* Ⓜ *Brochant.*

★ Marché aux Puces de St-Ouen
With 1,700 vendors spread over 17 acres at the northern edge of Paris, this is considered the largest antiques and secondhand market in the world. Dating back to 1885, the market has always felt far removed from posh, conservative Paris. The

divided into 14 smaller markets, where you can spend a whole day roaming through charming lanes teeming with crystal chandeliers, Belle Époque postcards, African masks, and countless bins of quirky odds and ends. Bypass the cheap clothing vendors you'll come across first to reach the real rabbit hole of the market, where you can embark on your own Alice in Wonderland-style adventure. ■TIP➜ Bring cash; many vendors still don't accept cards. ⊠ *Rue des Rosiers, Les Puces* ☎ *01–40–11–77–36* ⊕ *www. pucesparis.com* ✆ *Closed Tues.–Fri.* Ⓜ *Garibaldi, Porte de Clignancourt.*

★ Parc Clichy-Batignolles – Martin-Luther-King

Just behind the more classical Square des Batignolles is one of the city's newest and most avant-garde parks, occupying more than 12 acres along former train freight yards. Like its namesake, the park is rather daring by Parisian standards, a polar opposite of the manicured *jardin à la francaise*. Opened in two waves in 2007 and 2014 as an integral part of the new Clichy-Batignolles urban project, the relaxed green space has undulating knolls fringed with sheaths of wheat and wildflowers, a community vegetable garden, unique ecosystems, wind turbines, rain-water harvesting, an eccentric playground, and a skate park. ⊠ *147 rue Cardinet, Les Batignolles* Ⓜ *Brochant.*

Passage Geffroy-Didelot

After doing some food shopping on the Rue de Lévis, make a short detour to amble down this appealing pedestrian lane. Draped in flags and lined with colorful shop fronts, art studios, and cafés, the passage hasn't changed much since it opened in 1843, when Les Batignolles was just a tiny outpost at the fringes of town. ⊠ *90 bd. des Batignolles, Les Batignolles* Ⓜ *Villiers.*

Place du Dr Félix Lobligeois

Dating back to 1825, this charming square is the heart of the Batignolles and even today feels like part of a small French country town. Its centerpiece is the neoclassical Église Ste-Marie des Batignolles, flanked to the north by the splendid Square des Batignolles park and surrounded by shops and buzzing café terraces. ⊠ *Pl. du Dr Félix Lobligeois, Les Batignolles* Ⓜ *Rome.*

★ Square des Batignolles

When the Batignolles village became part of Paris in 1860, it fell under the jurisdiction of Napoléon III's garden planner, Jean-Charles Alphand, who created dozens of parks around the city, including the Buttes-Chaumont and subsequently, this sublime garden. Alphand turned away from the manicured style of the French jardin in favor of the more natural English style, embodied here with

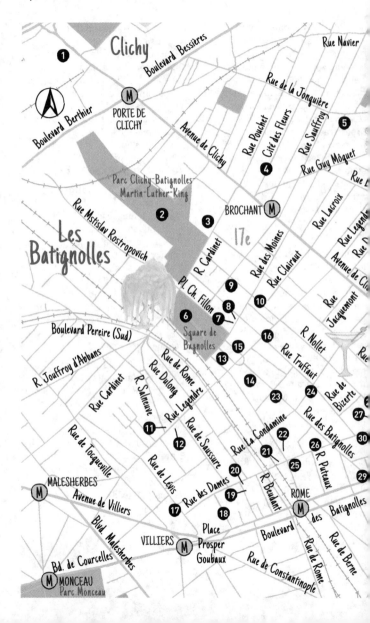

meandering lanes, giant 150-year-old trees, a lovely pond inhabited by ducks, and an old-fashioned carousel. ⊠ *Sq. des Batignolles, Les Batignolles* Ⓜ *Rome.*

Tribunal de Paris

Since 2018 the Porte de Clichy has been home to the city's new courthouse, a soaring 525-foot glass skyscraper and second tallest building in the city after the Tour Montparnasse. Designed by Renzo Piano, the co-architect of the Centre Pompidou, the building amasses the 25 courts of Paris under one shimmering roof. And it's not just any roof: the cutting-edge, eco-friendly structure features solar panels, rain collection facilities, and terraces covered with trees—with the whopping price tag of 2 billion euros. Architecture fans may prefer to get up close and explore (anyone can enter), but there's also a great view from Martin Luther King Park. ⊠ *Parvis du Tribunal de Paris, Les Batignolles* ☎ *01-44-32-51-51* ⊕ *www.tribunal-de-paris.justice.fr* ⓥ *Closed evenings, Sat. from 3 pm, Sun.* Ⓜ *Porte de Clichy.*

🛍 **Shopping**

Désordre Urbain

While the contents of these two shops on Rue Nollet don't necessary evoke "urban disorder," as their name indicates, they do have everything you need to become a cool Parisienne. Focused on local independent designers, the store has

GETTING HERE

Both Les Batignolles and Les Puces are on the outskirts of the city center. Take the métro to Rome or Villiers (lines 2 and 3) to reach Les Batignolles, but avoid Brochant and La Fourche, which fringe the sketchier areas of the 17e arrondissement. For Les Puces de St-Ouen, take line 4 to Porte de Clignancourt and walk straight north and under the overpass of the Peripherique expressway.

beautiful jewelry, leather clutches, suede heels, and cool-without-trying T-shirts. ⊠ *94–96 rue Nollet, Les Batignolles* ☎ *01-44-85-52-27* ⊕ *www.desordreurbain.fr* ⓥ *Closed Sun.* Ⓜ *Brochant.*

★ **Fédération Française de l'Apéro**

Pick up all you need for a DIY *apéro* (predinner drink or snack) at the second branch of this quirky speciality food shop. Stocking supplies found in all corners of the country, it's packed with artisanal pâtés, terrines, tapenades, wine, craft beer, *fromage* (cheese), and *saucisson* (dry-cured sausage). ⊠ *50 rue des Dames, Les Batignolles* ☎ *01-47-42-72-54* ⊕ *www.ffaperitif. com* ⓥ *Closed Sun.* Ⓜ *Rome.*

★ **French Touche**

One of the first concept stores to open in Les Batignolles, this eclectic boutique has an impressive and varied range of designer items that are 100% made in France. You may just need an extra suitcase to carry home the wide selection of funky totes, oddball cushions, vibrant scarves, and hip handbags you'll find. ⊠ *90 rue Legendre, Les Batignolles* ☎ *01-42-63-31-36* ⊕ *www.french-touche.com* ⊙ *Closed Sun. and Mon., Aug.* Ⓜ *Rome, La Fourche.*

L'Atelier Haut Perché

Find perfect Parisian accessories at the workshop of young jewelry designer Aliénor Frolet. Contemporary and trendy, Aliénor's designs range from playful Packman earrings to custom-order gemstone rings. They're all made in the atelier section of her boutique, which you can discover firsthand during her private jewelry design workshops. ⊠ *29 rue des Dames, Les Batignolles* ☎ *01-44-70-03-76* ⊕ *www.atelier-hautperche.com* ⊙ *Closed Sun. and Mon.* Ⓜ *Rome, Place de Clichy.*

Marché Biologique des Batignolles

Every Saturday until 3 pm the tree-lined promenade along Boulevard des Batignolles overflows with the green goodness of one of Paris's three dedicated organic open-air markets. Enjoy a stroll among stalls of seasonal farmers' produce, wildflower honey, multigrain breads, fresh juices, and takeaway foods prepared with love and quality all-organic ingredients. ⊠ *34 bd. des Batignolles, Batignolles* ⊙ *Closed weekdays and Sun.* Ⓜ *Place de Clichy, Rome.*

Rue de Lévis

One of the oldest market streets in Paris, the charming Rue de Lévis is lined with top-quality purveyors of produce, meat, cheese, wine, and more. Come here to stock up on provisions for a picnic or simply to ogle at the piles of bright fruit and breathe in aromas of fresh bread, pungent fromage, and fresh flowers—the unique *parfum de Paris*. ⊠ *Rue de Lévis, Les Batignolles* Ⓜ *Villiers.*

Wenhua Duvergé

Since 2014 this talented designer has been dressing eco-conscious Parisians with her slow-fashion creations. Made of 100% organic cotton or recycled material, her boutique-workshop features superior-quality basics, from ultracomfy T-shirts to simple, chic straight-legged pants that perfectly embody Parisians' relaxed elegance. ⊠ *31 rue Legendre, Les Batignolles* ☎ *01-45-75-09-07* ⊕ *www.wenhuaduverge.com* Ⓜ *Villiers, Rome.*

☕ Coffee and Quick Bites

A la Volée

$ | **Bakery.** A neighborhood gem, this cozy café and bakeshop on buzzing Rue des Dames is the perfect place for lunch, brunch, or an afternoon snack. The sweet and savory delicacies are all made in-house and best enjoyed in the park up the street if there are no seats left inside. **Known for:** tarts and quiches; friendly staff; popular weekend brunch. *Average main: €3* ⊠ *21 rue des Dames, Les Batignolles* ☎ *01-42-93-76-02* ⊙ *Closed Mon. and Tues.* Ⓜ *Place de Clichy, Rome.*

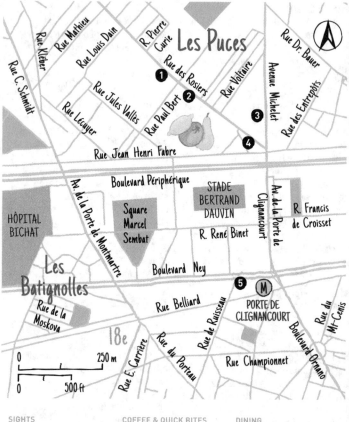

TOP PICKS AT THE MARCHÉ AUX PUCES

The vast flea market can be somewhat overwhelming. Peruse it with an open mind, an idea of what you are looking for, and the readiness to bargain. Of the many choices you'll have, here are a few top picks from Paris-based designer and fashion specialist Kasia Dietz, who also offers insider tours.

Marché Vernaison: The most eclectic and characteristic of the 14 markets is also the oldest. Here you can pick up a real piece of French history, ranging from antique prints to Limoges tableware.

Marché Serpette: You'll find dazzling vintage jewelry, including pieces by Chanel and Schiaparelli, in a collection by Olwen Wilson at this market (allée 3, stand 5). For the best in vintage apparel, head to Patricia Attwood (allée 2, stand 7) and complete the look with luxury bags at Le Monde du Voyage (allée 3, stand 15).

Marché Paul Bert: Modern art mingles with mid-century modern at this market, where you can find the perfect artful souvenir.

Bodrum

$ | Fast Food. Turkish *döner* kebabs are one of Parisians' favorite late-night snacks, and this joint serves one of the best in the city. Decide for yourself whether it's the secret mix of spices or the quality meat that keeps people coming back for the greasy delights—after you've waited in the ever-present line, that is. **Known for:** signature sandwich-frites; 100% veal meat kebabs; local favorite for late-night snacks. *Average main: €6 ⊠ 45 rue des Batignolles, Les Batignolles ⊙ Closed Sun. ⊟ No credit cards Ⓜ Rome.*

★ Interfabric

$ | Contemporary. Enjoy a healthy and delicious break from standard French fare at this hip, mostly vegetarian local lunch spot. Its stripped walls and simple furniture are no reflection of the abundant flavors found in its vegetarian dishes, soups, and range of sandwiches on homemade buns. **Known for:** daily specials; reasonable prices for eating in or takeaway; young, cool local crowd. *Average main: €9 ⊠ 46 rue Legendre, Les Batignolles ☎ 06-95-96-85-61 ⊙ Closed weekends, 3 wks in Aug. Ⓜ Rome, Villiers.*

La Chope des Puces

$ | French. Located within the flea markets of Les Puces, this former haunt of jazz star Django Reinahrdt opened in 1963 and recalls the days when the markets were filled with outdoor music bars. Stop in on weekend afternoons for a drink or casual bite served with a side of live music. **Known for:** lively atmosphere; free live jazz; convenient location in the market. *Average main: €5 ⊠ 22 rue des Rosiers, Les Puces ☎ 01-40-11-28-80 ⊕ www.lachopedespuces.fr ⊙ Closed Tues. and Wed. Ⓜ Porte de Clignancourt.*

La REcyclerie

$$ | **Vegetarian.** Overlooking an old railway, this converted train station is more than just a trendy café draped in greenery—it's also an eco-conscious community center with a garden and a secondhand clothing market. Located outside of the city center, it's a good stop for brunching with locals before hitting the nearby Marché aux Puces de St-Ouen. **Known for:** weekend brunch; views of a former railway; eco-friendly concept. *Average main: €22 ⌧ 83 bd. Ornano, Les Puces ☎ 01-42-57-58-49 ⊕ www.larecy-clerie.com Ⓜ Porte de Clignancourt.*

Pistache, le Petit Apéro

$ | **Modern French.** If you're craving a casual bite or a glass of wine after a long day of exploring, make your way to this friendly café where natural light pours in from the back terrace. Its all-organic menu show-cases original salads, specials of the day, and omnivore small-plates designed for apéro. **Known for:** bite-size snacks; stir-fry of the day; convenient takeaway, perfect for a picnic. *Average main: €12 ⌧ 24 rue Boursault, Les Batignolles ☎ 06-74-15-37-11 ♥ Closed Sun. Ⓜ Rome.*

Sitron

$ | **French.** As you sink your teeth into the divine madeleines, tarts, and cakes at this tiny bakery, you'd never guess that they are all gluten free (and many are also lactose free). Proving to be as popular as their first shop in the Montorgueil area, this branch serves a reduced yet equally delicious range of

ART IN THE WILD

Although not typically known for its street art, the Batignolles area has two hot spots. Amble down lively **Rue Biot**, where you can admire a vast wall where many artists have left their mark, then head a few blocks away to the **Galerie Ligne 13** (⌧ 3 rue la Condamine), one of Paris's only galleries fully dedicated to street art.

sophisticated goodies that you can snack on while wandering the area. **Known for:** signature citron (lemon) tart; chocolate-lovers' Lotus Noir; dairy-free flan. *Average main: €5 ⌧ 59 rue des Batignolles, Les Batignolles ☎ 01-53-11-44-44 ⊕ sitron-sansgluten.com ♥ Closed Sun. and Mon. Ⓜ Rome, La Fourche.*

Super Vegan

$ | **Fast Food.** Fast food can indeed be vegan, as evidenced by this playful eatery a few blocks from the Martin Luther King Park. Two young French entrepreneurs and comic book fans dreamed up the menu, which features meat- and dairy-free equivalents to burgers and kebabs that might even fool staunch carnivores. **Known for:** vegan kebab sandwich; veggie burgers; fun and friendly vibe. *Average main: €7 ⌧ 118 rue des Moines, Les Batignolles ☎ 09-51-56-99-16 ⊕ supervegan.fr ♥ Closed Wed. Ⓜ Brochant, Guy Môquet.*

🍴 Dining

Brutus

$ | French. One of France's most beloved traditional specialties, the crêpe, gets a modern makeover at this contemporary crêperie and cider bar on bustling Rue des Dames. The minimalist decor reflects the modernity of the deluxe crêpes, made with buckwheat flour from the venue's own mill in Brittany. **Known for:** truffle, mushroom, and Beaufort cheese crêpe; craft cider list; creative cocktails. *Average main: €12* ⊠ *99 rue des Dames, Les Batignolles* ☎ *09–86–53–44–00* ⊕ *www.brutus-paris.com* ⏾ *No dinner Sun., closed 2 wks in Aug.* Ⓜ *Rome.*

Chez Louisette

$ | French. Immerse yourself in the Marché aux Puces with a lunch break at this legendary institution at the edge of the Vernaison Market. A singer belting out the best of Edith Piaf and Yves Montand will guide you to the hidden gem, where you can squeeze into one of the communal tables and order *tête de veau* (calf's head) and a carafe of cheap wine as you sing along. **Known for:** old-school French ambience; hearty boeuf Bourguignon; a sense of kitsch that's part of the fun. *Average main: €13* ⊠ *130 av. Michelet, Les Puces* ☎ *01–40–12–10–14* ⏾ *Closed Tues.– Fri., nights* Ⓜ *Porte de Clignancourt.*

★ Comme Chez Maman

$$$ | Modern French. With its simple wooden tables, friendly welcome, and chalkboard menu scrawled with delectable dishes, this locally loved bistro will make you feel right at home. Its chef, who gained Michelin-level chops with gastronomic heavyweights, impressively reinvents French classics that would make any *maman* proud. **Known for:** great value prix-fixe lunch menu; locally sourced ingredients; heavenly waffles, a nod to the chef's Belgian roots. *Average main: €25* ⊠ *5 rue des Moines, Les Batignolles* ☎ *01–42–28– 89–53* ⊕ *comme-chez-maman.com/en* Ⓜ *Brochant, Rome.*

★ Coretta

$$$$ | Contemporary. Facing the avant-garde Martin Luther King Park is this equally modern neo-bistro, named in honor of the wife of the American Civil Rights leader. Daring, impeccable dishes from the talented chef Beatriz Gonzalez are served in an airy two-story dining room overlooking the park. **Known for:** gorgeous presentation; monthly changing menu; French toast– style brioche. *Average main: €35* ⊠ *151 rue Cardinet, Les Batignolles* ☎ *01–42–26–55–55* ⊕ *www.restau-rantcoretta.com* Ⓜ *Brochant.*

Formaticus

$$ | French. Cheese lovers will be in unpasteurized seventh heaven at this trendy cheese bar and restaurant on the up-and-coming Rue Brochant. Appealing to the neighborhood's increasing population of bobos, the sophisticated menu includes a refined range of cheese plates accented by a selection of wines and small bites, also available to go. **Known for:** 80 varieties of cheese; hip crowd; The Fontainebleau of my Childhood, a cheese dessert with whipped cream. *Average main: €18* ⊠ *16 rue Brochant, Les Batignolles* ☎ *01–42–28–77–36* ⊕ *www.restaurant-format-icus.fr* ⊗ *Closed Sun. and Mon.* Ⓜ *Brochant.*

Gare au Gorille

$$ | **Modern French.** Hugging the St-Lazare train tracks, this sleek restaurant with a contemporary industrial aesthetic serves no mere "train station" food as its name might suggest. Instead, young chef Marc Cordonnier applies his experience from gastronomic doyens Agapé, Arpège, and Septime to his own ingenious Italian-influenced tapas, best accompanied by a glass of natural wine. **Known for:** unusual but delightful fusions; Italian cheeses; friendly albeit noisy atmosphere. *Average main: €20* ⊠ *68 rue des Dames, Les Batignolles* ☎ *01–42–94–24–02* ⊕ *gareaugorille.fr* ⊗ *Closed weekends, Aug.* Ⓜ *Rome.*

Les Poulettes Batignolles

$$ | **Modern French.** A gust of Spanish flair has drifted all the way to Les Batignolles via this attractive neighborhood bistro. After years working in the land of tapas and paella, husband and wife team chef Ludovic Dubois and sommelier Judith Cercós now seduce Parisians with their inventive bistronomie menu bearing noticeable, and tasty, influences from the Iberian Peninsula. **Known for:** signature "Les Poulettes" crispy organic egg starter; products imported from Spain; authentic seafood paella. *Average main: €20* ⊠ *10 rue de Cheroy, Les Batignolles* ☎ *01–42–93–10–11* ⊕ *www.lespoulettes-batignolles.fr* ⊗ *Closed Sun. and Mon., Aug.* Ⓜ *Rome.*

Ma Cocotte

$$ | **French.** Take a break from shopping and refuel at this stylish eatery in the center of Le Marché aux Puces. French designer Philippe Starck decorated the place with colorful sofas, mismatched chairs, and oddball artwork he collected around the market. **Known for:** designer influence on decor, not food; little surprises on the tableware; excellent people-watching. *Average main: €24* ⊠ *106 rue des Rosiers, Les Puces* ☎ *01–49–51–70–00* ⊕ *www.macocotte-lespuces. com* Ⓜ *Porte de Clignancourt.*

Mamma Primi

$$ | **Italian.** You'll forget about the long wait at this trendy Italian restaurant from Big Mamma Group as soon as you dig into its seasonal antipasti, house-made pasta, and Neapolitan-style pizzas. The venue's sublime dining room is decked out in rustic gilded mirrors, marble tables, and cascading vines. **Known for:** high-quality imported Italian ingredients; friendly waiters; no reservations (come before opening or have a drink while you wait). *Average main: €18* ⊠ *71 rue des Dames, Les Batignolles* ☎ *01–47–42–*

33–31 ⊕ www.bigmammagroup.com
Ⓜ Rome.

Ⓨ Bars and Nightlife

★ Le Cyrano
A few steps from brash Place de
Clichy is this friendly neighborhood
watering hole, one of the oldest
bars of Les Batignolles. With its
zinc counter, gorgeous oval mirrors,
and glittering mosaics, the decor
doesn't seem to have changed
since it opened in 1914—and luckily
the prices haven't changed much
either. Mingle with the locals over a
glass of wine, cool beer, or planche
(board) of small bites. ⊠ 3 rue Biot,
Les Batignolles ☎ 01-45-22-53-34
Ⓜ Place de Clichy.

Le Felixio
With a prime location on the corner
of Place du Dr Félix Lobligeois
and the Square des Batignolles,
this is the perfect place for a
casual drink in the central hub of
Les Batignolles. While the food is
nothing special, its star feature is
a highly coveted terrace where you
can sip a glass of wine and watch
the comings and goings around this
busy spot—there's no need to be in
a rush yourself, especially on weekends when it's open late. ⊠ 75 pl. du
Dr Félix Lobligeois, Les Batignolles
☎ 01-42-26-14-53 ⊕ le-felixio.
lafourchette.rest Ⓜ Brochant, Rome.

Le Petit Village
The little village spirit of Les
Batignolles lives on at this friendly,
nocturnal neighborhood hangout.

Share a few cheap pints or some
homemade punch with the area's
young hip crowd, which spills onto
the street most nights, but especially on weekends, when guest DJs
turn the bar's fun meter up several
notches. ⊠ 58 rue La Condamine,
Les Batignolles ☎ 06-28-01-82-77
Ⓜ Rome, La Fourche.

★ Les Caves Populaires
It seems all Batignolles night
owls stop in at this favorite local
wine bar, sporting a very fitting
red mosaic facade with dangling
bunches of grapes. Sit at the zinc
bar to watch the action, make new
friends over a game of chess, or
settle into a simple wooden chair
for a very reasonably priced glass
of St-Émilion and plate of charcuterie and fromage. ⊠ 22 rue des
Dames, Les Batignolles ☎ 01-53-04-
08-32 Ⓜ Place de Clichy, Rome.

Les Paresseux
Make like the name of this tiny,
stylish tapas bar (it translates
to "the sloths") and enjoy a lazy
apéro on the busy Rue des Dames.
Featuring a wall of faux foliage, intimate seating, and a packed crowd of
locals, the family-run venue serves
rillettes (similar to pâté), spicy Asian
small plates, and an admirable list
of independent wines. ⊠ 24 rue des
Dames, Les Batignolles ☎ 01-42-93-
03-53 ⊕ www.lesparesseux.fr Ⓜ Place
de Clichy, Rome.

Société Parisienne de Bière
The 17e arrondissement's
premier craft beer venue, Société
Parisienne de Bière began brewing

its own beer, la Bière Batignolle, in 2018. Sample it, as well as more than 30 other French-made beers and a selection of foreign brews, at their handful of tall tables, or create your own mix-and-match six-pack to go. ⊠ *5 rue des Moines, Les Batignolles* ☏ *07–64–09–92–27* ⊕ *societeparisiennedebiere.fr* ☞ *Closed Sun. and Mon.* Ⓜ *Rome, Brochant.*

🎟 Performing Arts

Le Cinéma des Cinéastes
One of the coolest art house cinemas in Paris is oddly located between cheap clothing shops on the gritty Avenue de Clichy. Occupying the former 19th-century Cabaret du Père Lathuille, the gorgeous building was refurbished in the 1990s thanks to famous French actress Fanny Ardant— whom you just may see in its vast screening room or having a glass of wine in the cinema's artsy bar. ⊠ *7 av. de Clichy, Les Batignolles* ☏ *08–92–68–97–17* ⊕ *cinema-des-cineastes.fr* ☞ *Restaurant-bar closed Aug.* Ⓜ *Place de Clichy.*

LES PUCES

ÉPINETTES

CLIGNAN-COURT

LA CHAPELLE

LA VILLETTE

LES BATIGNOLLES

MONTMARTRE

PIGALLE

TERNES

MONCEAU

LES GRANDS BOULEVARDS

SENTIER

CANAL ST-MARTIN

BELLEVILLE

CHAILLOT

CHAMPS-ÉLYSÉES

TROCADÉRO

PALAIS-ROYAL

LES HALLES

LE MARAIS

OBERKAMPF

MÉNILMONTANT

PÈRE-LACHAISE

BOIS DE BOULOGNE

PASSY

AUTEUIL

LES INVALIDES

LES ÎLES

ST-GERMAIN-DES-PRÉS

BASTILLE

CHARONNE

VAUGIRARD

QUARTIER LATIN

BERCY

BEL-AIR

JAVEL

MONTPARNASSE

BUTTE-AUX-CAILLES

AUSTERLITZ

SEINE

BOIS DE VINCENNES

ST-LAMBERT

MONTROUGE

MAISON BLANCHE

Even more charming than what you might recall from the French film Amélie, Montmartre is one of the hilliest parts of Paris, known for its old-world village feel and neighborhood vibe. Once an artist's enclave more affordable for those on painter's and poet's wages, it's now drawing a new influx of young creatives that have managed to keep it from feeling at all suburban. With unique shops, bistros, and galleries, as well as some snap-worthy street art, Montmartre and Pigalle are both heavy on history. At the Sacré-Coeur, you'll understand why visitors flock here to see Paris the way the birds do at the butte of Montmartre. Skip the cheesy showgirl shenanigans at the Moulin Rouge, but do stroll through the seedy-sexy side of Pigalle. Wear flats and comfortable shoes to glide over cobblestone streets and up the many staircases.—by Georgette Moger

◉ Sights

★ Basilique du Sacré-Coeur

Climb the steps or hop in the funicular to the Butte de Montmartre to behold the majestic Basilique du Sacré-Coeur. Its construction began in 1875, after the Franco-Prussian War, and was completed in 1914, a time of massive division between devout Catholics, socialists, and radicals. Today, it stands as homage to the lives of priests, nuns, and seminaries lost in two world wars, a place of reverence for those who've come to worship, and arguably the best view of the entire city. Within the gardens of the complex is a meditation sanctuary open to the public, while inside the basilica you can climb the 300 steps to the southernmost side for the ultimate panoramic view of Paris. If you do enter the church, dress appropriately, keep voices to a hush, and don't even think about snapping a selfie. ⊠ 35 rue du Chevalier de la Barre, Montmartre ☎ 01-53-41-89-00 Ⓜ Abbesses.

Bateau-Lavoir (Wash-barge)

The birthplace of Cubism isn't open to the public, but a display in the front window details this unimposing spot's rich history. Montmartre poet Max Jacob coined the name because the original structure here reminded him of the laundry boats that used to float in the Seine, and he joked that the warren of paint-splattered artists' studios needed a good hosing down (wishful thinking, because the building had only one water tap). It was in the Bateau-Lavoir that, early in the 20th century, Pablo Picasso, Georges Braque, and Juan Gris made their first bold stabs at Cubism, and Picasso painted the groundbreaking Les Demoiselles d'Avignon in 1906–07. The experimental works of the artists weren't met with open arms, even in liberal Montmartre. All but the facade was rebuilt after a fire in 1970. Like the original building, though, the current incarnation houses artists and their studios. ⊠ *13 pl. Émile-Goudeau, Montmartre* Ⓜ *Abbesses.*

Cimetière de Montmartre

With sandwich in hand, stroll through the bucolic resting place of such grand personas as Berlioz, Degas, and Truffaut. While a formal picnic sprawl is verboten, it is possible to pause between headstones and pay respects to the deceased thinkers, writers, and artists—even though Foucault, with his disdain for photos and simula-crum, would grumble in ire. ⊠ *20 av. Rachel, Montmartre* ☎ *01-53-42-36-30* Ⓜ *Place de Clichy.*

Espace Dalí

Located 1,600 feet from Salvador and Gala Dalí's apartment at 7 rue Becquerel, this intimate museum of original Dalí sculptures, surrealist furniture, etchings, paintings, and graphic artworks houses the largest private collection of the artist's creations in France. Because of its small size, you can cover the whole experience in about an hour. ◼ TIP➔ Book tickets online and skip the line. ⊠ *11 rue Poulbot, Montmartre* ☎ *01-42-64-40-10* ⊕ *www.daliparis.com* Ⓜ *Abbesses.*

Halle St-Pierre

The elegant iron-and-glass, 19th-century market hall at the foot of Sacré-Coeur stages dynamic exhibitions of *art brut,*

"raw" or outsider and folk art. The international artists featured are contemporary in style and outside the mainstream. There's also a good bookstore and a café serving light, well-prepared dishes, such as savory tarts and quiches with salad on the side, plus homemade desserts. ⊠ *2 rue Ronsard, Montmartre* ☎ *01-42-58-72-89* ⊕ *www.hallesaintpierre. org* ⌑ *Museum €9* ⊙ *Closed Aug.* Ⓜ *Anvers.*

Le Clos Montmartre

The only remaining vineyard in Paris, the pastoral sprawl of vines has been maintained and harvested since 1934. Every October 1,000–1,500 bottles are auctioned off at a harvest festival, with proceeds benefiting charity (prices are typi-cally €20 to €40 per bottle). While the wines themselves probably won't be taking home 100-point ratings, seeing a miniature vineyard in the city is worth the detour if you're in the area. ⊠ *Rue des Saules, Montmartre* ☎ *01-46-06-00-32* Ⓜ *Lamarck–Caulaincourt.*

Marché St-Pierre

This self-described "fabric kingdom" has been selling Parisians their curtains for more than 60 years. With five floors, it actually stocks a lot more than draperies, including bolts of fine silk, feather boas, and spangled cushions. Among the regulars here are the designers who create the famous windows at Hermès. The Marché anchors a fabric district that extends to the neighboring streets; each shop is a bit different from

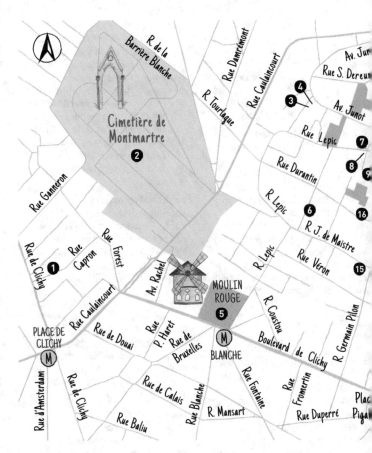

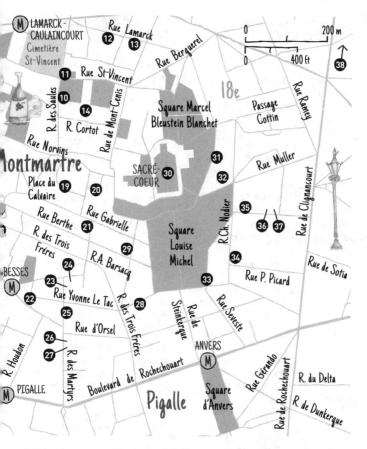

the next. ✉ *2 rue Charles Nodier, Montmartre* ☎ *01–42–06–92–25* ⊕ *www.marchesaintpierre.com* ⊘ *Closed Sun.* Ⓜ *Anvers.*

Moulin de la Galette

Of the 14 windmills (*moulins*) that used to sit atop this hill, only two remain. They're known collectively as Moulin de la Galette, a name taken from the bread the owners once produced. The more storied of the two is Le Blute-Fin: in the late 1800s there was a dance hall on the site, famously captured by Renoir (you can see the painting in the Musée d'Orsay). A face-lift restored the windmill to its 19th-century glory; however, it is on private land and can't be visited. Down the street is the other moulin, Le Radet. ✉ *Le Blute-Fin, corner of Rue Lepic and Rue Tholozé, Montmartre* Ⓜ *Abbesses.*

Moulin Rouge

When this world-famous cabaret opened in 1889, aristocrats, professionals, and the working classes alike all flocked to ogle the scandalous performers (the cancan was considerably kinkier in Toulouse-Lautrec's day, when girls kicked off their knickers). There's not much to see from the outside except for tourist buses and sex shops; if you want to catch a show inside, ticket prices start at €112. Souvenir seekers should check out the Moulin Rouge gift shop (around the corner at 11 rue

GETTING HERE

Located in the 18e arrondissement, hilly Montmartre is serviced by several métro stations. Take line 2 to the Anvers stop and then the funicular up to the Sacré-Coeur, or take the 12 line to the Abbesses stop—but beware the obligatory 200 stairs up to the ground level. An easier stop on the 12 line is Jules Joffrin, where you can take the public Montmartrobus on a scenic tour for the price of one métro ticket. Neighboring Montmartre to the south, in the 9e arrondissement, Pigalle is serviced by a métro stop of the same name on lines 2 and 12.

Lepic), which sells official merchandise, from jewelry to sculptures, by reputable French makers. ✉ *82 bd. de Clichy, Montmartre* ☎ *01–53–09–82–82* ⊕ *www.moulinrouge.fr* Ⓜ *Blanche.*

Musée de Montmartre

During its turn-of-the-20th-century heyday, this building—now home to Montmartre's historical museum—was occupied by painters, writers, and cabaret artists. Foremost among them was Pierre-Auguste Renoir, who painted *Le Moulin de la Galette* (an archetypal scene of sun-drenched revelers) while living here. Recapping the area's colorful past, the museum has a charming permanent collection, which includes many Toulouse-Lautrec posters and original Eric Satie scores. An ambitious renovation, completed in 2014, doubled its space by incorporating both the studio-apartment once shared by mother-and-son duo Suzanne Valadon and Maurice Utrillo (now fully restored) and the adjoining Demarne Hotel (which has been redesigned to house temporary exhibitions). The lovely surrounding gardens—named in honor of Renoir—have also been revital-ized. An audioguide is included in the ticket price. ⊠ *12 rue Cortot, Montmartre* ☎ *01–49–25–89–39* ⊕ *www.museedemontmartre.fr* 🎫 *€10* Ⓜ *Lamarck–Caulaincourt.*

Place des Abbesses

After climbing the 200 mural-illustrated stairs of the Abbesses stop on line 12 of the métro, emerge under the glass-covered Guimard awning into the triangle of Place des Abbesses, a plaza surrounded by cafés and boutiques. You'll walk nearly straight into the serene Church of St-Jean de Montmartre, flush with Art Nouveau flourishes and a smattering of stained-glass windows. Nearby is the square of Jehan Rictus, abloom with cherry blossoms and verdant ancient shrubs in spring. Admire the mur des je t'aime, or I Love You Wall, and take a turn on the ornately painted equines of one of the few carousels permitting adults before beginning your day in this impos-sibly charming, village-feeling part of Paris. ⊠ *Pl. des Abbesses, Montmartre* Ⓜ *Abbesses.*

Place du Tertre

Artists have peddled their wares in this square for centuries. Busloads of tourists have changed the atmo-sphere, but if you come off-season—

VIEWFINDER

Everyone goes to the Sacré-Coeur for the best view of Paris, but what about the best view of the Sacré-Coeur? Surprisingly, it can be found at street level, at Rue Lafitte between Rue Chateaudun and Rue la Fayette. Aim to arrive just after sunset, when the sky is ablaze in lavender and orange.

Share your photo with us!
@FodorsTravel #FodorsOnTheGo

when the air is chilly and the streets are bare—you can almost feel what is was like when up-and-coming Picassos lived in the houses that today are given over to souvenir shops and cafés. ⊠ *East end of Rue Norvin, Pl. du Tertre, Montmartre* Ⓜ *Abbesses.*

🛍 Shopping

A.P.C. Surplus

This is sartorial minimalism made French. Here you'll find a shop full of markdowns on the effortlessly cool, albeit modestly spendy brand,

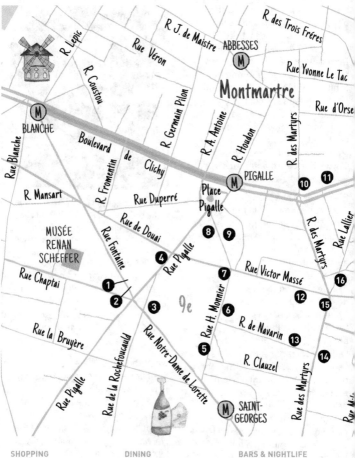

A.P.C. On rotation are boxy, polished dresses and jumpers for Francophile femmes, basics for hommes, and jeans and cords you'll wear for years. Score a steal on the trench coat of your dreams, a pair of oxfords to wear *sans chaussettes* , or a pair of precious, made-in-Italy Mary Janes from last fall. ⊠ *20 rue André Del Sarte, Montmartre* ☎ *01–42–62–10–88* ⊕ *www.apc.fr* Ⓜ *Anvers.*

Chinemachine

Walk through the electric-blue storefront, be greeted by one of the shop's friendly faces, and behold deals in every organized nook— think vintage Christian Dior ties for €15 and Acne sweaters for €25 mingling among preloved Lanvin, Gucci, and Louboutins. Downstairs is a well-curated cave of vintage and new-school mens' digs. ⊠ *100 rue des Martyrs, Montmartre* ☎ *01–80–50–27–66* ⊕ *www.chinemachinevintage.com* Ⓜ *Abbesses, Anvers.*

Galerie Belle de Jour

Before you ascend the stairs of the Sacré-Coeur, lose yourself in this hypnotic shop-gallery celebrating a history of olfactory offerings. Admire the intoxicating illustrations of vintage perfume ads—some for sale and some for display—sniff fragrances of eras long past, or splurge on a meticulously restored Belle Époque–era atomizer, an Art Deco powder box, or perhaps a bottle from Baccarat's bohemian moment. ⊠ *7 rue Tardieu, Montmartre* ☎ *01–46–06–15–28* ⊕ *www.belle-de-jour.fr* ⊙ *Closed Sun. and Mon.* Ⓜ *Abbesses, Anvers.*

Le Rideau de Fer

Lose yourself in this tightly packed record shop flush with modern indie, folk, punk, and '60s French pop. Well-organized red bins line an enclave that feels like a cool big brother's room (prices hover around €8–€10). Comic collectors, save some suitcase real estate for stacks of inevitable splurges. ⊠ *12 rue André Del Sarte, Montmartre* ☎ *01–42–55–66–40* ⊙ *Closed Sun. and Mon.* Ⓜ *Anvers, Château Rouge.*

L'Objet Qui Parle

If it comes from France and it's dead, religious, creepy, or all of the above, chances are it's found a second home in this packed curio parlor. A veritable goldmine of antiques, flags, and all manner of religious kitsch, this is the spot to score a magician's cape from the 1940s, a glass-enclosed diorama of undersea creatures, or a roll of beautifully printed wallpaper. Claustrophobes beware—quarters are tight. ⊠ *86 rue des Martyrs, Montmartre* ⊕ *lobjetquiparle.fr* ⊙ *Closed Sun.* Ⓜ *Anvers.*

Myrtille Beck

Here you'll find sophisticated bijoux for the minimalist with a penchant for vintage. For those teetering on betrothal, consider Myrtille Beck's sweetly stackable engagement and wedding bands, along with finely crafted, understated bands for the groom-to-be. Delicate earrings and sweetly simple bracelets are also an irresistible splurge. ⊠ *20 rue Henri Monnier, Pigalle* ☎ *01–40–23–99–84* ⊙ *Closed Sun. and Mon.* Ⓜ *Pigalle, St-Georges.*

Spree

A clubhouse for designers like Isabel Marant, Helmut Lang, and Vanessa Seward, this spacious, white shop presents dresses, blouses, and coats on suspended racks. Peruse an abundant offering of jewel-tone Comme des Garçons wallets, Illestevac shades, and delicate baubles from Pamela Love. Spree's signature ballet flats are available in shades both vibrant and neutral. ⊠ 16 rue la Vieuville, Montmartre ☎ 01–42–23–41–40 ⊕ www.spree.fr ⊘ Closed Mon. Ⓜ Abbesses.

🍴 Coffee and Quick Bites

Boulangerie Raphaëlle

$ | Café. Brave the line at locally loved Boulangerie Raphaëlle and exit with the ultimate walking companion: a perfect ham and cheese sandwich bound by a still-warm, crispy, chewy baguette. Sure, there are salads and savories worthy of mention, but the award-winning breads of every breed and bake (including gluten-free options) are the real show-stealers at this long-standing favorite. **Known for:** award-winning baguettes; takeaway options; oven-warm carb comforts. *Average main:* ⊠ 1 rue Feutrier, Montmartre ☎ 06–99–34–81–61 ⊕ boulangerieraphaelle.fr ⊘ Closed Wed. Ⓜ Château Rouge, Anvers.

Café Lomi

$ | Café. The long list of beans and brews at Lomi is almost as intimi-dating as the hike up Montmartre's hill, but the rocket fuel you'll order is well worth it. Let the friendly staff guide you to a perfectly bespoke blend, and if you've got time, consider a tasting class offered in the late afternoon. **Known for:** serious coffee worth the walk (and wait); chic chem-lab aesthetic; crowd of book-worms on weekends. *Average main:* €10 ⊠ 3 ter rue Marcadet, Montmartre ☎ 09–80–39–56–24 Ⓜ Marcadet–Poissonniers, Marx Dormoy.

Café Marlette

$ | Café. What began as an organic bread and cake mix brand baked up by two sisters manifested into Marlette, a mirthful, exposed-brick and foliage-dotted brunch spot. On a sunny day, settle in for a relaxing breakfast on the patio, or relax into a window seat with a flat white on a rainy day and catch up on some emails. **Known for:** fluffy pancakes and pastries (gluten-free available); strong coffee; soft-boiled eggs with golden, runny yokes. *Average main:* €8 ⊠ 51 rue des Martyrs, Pigalle ☎ 01–48–74–89–73 ⊕ www.marlette.fr Ⓜ St-Georges, Anvers.

Café Miroir

$$$ | Bistro. At breakfast, Miroir is the sort of place where you can cozy up with a book or a crinkly news-paper, order a strong coffee, and surrender to the pillowy French toast drizzled with caramel. Later in the day, dishes are built to share, such as plates of pâté and sausages, plucky salads, octopus ravioli, or a rib eye for two that could feed four. **Known for:** affordable; breakfast, lunch, and dinner; sharing plates. *Average main:* €25 ⊠ 94 rue des Martyrs, Montmartre ☎ 01–46–06–50–73 ⊕ www.cafemiroir.com ⊙ *Closed Sun. and Mon.* Ⓜ *Abbesses*.

Gilles Marchal

$ | Café. Hailing from Alsace, home of the madeleine, pastry chef Gilles Marchal helms this gilded sweet shop that reads like the Cartier of cake indulgences. Fill a takeaway bag with glazed lemon madeleines and pluck a crisp caramel-and-custard *canelé* from a pin-straight row of baby bundts. **Known for:** excellent madeleines; canelés; Paris-Brest éclairs. *Average main:* €5 ⊠ *9 rue Ravignan, Montmartre* ☎ *01–85–34–73–30* ⊕ *gillesmarchal. com* ⊙ *Closed. Mon. and Tues.* Ⓜ *Abbesses*.

Hardware Société

$ | French. Butterfly wallpaper and a kaleidoscope of colorful kitchenware fills the dining room of Hardware Société. The menu is a remix of Aussie and French favorites, like crumbled black pudding on your boiled *oeufs* , baked eggs that arrive in a mini cast-iron pot, fancy jams to top a flaky, pillowy croissant, and exhibit-worthy latte art. **Known for:** ultratwee aesthetic; darling, decadent brunch options; photogenic latte art. *Average main:* €5 ⊠ *10 rue Lamarck, Montmartre* ☎ *01–42–51–69–03* ⊙ *Closed Tues. and Wed.* Ⓜ *Anvers*.

KB CaféShop

$ | Café. KB stands for kookaburra, just one indication you're at an Aussie-inspired coffee shop, and the serious selection of coffee beans here are sourced from Kenya to Costa Rica. Come for the flat whites, and stay to relish a scone or spiced tea cake while getting some quality laptop time. **Known for:** globe-spanning beans; laptop-wielding freelancers; AC when you want it, toasty temps when you don't. *Average main:* €10 ⊠ *53 av. Trudaine, Montmartre* ☎ *01–56–92–12–41* ⊕ *www.kbcafe-shop.com* Ⓜ *Anvers, Pigalle*.

Pain Pain

$ | Café. This is an impossibly adorable destination for arguably the best *chouquettes* (sugar-topped pastry puffs) in Paris, along with Technicolor tarts, creative quiches, and flaky, powdery almond croissants in all their pull-apart glory. Score a tiny window table in the corner, or take a coffee and your breakfast with you to power your walk along Rue des Martyrs. **Known for:** joyful little chouquettes; perfect pain au chocolat; dreamy almond croissants. *Average main:* €4 ⊠ *88 rue des Martyrs, Montmartre* ☎ *01–42–23–62–81* ⊕ *www.pain-pain.fr* ⊙ *Closed Mon.* Ⓜ *St-Georges, Anvers*.

Rose Bakery

$ | Café. No mere boulangerie, Rose Bakery has a counter of tempting savory items in addition to its baked beauties, including whimsical salads, roasted vegetables, and quiches that you can relish on-site or take away. The warm and jovial owner also maintains a grocery store around the block that stocks all of her favorite English imports, choice organic fruits, and vegetables, along with an impressive selection of *fromage* (cheese). **Known for:** friendly owner; takeaway delicacies; legendary carrot cake. *Average main:* €4 ⊠ *46* *rue des Martyrs, Pigalle* ☎ *01-42-82-12-80* ⊕ *www.rosebakery.fr* Ⓜ *St-Georges, Anvers.*

🍴 Dining

★ Bal Café

$ | **Café**. Set in a bright, modern space on a tiny street in the lower reaches of Montmartre, the popular Bal Café caters to a diverse clientele who come for the great coffee, delicious homey food, lively crowd, and the art gallery–bookstore. British–French-inspired cuisine with far-flung influences (like kedgeree, a Scottish–Indian rice-and-smoked-haddock dish), tender pancakes, fried eggs with ham and roasted tomatoes, and buttery scones with jam represent some the best comfort food in town. **Known for:** great brunches and reliably good coffee; art gallery on the premises; outdoor terrace on a quiet passageway. *Average main: €12* ⊠ *6 impasse de la Défense, 18e, Montmartre* ☎ *01-44-70-75-51* ⊕ *www.le-bal.fr* ☾ *Closed Mon. and Tues. No dinner Sun.* Ⓜ *Place de Clichy.*

Guilo Guilo

$$$ | **Japanese**. Already a star in Kyoto, Eiichi Edakuni created a sensation with his first Parisian restaurant, where 20 diners seated around the black horseshoe bar can watch him at work each night. The €55 set menu is a bargain given the quality and sophistica-tion of the food. **Known for:** reliably good Japanese cuisine with French accents; signature foie-gras sushi; buzzy, sometimes chaotic atmo-

sphere. *Average main: €27* ⊠ *8 rue Garreau, 18e, Montmartre* ☎ *01-42-54-23-92* ☾ *Closed Sun. and Mon. No lunch* Ⓜ *Abbesses.*

Ito Chan

$ | **Japanese**. The next-door sister restaurant of Ito Izakaya is adored by ramen enthusiasts who flock here for bowls of rich, dark broth, perfectly seasoned beef, and springy noodles for a scant €11. Other wallet-friendly offerings in this comforting canteen include a €12 bento duo and €7 bao, and an extensive list of sake is available by the glass, carafe, or bottle. **Known for:** cult-status ramen; budget bao and bento; sake to savor. *Average main: €11* ⊠ *2 rue Pierre Fontaine, Montmartre* ☎ *09-51-71-95-44* ⊕ *www.itoeats.fr/itochan* ☾ *Closed Sun. and Mon.* Ⓜ *Pigalle, Blanche.*

Ito Izakaya

$$$ | **Japanese**. This miniscule spot for tiny, beautifully presented Japanese tapas has a constantly changing set menu—though crowd-pleasing miso soup and *aubergine dengaku* (grilled eggplant) are permanent fixtures, for good reason. The late-night option is ideal for snacky groups looking to soak up the evening's cocktails, though even if you're ordering à la carte, the bill quickly adds up. **Known for:** late-night Japanese; sharable tapas; set menus. *Average main: €25* ⊠ *4 rue Pierre Fontaine, Pigalle* ☎ *09-52-91-23-00* ⊕ *www.itoeats. fr/menus* ☾ *Closed Sun.* Ⓜ *Pigalle, Blanche.*

★ L'Arcane

$$$ | **French.** Once a well-guarded foodie secret, a Michelin star brought this cozy restaurant tucked behind the Sacré-Coeur richly deserved acclaim. Now the intimate 14-seat dining room is packed with diners enjoying impeccable contemporary French cuisine that's gorgeously presented and full of flavor. **Known for:** three-course "surprise" menu; location near the Sacré-Coeur; online reservations needed. *Average main: €26* ⊠ *9 rue Lamarck , 18e, Montmartre* ⊕ *www.restaurantlarcane. com* ✆ *Closed Sun. and Mon. No lunch Tues.* Ⓜ *Lamarck-Cauliancourt.*

La Fourmi

$ | **Bistro.** All the reliable comforts of pub food are made classy in this buzzy bistro bar that's loved by Montmartre locals. Friendly servers and bartenders welcome you into a wood-paneled room with steampunk finishes, where you can choose from an affordable menu of beer, wine, and cocktails as well as salads, sandwiches, and charcuterie spreads to offset your nightcap or pregame tipple. **Known for:** lively and local; budget-friendly beer, wine, and cocktails; unfussy snacks and daily specials. *Average main: €13* ⊠ *74 rue des Martyrs, Pigalle* ✆ *01-42-64-70-35* Ⓜ *Pigalle.*

Le Botak Café

$ | **Café.** On the eastern side of Sacré-Coeur, at the bottom of the stairs, you'll find the leafy Square Louise Marie and this little café, which serves a small, ever-changing menu of French home cooking.

The daily lunch specials (€16 for two courses and a glass of wine) are a great deal, but service can sometimes be slow when it's busy. *Average main: €17* ⊠ *1 rue Paul Albert, Montmartre* ✆ *01-46-06-98-30* ✆ *Closed Sun. nights in winter* Ⓜ *Anvers, Château Rouge.*

★ Le Coq Rico

$$$$ | **Bistro.** Chef Antoine Westermann's polished Montmartre flagship is known as the "bistro of beautiful birds." The chef incorporates his signature poaching-roasting expertise in succulent *poulet* offerings, encouraging whole-bird dining as a tribute both to the bird and to the communal bond between you and your dining partner(s). For lunch, bargains abound with a set menu for €27 or a revolving plat du jour for €15. **Known for:** poultry-centric bistro; whole-bird dining; modestly priced set lunch menu. *Average main: €35* ⊠ *98 rue Lepic, Montmartre* ✆ *01-42-59-82-89* ⊕ *www.lecoqrico. com* Ⓜ *Abbesses.*

Le Moulin de la Galette

$$$ | **Bistro.** One of two remaining windmills left in Montmartre, immortalized on canvas by the likes of van Gogh, Toulouse-Lautrec, Picasso, and Renoir, is now home to a remarkably unkitsch and surprisingly nontouristy bistro. Drop into the bar for a glass of rosé, or stay for a set lunch on the ivy-covered terrace. **Known for:** located in a windmill; coal-oven-cooked meats; set menus. *Average main: €31* ⊠ *83 rue Lepic, Montmartre* ✆ *01-46-06-*

84–77 ⊕ www.lemoulindelagalette.fr
Ⓜ Abbesses.

Le Pantruche

$$$ | Bistro. Simple, artfully composed bistro comforts are masterfully swirled into two afford-able menus for day and night (€17 and €34, respectively). The space's aged oak and mirrors aestheti-cally defy its small square footage, but the closely arranged tables fill quickly, so secure a reservation before going. **Known for:** cozy and romantic 1940s-inspired dining room; wallet-friendly set menus; legendary Grand Mariner soufflé. *Average main: €34* ⊠ *3 rue Victor Masse, Pigalle* ☎ 01-48-78-55-69 ⊘ *Closed weekends* Ⓜ *Pigalle.*

★ L'Epuisette

$$$$ | Seafood. Outfitted in ikat and rattan, with a name loosely translating to "the landing net," L'Epuisette plays the best seafood game in town. Ever reliable for quality *fruit de mer* sourced from the iconic fishmonger Reynaud at the Rungis Market, L'Epuisette serves sweet and salty *huîtres* (oysters), even in months not ending in "r" (a belief still strongly held in France). *Langoustines à la plancha* (on the griddle) are lavished in piquant pepper and basil, and razor clams in a parsley garlic sauce meet a pillowy baguette. **Known for:** creatively interpreted ocean fare; criminally delicious sweet potato fries; oysters for all seasons. *Average main: €50* ⊠ *73 rue de Rochechouart, Pigalle* ☎ 01-53-21-02-87 ⊕ www.l-epuisette.fr Ⓜ *Anvers.*

Les Affranchis

$$$$ | Bistro. Like being in the pres-ence of a warm Italian godfather (as the restaurant's name implies), the calming ambience of this elegant space is a standout among the gritty bustle of Pigalle. Les Affranchis offers an exceptional tasting menu of options for lunch or dinner. **Known for:** stellar service; elegant tasting menus; decon-structed carbonara. *Average main: €52* ⊠ *5 rue Henry Monnier, Pigalle* ☎ 01-45-26-26-30 ⊘ *Closed Mon.* Ⓜ *St-Georges, Pigalle.*

Maison Lautrec

$$ | Bistro. The romantic Art Deco–inspired dining room of Maison Lautrec swells with exotic flora and lush fabrics. The made-for-sharing plates are a celebration of small-batch produce grown by the owners, while all creatures, from a Landes chicken oozing with hazelnuts and spinach to the plancha-cooked ox sirloin, are sustainably sourced from organic farms. **Known for:** Art Deco design; seasonal, small-batch produce; garden-to-glass cocktails. *Average main: €18* ⊠ *63 rue Jean-Baptiste, Pigalle* ☎ 01-53-21-07-78 ⊕ www.maisonlautrec.fr ⊘ *Closed Sun. and Mon.* Ⓜ *Pigalle.*

Marcel

$$ | Fusion. Revel in a sublime breakfast of fluffy waffles with strawberries and Chantilly cream or a late-night pulled pork burger at this restaurant. Marcel is easy like Sunday morning every day of the week, but especially on weekends, with a lox and bagel spread to rival any Brooklyn haunt.

Known for: Manhattan meets Manchester by way of Montmartre; casual breakfast; weekend brunch decadence. *Average main: €18 ⊠ 1 Villa Léandre, Montmartre* ☎ *01–46–06–04–04* ⊕ *www.restaurantmarcel.fr* Ⓜ *Lamarck–Caulaincourt.*

★ Soul Kitchen

$ | Café. Run by three friendly young women, the snug Soul Kitchen unites a pleasantly homey decor and welcoming atmosphere with the kind of Anglo-French all-organic comfort food that soothes body and soul. Choose from gruyère mac and cheese, chèvre and leek tarts, house-made foie gras, and a pastry counter laden with treats like homemade scones, cheese-cake, tiramisu, and rich mousse au chocolat. **Known for:** charming atmosphere; delicious coffee and fresh juices; range of homemade dishes and desserts made fresh daily. *Average main: €12 ⊠ 33 rue Lamarck, 18e, Montmartre* ☎ *01–71–37–99–95* ⊙ *Closed Mon.* Ⓜ *Lamarck-Caulaincourt.*

Ⓨ Bars and Nightlife

★ Au Lapin Agile

An authentic survivor from the 19th century, Au Lapin Agile considers itself the doyen of cabarets. Founded in 1860, it inhabits the same modest house that was a favorite subject of painter Maurice Utrillo. It became the home-away-from-home for Braque, Modigliani, Apollinaire, and Picasso—who once paid for a meal with one of his paintings, then promptly exited and painted another that he named after this place. There are no topless dancers; this is a genuine French cabaret with songs, poetry, and humor (in French) in a publike setting. Entry is €28. ⊠ *22 rue des Saules, 18e, Montmartre* ☎ *01–46–06–85–87* ⊕ *www.au-lapin-agile.com* Ⓜ *Lamarck–Caulaincourt.*

Bar Le Très Particulier

Tucked discreetly in the refined verdant wilds of the Hôtel Particulier is this provocative jewel box of a bar. Through a glass-enclosed, checkered-tile veranda, flush with red velvet thrones and exotic foliage, you'll enter a drinking den papered in enchanted forest murals. Dim golden light reflects off bottles both curious and compelling. Order from such cockails as the Darjeeling Ltd—a spicy and sweet, clear-as-crystal milk punch—and the Seven Mercenaries, a pine-scented scotch nightcap that will immerse you further in the all-encompassing forest. ⊠ *Pavillon D, 23 av. Junot, Montmartre* ☎ *01–53–41–81–40* Ⓜ *Lamarck–Caulaincourt.*

★ Dirty Dick

The risqué name of this tiki bar is a nod to the history of the house as a hostess bar. Today, the mood is that of an unplugged punk-rock luau, with a menu of ever-evolving libations, flaming large-format punches served in oversized conch shells, grandly garnished moas, and a rum list that runs from entry-level to connoisseur league. Don some aloha-wear, come with friends, mingle with the expats, and stay late. ✉ *10 rue Frochot, Pigalle* ☎ *01-48-78-74-58* Ⓜ *Pigalle.*

★ Glass

From the team behind some of Paris's most-adored cocktail haunts—Candelaria, Mabel, Hero, Le Mary Celeste—Glass is a gritty departure. Here, you can shimmy off residual jetlag on a tiny, glowing-tile dance floor crammed with stylish locals while sipping cocktails with names like Black Panties, Glitterball, and Patti & Robert. Take in a set from your next favorite under-the-radar DJ and surrender to an impending hangover. Arrive on the early side for the mellow preparty vibes and to secure a table of your own for when the fête hits the fan. ✉ *7 rue Frochot, Pigalle* ☎ *09-80-72-98-83* ⊕ *www.quixotic-projects.com/venue/glass* Ⓜ *Pigalle.*

Grand Pigalle Hotel Bar

From the fine folks who practically brought the dawn of craft cocktails to Paris, Experimental Cocktail Club, comes this "bed & beverage" hotel and its respective libation lounge. The bar reads as Art Deco on a minimalist mission. Take it all in with a calvados-based and absinthe-spritzed PanAmerican Clipper (€13) or the Dame Blanche, a gin sipper of pressed lemon and orange essences and the inviting perfume of vanilla (€13). ✉ *29 rue Victor Massé, Pigalle* ☎ *01-85-73-12-02* ⊕ *www.grandpigalle.com* Ⓜ *Pigalle.*

Le Bâton Rouge

Joseph Biolatto sends *bisous* to the bayou in a bar primed to satiate cravings for bottle-aged Vieux Carres, masterfully rendered sazeracs, or any number of other French Quarter classics—along with po'boys and juicy grilled pork ribs. Palm fronds, Mardi Gras beads, and paper lanterns add to the quirky feel of a wild night in New Orleans. Stray from the classics with the innovative Nola Fizz (a high-octane sipper of Plymouth gin, lemon juice, Bols Yogurt Liqueur, and blood-orange liqueur). ✉ *62 rue Notre Dame de Lorette, Montmartre* ☎ *06-52-90-36-42* Ⓜ *Pigalle, St-Georges.*

Le Rendez-Vous des Amis

This makes an intriguing midway breather if you climb the hill of Montmartre by foot. Le Rendez-Vous des Amis has a jovial staff, eclectic music, and a century's worth of previous patrons immortalized in photos. ✉ *23 rue Gabrielle, 18e, Montmartre* ☎ *01-46-06-01-60* Ⓜ *Abbesses.*

Le Sancerre

Café by day, Le Sancerre turns into an essential watering hole for Montmartrois and artists at night, with Belgian beers on tap and an impressive list of cocktails. Locals love its traditional old-school vibe. ✉ *35 rue des Abbesses, 18e, Montmartre* ☎ *01-42-58-08-20* Ⓜ *Abbesses.*

Restaurant Amour

Take a detour for an afternoon aperitif and snack in the lush gardens of the Hôtel Amour, a prime spot for people-watching. Settle into the tiny Eden for crudités, a tartare, or a terrine to accompany a spritz or the house favorite cocktail, the

S.O.S. Mademoiselle—a mélange of mezcal, tequila, agave, orange zest, lime, and Fever Tree tonic. ✉ *8 rue de Navarin, Pigalle* ☎ *01–48–78–31–80* ⊕ *www.hotelamourparis.fr* Ⓜ *Pigalle, St-Georges.*

🎭 Performing Arts

Galerie Chappe
Many an underground musician and legendary artist have made their debut or surfaced from obscurity at Galerie Chappe. The oldest art space in Montmartre is part music venue, part gallery, with previous musician appearances including Cat Power and Devendra Banhart. Jarvis Cocker even moved in for a week for a performance installation. ✉ *4 rue André Barsacq, Montmartre* ☎ *01–42–62–42–12* ⊕ *galeriechappe.org* Ⓜ *Abbesses.*

★ La Cigale
Artists like Maurice Chevalier and Arletty were once a staple of this small concert hall in the storied Pigalle neighborhood before cabaret and vaudeville moved in. Today it's one of Paris's top pop and contemporary music venues, featuring such acts as Adele and Coldplay. ✉ *120 bd. de Rochechouart, 18e, Montmartre* ☎ *01–49–25–89–99* ⊕ *www.lacigale.fr* Ⓜ *Pigalle, Anvers.*

★ Le Louxor
First opened in 1921, Le Louxor has since been returned to its original Egyptian-themed splendor. Now the city's grandest cinema, this Art Deco beauty is gorgeously appointed—all in rich ocher with jewel-tone velvet seating—and shows a roster of contemporary international art films in three cinemas. Have a drink at the top-floor bar or balcony for spectacular views of the neighborhood and Sacré-Coeur. ✉ *170 bd. Magenta, 10e, Montmartre* ☎ *01–44–63–96–96* ⊕ *www.cinemalouxor.fr* Ⓜ *Barbès–Rochechouart.*

Studio 28
This little movie house has a distinguished history: when it opened in 1928, it was the first theater in the world purposely built for *art et essai*, or experimental film (Luis Buñuel and Salvador Dalí's *L'Age d'Or* caused a riot when it premiered here). Through the years artists and writers came to see "seventh art" creations by directors such as Jean Cocteau, François Truffaut, and Orson Welles. Today it's a repertory cinema, showing first-runs, just-runs, and previews—usually in their original language. Movies are screened from 3 pm daily, and tickets cost €9. In the back of the movie house is a cozy bar and café that has a quiet outdoor terrace decorated with murals of film stars. Oh, and those charmingly bizarre chandeliers in the *salle*? Cocteau designed them. ✉ *10 rue Tholozé, Montmartre* ☎ *01–46–06–47–45* ⊕ *www.cinema-studio28.fr/en* 🎟 *Movie tickets €9* Ⓜ *Abbesses.*

LES
PUCES

CLIGNAN-
COURT

ÉPINETTES

LA
CHAPELLE

LA VILLETTE

LES
BATIGNOLLES

MONTMARTRE

TERNES

MONCEAU

PIGALLE

BELLEVILLE

CHAILLOT

LES GRANDS
BOULEVARDS

SENTIER

CANAL
ST-MARTIN

CHAMPS-
ÉLYSÉES

BOIS DE
OULOGNE

TROCADÉRO

PALAIS-
ROYAL

LES
HALLES

LE
MARAIS

OBERKAMPF

MÉNILMONTANT

PÈRE-
LACHAISE

PASSY

LES
INVALIDES

LES ÎLES

CHARONNE

AUTEUIL

VAUGIRARD

ST-GERMAIN-
DES-PRÉS

BASTILLE

BEL-AIR

QUARTIER
LATIN

BERCY

JAVEL

MONTPARNASSE

BOIS DE
VINCENNES

ST-LAMBERT

BUTTE-AUX-
CAILLES

AUSTERLITZ

SEINE

MONTROUGE

MAISON
BLANCHE

tseeing ★★★☆☆ | Shopping ★★★★☆ | Dining ★★★★☆ | Nightlife ★★★★★

Canal St-Martin is one of the trendiest spots in Paris right now—and it's a true Cinderella story. Linking the Seine to Paris's northeastern neighborhoods, Napoléon's 19th-century canal was carved out to carry fresh water into the city. The working class once dominated the industrial quartier, whose workshops and warehouses were the sole attractions, and the terms "shabby" and "chic" weren't combined. Now crumbling buildings have blossomed into some of the city's sleekest craft cocktail bars, art spaces, and even designer hostels on par with boutique hotels in the neighboring Marais. The main difference? Canal St-Martin never lost its village spirit (though it cleaned up its act and acquired a slew of street art along the way). This sliver of Old Paris remains trapped in time. Sure, gluten-free boulangeries and craft coffee shops may have moved in, but the main selling factor is still a stroll along the canal's Venetian-esque footbridges, where Amélie famously skipped stones in the French cult classic. Follow the locals' lead snagging artisanal baguettes and farm-fresh fromage (cheese) from one of the canal's haute épiceries before taking a seat and surveying the scene picnic-style along the banks.—by Lane Nieset

◉ Sights

★ Canal St-Martin

This once-forgotten canal has morphed into one of the city's trendiest places to wander. A good time to come is Sunday afternoon, when the Quai de Valmy is closed to cars and some of the shops are open. Rent a bike at any of the many Vélib' stations, stroll along the banks, or go native and cuddle quai-side in the sunshine with someone special.

In 1802 Napoléon ordered the 4.3-km (2.7-mile) canal dug as a source of clean drinking water after cholera and other epidemics swept the city. When it finally opened 23 years later, it extended north from the Seine at Place de la Bastille to the Canal de l'Ourcq, near La Villette. Baron Haussmann later covered a 1.6-km (1-mile) stretch of it, along today's Boulevard Richard Lenoir. It nearly became a highway in the 1970s, before the city's urban planners regained their senses. These days you can take a boat tour from end to end through the canal's nine locks: along the way, the bridges swing or lift open. The drawbridge with four giant pulleys at Rue de Crimée, near La Villette, was a technological marvel when it debuted in 1885.

In recent years gentrification has transformed the once-dodgy canal, with artists taking over former industrial spaces and creating studios and galleries. The bar and restaurant scene is hipster central, and small designers have arrived, fleeing expensive rents in the Marais. To explore this evolving *quartier,* set out on foot. Start on the Quai de Valmy at Rue Faubourg du Temple (use the République métro stop). Here, at Square Frédéric Lemaître facing north, there is a good view of one of the locks (behind you the canal disappears underground). As you head north, detour onto side streets like Rue Beaurepaire, a fashionista destination with several "stock" (or surplus) shops for popular brands, some open on Sunday. Rues Lancry and Vinaigriers are lined with bars, restaurants, and small shops.

A swing bridge across the canal connects Lancry to the Rue de la Grange aux Belles, where you'll find the entrance to the massive Hôpital Saint-Louis, built in 1607 to accommodate plague victims and still a working hospital today. In front of you is the entrance to the chapel, which held its first Mass in July 1610, two months after the assassination of the hospital's patron, Henry IV. Stroll the grounds, flanked by the original brick-and-stone buildings with steeply sloping roofs. The peaceful courtyard garden is a neighborhood secret.

Back on Quai Valmy, browse more shops near the Rue des Récollets.

Nearby is the Jardin Villemin, the 10e arrondissement's largest park (4½ acres) on the former site of another hospital. The nighttime scene, especially in summer, is hopping with twentysomethings spilling out of cafés and bars and onto the canal banks. If you've made it this far, reward yourself with a fresh taco or burrito at the tiny and authentically Mexican El Nopal taqueria at 3 rue Eugène Varlin. Farther up, just past Place Stalingrad, is the Rotonde de la Villette, a lively square with restaurants and twin MK2 cinemas on either side of the canal, plus a boat to ferry ticket holders across. Canauxrama (www.canauxrama. com) offers 2½-hour boat cruises through the locks (€18). Embarkation is at each end of the canal: at Bassin de la Villette or Port de l'Arsenal. ⊠ *Canal St-Martin* Ⓜ *Jaurès (north end), République (south end), Gare de l'Est (middle).*

Hôtel du Nord

This hotel—which starred in the classic Marcel Carné film of the same name—has been spiffed up but still maintains its cool with a vibrant lounge-bar (and restaurant) scene in the buzz-worthy Canal St-Martin district. ⊠ *102 quai de Jemmapes, 10e, Canal St-Martin* ☎ *01-40-40-78-78* ⊕ *www.hoteldu-nord.org* Ⓜ *Goncourt.*

Jardin Villemin

A neighborhood garden with a walking path winds among the Avenue de Verdun, Rue des Récollets, and the Canal St-Martin, providing a peaceful break from city

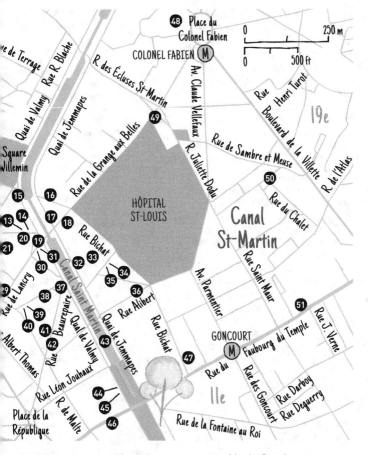

life. Full of chestnut and oak trees, the park offers up space for activities like handball and basketball, but the garden's true purpose is more community focused, with shared garden plots lining either side of the pathway. Check out the 19th-century gate to the old military hospital still crowning one of the four entrances. ⊠ *14 rue des Récollets, Canal St-Martin* Ⓜ *Gare de l'Est*.

Passage Brady

Paris's "Little India" is housed in the two historic arcades of Passage Brady, divided by the Boulevard de Strasbourg. Enter the open-air section of Indo-Pakistani, Mauritian, and Réunion businesses from Rue du Faubourg St-Martin, or step inside the glass-roofed passage along Boulevard de Strasbourg. Here, you'll find shops selling an array of hard-to-source spices, vibrant clothing, and ayurvedic medicine, as well as restaurants whipping up classic (and cheap) Indian dishes like chicken tandoori and tikka masala (with lunch specials as low as €5). ⊠ *46 rue du Faubourg St-Denis, Canal St-Martin* ☎ *07–83–66–98–24* Ⓜ *Château d'Eau, Strasbourg–St-Denis*.

🛍 Shopping

Antoine & Lili

This bright, fuchsia-color store is packed with an international assortment of eclectic objects and items from Antoine & Lili's own clothing line. There's an ethnic-rummage-sale feel, with

GETTING HERE

Hop on métro line 5 to Jacques Bonsergent, which will drop you in the heart of the neighborhood. Another major station servicing Canal St-Martin: République (serving lines 3, 5, 8, 9, and 11). If you're arriving by bus, the 75 conveniently stops right along the canal. Vélib' also has stations set up throughout the quartier, where you can pick up or return one of the public bikes.

old Asian posters, small lanterns, and basket upon basket of inexpensive doodads, baubles, and trinkets for sale. The clothing itself has simple lines, and there are always plenty of raw-silk pieces to pick from. ⊠ *95 quai de Valmy, 10e, Canal St-Martin* ☎ *01–40–37–41–55* ⊕ *www.antoineetlili.com* Ⓜ *Jacques-Bonsergent*.

Artazart

Librairies, or bookstores, are as typically French as fromage and baguettes. While you can find classics at the landmark Shakespeare and Company and coffee-table books at Assouline, Artazart fills the gap in between with design-centric books, photography-focused magazines, and a concept shop where you can buy Polaroid cameras and legendary Lampes Gras lighting. ⊠ *83 quai de Valmy, Canal St-Martin* ☎ *01–40–40–24–00* ⊕ *www.artazart. com* Ⓜ *Jacques Bonsergent, Gare de l'Est, Goncourt*.

Atelier Couronnes

Créatrices Louise Damas (known for her eponymous jewelry brand) and Claire Rischette (of leather brand Fauvette Paris) partnered up to open concept shop and workshop Atelier Couronnes. In addition to crafting and selling their own designs, the duo source a mix of gilded decor, stationery, and specialty chocolate bars by French favorites like Papier Tigre and Le chocolat des Français. ✉ *6 rue du Château d'Eau, République* ☎ *01-40-37-03-54* ⊘ *Closed Sun. and Mon.* Ⓜ *Jacques Bonsergent.*

★ Centre Commercial

Exposed concrete walls and geometric neon light fixtures set the tone for the sustainable-chic Centre Commercial concept shop, tucked between major marques like A.P.C. and Maje along the Rue de Marseille. The founders started environmentally friendly sneaker line Veja, which you can find scattered around the store alongside a mix of harder-to-source brands and award-winning designers like Valentine Gauthier. ✉ *2 rue de Marseille, Canal St-Martin* ☎ *01-42-02-26-08* ⊕ *www.centrecommercial. cc* ⊘ *Closed weekends* Ⓜ *Jacques Bonsergent.*

Des Petits Hauts

This poetic brand charmed its way into the local fashion idiom with chic yet beguilingly feminine styles. Fabrics are soft, and styles are casual with a tiny golden star sewn into each garment for good luck. ✉ *21 rue Beaurepaire, 10e, Canal St-Martin* ☎ *01-75-44-05-83* ⊕ *www. despetitshauts.com* Ⓜ *République.*

Jamini

Pulling inspiration from her home state of Assam in northeastern India, Usha Bora blends the best of the region's textiles and traditional weaving techniques with more contemporary French touches for her lifestyle brand, Jamini. Handwoven Indian *charpoy* beds, *eri* silk (peace silk) scarves, and *dabu* block-printed tote bags are just a few of the treasures you'll find at the Canal St-Martin concept shop. ✉ *10 rue du Château d'Eau, Canal St-Martin* ☎ *09-83-88-91-06* ⊕ *www. jaminidesign.com/en* ⊘ *Closed weekends* Ⓜ *République, Gare de l'Est.*

★ La Trésorerie

Simply calling La Trésorerie a concept shop doesn't do it justice. Every aspect, from the collection of housewares to the skylight-flooded space (formerly a treasury building), is curated as carefully as a gallery. Furniture leans heavily on the Scandinavian side, as does the neighboring Swedish café, Smörgås, where you can take a shopping break and post up with a cup of Belleville Brûlerie–roasted coffee and namesake *Smörgås* (open-face sandwich). ✉ *11 rue du Château d'Eau, Canal St-Martin* ☎ *01-40-40-20-46* ⊕ *www.latresorerie.fr* ⊘ *Closed Sun. and Mon.* Ⓜ *Jacques Bonsergent, République, Château d'Eau.*

Médecine Douce

Sculptural pieces that combine leather, suede, rhinestones, agate, or resin with whimsical themes can be found at Médecine Douce. The wildly popular lariat necklace can be looped and dangled according to your mood du jour. ✉ 10 rue de Marseille, 10e, Canal St-Martin ☎ 01-82-83-11-53 ⊕ www.bijouxmedecinedouce.com Ⓜ République.

Patricia Blanchet

Do not hesitate to run for that taxi in a pair of superchic pumps, flats, or yummy booties from Patricia Blanchet, which are neither too high nor too low but just the right height. Though the designer doesn't swerve from her five or six basic styles, her beautifully hued leathers, including metallics and exotic skins like pony and stingray, change with the season. Booties may come with metallic piping or colorful insets and cutouts, and are cut low for a sexy peek at the ankle. ✉ 20 rue Beaurepaire, 10e, Canal St-Martin ☎ 01-42-02-35-85 ⊕ www.patriciablanchet.com Ⓜ République.

☕ Coffee and Quick Bites

Bob's Juice Bar

$ | Café. For years, the only juice you'd see on a menu in Paris was the typical orange, but that all changed when an American in Paris, Marc Grossman, opened up shabby-chic Bob's Juice Bar along the Canal St-Martin in 2006. Now Parisians get their health fix with freshly bottled cold-pressed juices and grab-and-go vegetarian fare (from colorful salads to bagel sandwiches) on par with what you'd find stateside. Known for: New York–style bagels; soups du jour; vegan desserts. Average main: €10 ✉ 15 rue Lucien Sampaix, Canal St-Martin ☎ 09-50-06-36-18 ⊕ www.bobsjuicebar.com ⊘ Closed Sun. Ⓜ Jacques Bonsergent, Château d'Eau, Gare de l'Est.

Café A

$ | French Fusion. The Maison de l'Architecture—a center for architectural advancement—occupies a onetime monastery near the Canal St-Martin. Inside its Renaissance courtyard, Café A offers a seasonal menu at prices that are reasonable for this ever-gentrifying area. Average main: €15 ✉ 148 rue du Faubourg St-Martin, Canal St-Martin ☎ 09-81-29-83-38 ⊕ www.cafea.fr Ⓜ Gare de l'Est.

Café Craft

$ | Café. Billing itself as the "first café dedicated to independent creatives," Craft has helped make coworking in Paris cool. A communal table dominates the sleek interior, offering plenty of space and electrical outlets for freelancers to set up shop, but even if you're not working, Craft guarantees a calm escape from the bustling city—and only costs a coffee or €3 coworking fee per hour. Known for: flat white; reliable Wi-Fi; quiet-as-a-mouse setting. Average main: €6 ✉ 24 rue des Vinaigriers, Canal St-Martin ☎ 01-40-35-90-77 ⊕ www.cafe-craft.com Ⓜ Jacques Bonsergent, Gare de l'Est.

★ Du Pain et Des Idées

$ | Bakery. Fashion-industry-exec-turned-baker Christophe Vasseur returned a 19th-century bakery to its traditional roots with Du

Pain et Des Idées, which operates just as much as a boutique as a boulangerie. Made by perhaps the best baker in Paris, these sourdough loaves may be crafted with traditional techniques, but they're anything but ordinary. **Known for:** buttery croissants; namesake flatbread; puff pastries. *Average main: €3 ⊠ 34 rue Yves Toudic, Canal St-Martin ☎ 01-42-40-44-52 ⊕ www.dupainetdesidees.com ۞ Closed weekends Ⓜ République.*

IMA

$ | Mediterranean. Vegetarian eatery IMA, which means mother in Hebrew, is by no means your standard salad bar. Chef Victoria Werlé's vibrant salads change daily and are served alongside homemade pita for a stylish (and modern) version of Middle Eastern fare. **Known for:** homemade pastries; Belleville Brûlerie–roasted coffee; vegan and gluten-free breakfast fare. *Average main: €12 ⊠ 39 quai de Valmy, Canal St-Martin ☎ 01-40-36-41-37 ⊕ www.ima.paris Ⓜ République, Goncourt.*

LIBERTÉ

$ | Bakery. Beautifully decorated pastries and masterfully baked baguettes contrast with the raw, exposed walls of the industrial-inspired LIBERTÉ. Operating as a boutique baking lab, the boulangerie not only displays its freshly baked goods like objets d'art along the marble countertop, but also allows you to catch a glimpse of behind-the-scenes action and watch the artisans in the workshop. **Known for:** light break-

fast; Parisian pastries; tarte citron (lemon tart). *Average main: €5 ⊠ 39 rue des Vinaigriers, Canal St-Martin ☎ 01-42-05-51-76 ⊕ www.liberte-patisserieboulangerie.com ۞ Closed Sun. Ⓜ Jacques Bonsergent, Gare de l'Est.*

Miznon

$ | Israeli. Israeli celeb chef Eyal Shani expanded his Miznon empire from the Marais to a two-story spot along the Canal St-Martin, with a street-food-inspired menu that wouldn't be out of place in Jerusalem's buzzing Mahane Yehuda market. Chaos is part of the charm, as names for orders are shouted out Starbucks-style and cooks break into song while prepping pitas behind the counter of the open kitchen. **Known for:** grilled cauliflower; French-style pitas; takeaway fare. *Average main: €10 ⊠ 37 quai de Valmy, Canal St-Martin ☎ 01-48-03-47-22 ⊕ www.facebook.com/miznonparis ۞ Closed Sat. Ⓜ République, Goncourt.*

Peonies

$ | Café. A café every bit as charming in person as it is on Instagram, this combination coffee-shop-florist features fresh flowers lining shelves near the entry, which can be ordered as part of a package with a shot of espresso. If you'd prefer your flowers served up in drinkable form, try one of the floral teas paired with an edible-petal-topped treat. **Known for:** matcha lattes and pancakes; salads and spring rolls; flower and photography workshops. *Average main: €9* ⊠ *81 rue du Faubourg St-Denis, Canal St-Martin* ⊕ *www.peonies-paris.com* ⊗ *Closed Mon.* Ⓜ *Château d'Eau.*

Radiodays

$ | Café. Coffee aficionados will recognize some of the more famous roasters, like Tim Wendelboe, making their way onto Radiodays's menu. Specialty craft coffee from a changing roster of guest roasters is one draw, but the daily selection of Lebanese-inspired sandwiches and salads (a nod to the owners' nationality) are also worth seeking out. **Known for:** lunch deals; American-style sweets; homemade granola. *Average main: €6* ⊠ *15 rue Alibert, Canal St-Martin* ⊕ *www.radiodays. cafe* Ⓜ *République, Goncourt, Colonel Fabien.*

The Sunken Chip

$ | British. At the Sunken Chip, the catch of the day is served in a style more typical of London than the Canal St-Martin. British duo Michael Greenwold and James Whelan source fish daily from Brittany for their refined pub fare, which includes crispy, beer-battered hake served with classic sides: chips (fries) and mushy peas. **Known for:** homemade batter and cornflake breadcrumbs; takeaway orders; fried seafood. *Average main: €14* ⊠ *39 rue des Vinaigriers, Canal St-Martin* ☎ *01–53–26–74–46* ⊕ *www.thesunkenchip.com* Ⓜ *Jacques Bonsergent, Gare de l'Est, République.*

⭐ Ten Belles

$ | Café. An oasis in a sea of funky boutiques and shops, the closet-sized Ten Belles is typically bustling, with a line patiently waiting as baristas whip up latte-art-topped cappuccinos and coffee to go. If you're lucky enough to snag a seat inside, the mezzanine is the perfect place to perch with a filtered coffee and English-style scone. **Known for:** specialty coffee; sandwiches; breakfast sweets. *Average main: €7* ⊠ *10 rue de la Grange aux Belles, Canal St-Martin* ☎ *01–42–40–90–78* ⊕ *www. tenbelles.com* Ⓜ *Colonel Fabien.*

🍴 Dining

⭐ Abri

$$ | Modern French. This tiny storefront restaurant's immense popularity has much to do with the fresh and imaginative food, the friendly servers, and great prices. The lauded Japanese chef works from a small open kitchen behind the zinc bar, putting forth skillfully prepared dishes like lemon-marinated mackerel topped with microthin slices of beet with honey vinaigrette, or succulent duck breast

with vegetables au jus. **Known for:** daily changing menu inventive French-Japanese cuisine; casual atmosphere and great prices; need to make reservations weeks in advance. *Average main: €23 ⊠ 92 rue du Faubourg-Poissonnière, 10e, Canal St-Martin* ☎ *01–83–97–00–00* ⊘ *Closed Sun., Mon., 1 wk at Christmas, and Aug.* Ⓜ *Poissonnière, Cadet.*

Bonhomie

$ | **Mediterranean.** Paris may be a few hours from the Mediterranean, but Bonhomie brings tapas-style sharing plates from the coast to the capital city. Since it was launched by the team behind beloved Parisian bars like Little Red Door and Lulu White, it's no surprise the restaurant (slash coffeehouse and cocktail bar) serves up libations just as gastronomic as its cuisine. **Known for:** seasonal cocktails; fresh-pressed and fermented juices; flavors teetering from Tunisian to Moroccan. *Average main: €16 ⊠ 22 rue d'Enghien, Canal St-Martin* ☎ *09–83–88–82–51* ⊕ *www.bonhomie. paris* Ⓜ *Bonne Nouvelle.*

Chez Casimir

$$ | **Bistro.** This easygoing bistro, run by Breton chef Thierry Breton, is popular with polished Parisian professionals and hipster foodies alike. The affordable set dinner menu covers lentil soup with fresh croutons, braised endive and andouille salad, and roast lamb on a bed of Paimpol beans, along with 12 different cheeses to choose from. **Known for:** excellent value wines by the glass; sidewalk dining; daily-changing blackboard menu. *Average*

main: €19 ⊠ 6 rue de Belzunce, 10e, Grands Boulevards ☎ *01–48–78–28–80* ⊘ *No dinner weekends* Ⓜ *Gare du Nord.*

★ Chez Prune

$ | **French.** Chez Prune has all the characteristics of a typical bistro (chalkboard menus, hearty French fare), but it has earned the reputation of hipster hangout, with a vibe just as buzzy during lunch as at cocktail hour later in the evening. The red-canopy-covered terrace is a favorite for people-watching along the Canal St-Martin, but inside is just as cozy, with banquette space perfect for groups to catch up over coffee or cocktails. **Known for:** great spot for an aperitif; platters of charcuterie and cheese; Sunday brunch. *Average main: €12 ⊠ 36 rue Beaurepaire, Canal St-Martin* ☎ *01–42–41–30–47* Ⓜ *Jacques Bonsergent, Goncourt.*

★ Holybelly

$ | **Café.** Don't mistake the airy bistro for an American diner—you won't find greasy-spoon fare here (though you will find pancakes and fried eggs served all day long). Responsible for bringing a Melbourne-style brunch scene to Paris in 2013, Holybelly now attracts a line stretching around the block nearly every day of the week. **Known for:** pancakes topped with bourbon butter; Australian-style coffee; daily specials crafted from local, seasonal ingredients. *Average main: €9 ⊠ 5 rue Lucien Sampaix, Canal St-Martin* ☎ *01–82–28–00–80* ⊕ *www.holybellycafe.com* Ⓜ *Jacques Bonsergent.*

Jules et Shim

$ | Korean. Designed as a takeaway shop, Jules et Shim (an Asian play on director François Truffaut's French flick *Jules et Jim*) offers a simple menu of picnic fare modeled after Korean street food staple bibimbap. The only decision you'll have to make is what type of meat and spicy sauce you'd like mixed into your rice bowl. **Known for:** quick service; origami-style takeout boxes; side of kimchi. *Average main: €10* ✉ *22 rue des Vinaigriers, Canal St-Martin* ☎ *01-58-20-17-91* ⊕ *www.julesetshim.com* Ⓜ *Jacques Bonsergent, Gare de l'Est, République.*

La Cantine de Quentin

$$ | Bistro. Part convivial café on the terrace, part wine cave and haute grocery shop in the cozy interior, this is the epitome of a modern-day French cantine. You can eat just as well as you can shop, then take your bottle to go. **Known for:** cheesecake; homemade plates that twist tradition; hand-picked French wines. *Average main: €18* ✉ *52 rue Bichat, Canal St-Martin* ☎ *01-42-02-40-32* ⊕ *www.lacantinedequentin.com* ⊘ *Closed Mon.* Ⓜ *Jacques Bonsergent, Gare de l'Est, Colonel Fabien.*

La Taverne de Zhao

$ | Chinese. After a recent renovation, the fire-engine-red-paneled restaurant reopened with a new look (sleek marble countertop, mint-green walls) and menu revolving around tried-and-tested specialties from chef and owner Zhao's home city, Xi'an. Think tradi-tional street food from the Shaanxi province (which marked the Silk Road's eastern end), in generous portions that make sharing all the more desirable. **Known for:** refined Chinese street food; reasonably priced dishes; momo (meat-stuffed bread). *Average main: €10* ✉ *49 rue des Vinaigriers, Canal St-Martin* ☎ *01-40-37-16-21* ⊕ *www.lataverne-dezhao.com* Ⓜ *Jacques Bonsergent, Gare de l'Est.*

Le Cambodge

$ | Cambodian. Prepare for a wait come lunchtime. This family-run Cambodian restaurant—now in its second generation with daughter Kirita and her husband taking the helm—serves up authentic plates in an unassuming space (think exposed concrete walls and dim lighting), placing all the emphasis on the food. **Known for:** no-frills, home-style cuisine; bo buns of all varieties ; generous portions (and an even more generous Southeast Asian sauce selection). *Average main: €14* ✉ *10 av. Richerand, Canal St-Martin* ☎ *01-44-84-37-70* ⊕ *www.lecambodge.fr* Ⓜ *Jacques Bonsergent, Goncourt.*

⭐ **Le Galopin**

$$ | Bistro. Across from a pretty square on the border of two up-and-coming neighborhoods, this light-drenched spot is one of Paris's standout gastrobistros. By adhering to a tried-and-true formula—meticulously sourced produce, natural wines, open kitchen—dishes here are small wonders of texture and flavor. **Known for:** daily changing, market-fresh gastronomic menu;

hip, laid-back atmosphere; veggie-centric dishes. *Average main: €22* ⊠ *34 rue Sainte-Marthe, 10e, Canal St-Martin* ☎ *01-42-06-05-03* ⊕ *www.le-galopin.com* ⊘ *Closed weekends. No lunch Mon.–Wed.* Ⓜ *Goncourt, Belleville, Colonel Fabien.*

Les Enfants Perdus

$$ | **French.** You probably wouldn't guess that a Michelin-starred chef is tucked away in the kitchen—no teeny-tiny portions on these plates! Named after '90s French flick *La Cité des Enfants Perdu*, the Villemin Garden–facing restaurant feels more like you're eating in a friend's living room than in a fine dining restaurant, with concrete and brick walls and simple, homey interior design. **Known for:** attentive servers; bottomless Sunday brunch; namesake brioche-based pain perdu (aka the original French toast). *Average main: €22* ⊠ *9 rue des Récollets, Canal St-Martin* ☎ *01-81-29-48-26* ⊕ *www.les-enfants-perdus.com* ⊘ *No dinner Sun.–Thurs.* Ⓜ *Gare de l'Est.*

★ Les Résistants

$$ | **French.** For the childhood friends behind Les Résistants, the restaurant's concept goes far beyond table service. Owner Florent Piard left his job to start this passion project, spending six months traveling across the country (with chef de cuisine Clément and chef de salle Yannick in tow) to create a Rolodex of "Résistants," more than 250 producers from all corners of France who are just as dedicated to terroir and tradition as the eatery's determined trio.

Known for: daily changing seasonal menu; French ingredients; hand-selected products. *Average main: €19* ⊠ *16–18 rue du Château d'Eau, Canal St-Martin* ☎ *01-42-06-43-74* ⊕ *www.lesresistants.fr* ⊘ *Closed Sun. and Mon.* Ⓜ *Château d'Eau, Jacques Bonsergent.*

Philou

$$ | **Bistro.** A neighborhood go-to, this wine bar and bistro is a favorite for its affordable natural vinos by the *verre* (that's glass) and hearty cuisine (think sweetbread and roast pigeon). Japanese chef Shin Maeda's refined French fare is such a hit, dishes du jour are quickly crossed off the chalkboard list one by one as the night wears on. **Known for:** reasonably priced set menus; buzzing dinner scene; seasonal ingredients. *Average main: €24* ⊠ *12 av. Richerand, Canal St-Martin* ☎ *01-42-38-00-13* ⊕ *www.restophilou.com* ⊘ *Closed Sun. and Mon., summer* Ⓜ *Goncourt.*

Siseng

$ | **Asian.** Paris has plenty of Asian restaurants (as well as its own Chinatown), but Siseng brings some of the more traditional flavors to the trendy Canal St-Martin, adding a hip (but somewhat pricey) spin to fusion fare. The tiny canal-side "food bar" fills up fast (and doesn't take reservations), but if you're dining solo, you may be lucky enough to squeeze into a seat at the long bar lining one side of the dimly lit, industrial-chic space. **Known for:** bao burgers; grandma's Laotian salmon tartare; Asian-liquor-based craft cocktails. *Average main: €15* ⊠ *82 quai*

de Jemmapes, Canal St-Martin
☎ *09–51–55–15–77* ⊘ *Closed Mon.*
Ⓜ *République, Jacques Bonsergent,*
Goncourt.

Sol Semilla

$$ | **Vegetarian.** Part canteen, part organic superfood shop, Sol Semilla hails the plant-based movement, serving up vegan dishes sans gluten and refined sugar. South American–harvested products work their way into everything from soups and juices to desserts, crafted on-site or commissioned from small, family-owned Parisian bakeries. **Known for:** raw vegan fare with flavor; sustainable setting; detox drinks and soups with herbs like Andean cat's claw. *Average main: €21* ⊠ *23 rue des Vinaigriers, Canal St-Martin* ☎ *01–42–01–03–44* ⊕ *www.sol-semilla.fr* ⊘ *Closed Mon.* Ⓜ *Jacques Bonsergeant, République, Gare de l'Est.*

Sur Mer

$$$ | **Seafood.** This new seafood bar may be shoebox-size with a five-seat counter and a few communal tables, but each plate packs a big punch. Seafood is seasonal and designed to be shared, with dishes organized by category: crustacean, *coquillage* (shellfish), and *poisson* (fish) that's some of the freshest you'll find along the Canal St-Martin. **Known for:** prix-fixe menu; sharing plates; seafood platters. *Average main: €32* ⊠ *53 rue de Lancry, Canal St-Martin* ☎ *01–48–03–21–38* ⊘ *Closed Tues.* Ⓜ *Jacques Bonsergent, Château d'Eau.*

🍸 Bars and Nightlife

Benichat

David Benichou (who cut his teeth at top bars including Clown Bar and Vivant) brought his natural wine background from some of the city's much-loved bistros to his new wine bar, tucked behind the Canal St-Martin. You'll often find his enormous, St. Bernard–size dog, Lago, holding court out front, while in-the-know locals squeeze inside the narrow bar, nibbling on charcuterie and sampling the latest batch of bottles. ⊠ *6 rue Bichat, Canal St-Martin* ☎ *01–42–08–61–10* Ⓜ *Goncourt, Hôpital Saint-Louis.*

★ Comptoir Général

Stepping into Comptoir Général is like entering Peter Pan's Neverland . The tucked-away bar-slash-museum is a beautifully curated clash of cultures, with African artifacts on display in themed corners and a wooden ship serving as a Caribbean cocktail bar. Swing by on Sunday to peruse the collections of records and books before brunch, and return later in the evening for the weekly film screening. ⊠ *80 quai de Jemmapes, Canal St-Martin* ☎ *01–44–88–24–48* ⊕ *www.lecomptoirgeneral.com* Ⓜ *République, Goncourt, Jacques Bonsergent.*

Gravity Bar

If there were a guide on how to build the quintessential hipster craft cocktail bar, Gravity would have followed all the rules to a T. Wavelike strips of light wood cascade down from the ceiling, coming to an abrupt halt behind the curved concrete slab of a bar. Scandinavian-style stools sidle up to intimate tables for two, where you can actually sit back and enjoy your long-awaited cocktail (and your equally well-crafted small plate of market-sourced cuisine). ✉ 44 rue des Vinaigriers, Canal St-Martin ☎ 06-98-54-92-49 Ⓜ Château d'Eau.

Khayma Rooftop at Generator Paris

Rooftop bars are slowly popping up around town, but while some charge prices on par with the view, designer hostel Generator Paris does just the opposite. Head up to the ninth floor and start your evening at Khayma, the canopy-covered rooftop that could easily be someone's backyard patio with its bean bag chairs and a plywood-covered bar—except for the views of Montmartre and the Sacré-Coeur sprouting up in the distance. ✉ 9–11 pl. du Colonel Fabien, Canal St-Martin ☎ 01-70-98-84-00 ⊕ www.generatorhostels.com Ⓜ Colonel Fabien.

La Fontaine de Belleville

This 1920s-era café serves stellar coffee (plus breakfast fare, a rarity in Paris) during the day and transitions to a cocktail bar come nightfall, complete with craft French beer and pâté from the épicerie down the street. It's no wonder the brews are so good: the café-bar was founded by Thomas Lehoux and David Flynn, the duo behind one of Paris's hottest coffee roasters, Belleville Brûlerie. ✉ 31–33 rue Juliette Dodu, Canal St-Martin ☎ 09-81-75-54-54 ⊕ www.lafontaine.cafesbelleville.com Ⓜ Colonel Fabien, Goncourt.

La Java

The spot where Piaf and Chevalier made their names has reinvented itself as a dance club with an emphasis on rock–pop, soul, and electro. It also hosts inexpensive performances by up-and-coming bands. ✉ 105 rue du Faubourg du Temple, 10e, Canal St-Martin ☎ 01-42-02-20-52 ⊕ www.la-java.fr Ⓜ Belleville, Goncourt.

La Patache

Among the bars and eateries lining Rue Lancry, you'll find La Patache. It has a wide selection of wines and a retro-inspired ambience fueled by a jukebox and candlelight that illuminates the vintage photos on the wall. ✉ 60 rue Lancry, 10e, Canal St-Martin ☎ 01-42-08-14-35 Ⓜ Jacques-Bonsergent.

Le Gibus

This is one of Paris's most famous music venues. More than 6,500 concerts (put on by the likes of Iggy Pop, The Clash, and The Police) have packed in fans for 30-plus years. Today the Gibus's cellars are the place for electro, techno, and hip-hop. ✉ 18 rue du Faubourg du Temple, 11e, Canal St-Martin ☎ 01-47-00-78-88 ⊕ www.gibus.fr Ⓜ République.

Le Verre Volé

$$ | Wine Bar. Cyril Bordarier blazed a path with this small bar à vins, which quickly became the ticket for hipsters seeking out exceptional, good-value

natural wines with food to match. Nowadays you're as likely to be seated next to a table of American tourists or expats as a bunch of French wine aficionados. *Average main: €24* ✉ *67 rue de Lancry, 10e, Canal St-Martin* ☎ *01–48–03–17–34* ⊕ *www.leverrevole.fr* Ⓜ *République*.

🎟 Performing Arts

Le Manoir de Paris

Let yourself be enchanted (and frightened) as 35 talented performers bring Paris legends to life. When you walk through this mansion, the history of the Bloody Baker, the Phantom of the Opera, and Catherine de Medici's hired assassin are acted out—on you! If you're in Paris during Halloween, this is just about the best game in town. On holiday weekends, you could wait hours to get in, but the tour-style performance itself lasts less than 60 minutes. ✉ *18 rue de Paradis, 10e, Eastern Paris* ☎ *06–70–89–35–87* ⊕ *www.lemanoirdeparis.fr* Ⓜ *Poissonniere, Gare de l'Est*.

Théâtre de la Renaissance

Belle Époque superstar Sarah Bernhardt (who was the manager from 1893 to 1899) put Théâtre de la Renaissance on the map. Big French stars often perform here. Note that the theater is on the second floor, and there's no elevator. ✉ *20 bd. Saint-Martin, 10e, Canal St-Martin* ☎ *01–42–02–47–35* ⊕ *www.theatredelarenaissance.com* Ⓜ *Strasbourg–Saint-Denis*.

11

Oberkampf and Bastille

LES PUCES

ÉPINETTES CLIGNAN-COURT LA CHAPELLE LA VILLETTE

LES BATIGNOLLES MONTMARTRE

TERNES MONCEAU PIGALLE

LES GRANDS BOULEVARDS SENTIER CANAL ST-MARTIN BELLEVILLE

CHAILLOT CHAMPS-ÉLYSÉES

BOIS DE BOULOGNE PASSY TROCADÉRO PALAIS-ROYAL LES HALLES LE MARAIS Oberkampf MÉNILMONTANT PÈRE-LACHAISE

LES INVALIDES LES ÎLES BASTILLE CHARONNE

VAUGIRARD ST-GERMAIN-DES-PRÉS QUARTIER LATIN BERCY BEL-AIR

JAVEL MONTPARNASSE BUTTE-AUX-CAILLES AUSTERLITZ BOIS DE VINCENNES

ST-LAMBERT MONTROUGE MAISON BLANCHE SEINE

AUTEUIL

The capital of gastronomy may be home to more than 70 Michelin-starred spots, but some of Paris's most prominent young chefs are looking to less-trodden parts of town as the locale for their latest endeavor. The perfect example: the Oberkampf and Bastille neighborhoods in the 11e arrondissement, the edgy little sisters of shining stars like the Marais, where backpackers brush elbows with the movers and shakers dominating Paris's culinary scene. Just east of the southern Marais sits Bastille, an area that has evolved enormously since its days as a Revolutionary hotbed and is now drawing first-time restaurateurs and young creatives. Just to the north, the former working-class Oberkampf quartier has long had a reputation as a dive bar haven, and while you can still find hidden holes-in-the-wall, a wave of more refined wine bars (driving the natural-vino trend, of course) and neo-bistros have set up shop in some of its shabbier spots. The grit is still there, but the thirtysomething set have taken over the area's two main drags—Rue Oberkampf and Rue de Charonne—adding a new coat of paint (in the form of street art) and transforming this northeastern neighborhood into the coolest place to drink, dine, and dance in Paris.—*by Lane Nieset and Erin Dahl*

◉ Sights

★ Atelier des Lumières

One of the most captivating new art spaces in Paris is entirely empty—floors, ceilings, beams, and all. But when the lights go out, the surfaces of the industrial space become canvases for artistic projections. Picture concentric circles of light dancing across walls and lavish golden branches twisting up from the floor—the experience is as immersive as it gets. ⊠ *38 rue St-Maur, Oberkampf* ☎ *01-80-98-46-00* ⊕ *www.atelier-lumieres.com* ⊠ *€15* Ⓜ *Voltaire, St-Maur, Père Lachaise.*

Coulée Verte René-Dumont/Promenade Plantée (*La Coulée Verte*)

Once a train line from the Paris suburbs to Bastille, this redbrick viaduct (often referred to as Le Viaduc des Arts) is now the green heart of the unpretentious 12e arrondissement. The rails have been transformed into a 4.5-km (2.8-mile) walkway lined with trees, bamboo, and flowers, offering a bird's-eye view of the stately Haussmannian buildings along Avenue Daumesnil. Below, the *voûtes* (arcades) have been transformed by the city into artisan boutiques, many focused on decor and design. All tenants are hand-picked. There are also temporary galleries showcasing art and photography. The Promenade, which gained fame as a setting in the 2004 film *Before Sunset,* was the inspiration for New York's High Line. It ends at the Jardin de Reuilly. From here you can continue your walk to the Bois de Vincennes. If you're hungry, grab a bite at L'Arrosoir, a cozy café under the viaduct at 75 avenue Daumesnil. ⊠ *1–129 av. Daumesnil, Bastille* ☎ *01-86-95-95-07* ⊕ *www.leviaducdesarts.com* Ⓜ *Bastille, Gare de Lyon.*

★ La Cité du Figuier

Once a pathway leading to the village of Mesnil-Maudan (now known as Ménilmontant), this 18th-century strip will turn you into a *flâneur* , the French term for someone who strolls. Admire the ancient artist ateliers (particularly the wooden teal and moss-color facades) and greenery-lined homes while walking along one of the *quartier's* most picturesque passages. ⊠ *104–106 rue Oberkampf, Oberkampf* Ⓜ *Ménilmontant, Rue St-Maur.*

Marché d'Aligre

Place d'Aligre boasts two of Paris's best markets: the lively outdoor Marché d'Aligre and the covered Marché Beauvau. Open every day but Monday, both are great places to pick up picnic essentials, which you can enjoy nearby in the small park at Square Trousseau or on the Promenade Plantée. The picturesque outdoor market has dozens of boisterous vendors, their stands laden with fresh fruits and vegetables, flower bouquets, and regional products such as jam, honey, and dried sausage. The best bargains are had just before closing time, and many vendors are happy to give you a taste of whatever they're selling. The covered market stocks everything from meats and cheeses to Belgian beer. Sunday morning, when the accompanying flea market is in full swing, is the liveliest time to visit. Don't forget your camera. Stop for a plate of *saucisse* and a glass of *rouge* (even on Sunday morning) at one of the city's quirkiest wine bars, Le Baron Rouge, 1 rue Théophile Roussel. ⊠ *Pl. d'Aligre, Bastille* ⊕ *www.equipement. paris.fr/marche-couvert-beauvau-marche-d-aligre-5480* ⊗ *Closed Mon.* Ⓜ *Ledru-Rollin, Bastille.*

Passage St-Maur

Keep an eye out for No. 81 along Rue St-Maur. Behind the blue door you'll find the start of the wood-paved passage St-Maur, a former industrial strip home to 19th-century couture ateliers that once connected L'Abbaye de St-Maur-des-Fosses in the east to the Basilique St-Denis in the north. ⊠ *81 rue St-Maur, 6 passage St-Ambroise, Oberkampf* Ⓜ *Rue St-Maur.*

Pavillon de l'Arsenal

A must for architecture lovers, this free museum and center for urban architecture takes visitors through the past, present, and future of architecture and landscapes in Paris. Temporary exhibits upstairs showcase new construction

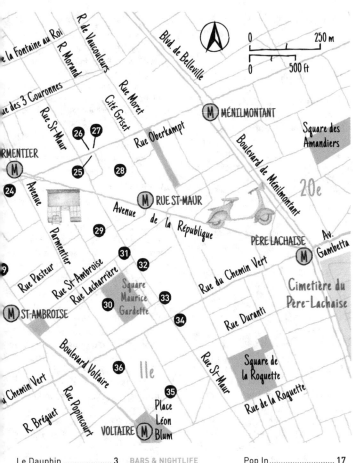

projects. ✉ *21 bd. Morland, Bastille*
☎ *01–42–76–33–97* ⊕ *www.pavillon-
arsenal.com/en* ⊗ *Closed Mon.*
Ⓜ *Sully-Morland.*

Place de la Bastille

Almost nothing remains of the infamous Bastille prison, destroyed more than 225 years ago, though tourists still ask bemused Parisians where to find it. Until the late 1980s, there was little more to see here than a busy traffic circle ringing the Colonne de Juillet (July Column), a memorial to the victims of later uprisings in 1830 and 1848. The opening of the Opéra Bastille in 1989 rejuvenated the area, however, drawing art galleries, bars, and restaurants to the narrow streets, notably along Rue de Lappe—once a haunt of Edith Piaf—and Rue de la Roquette.

Before it became a prison, the Bastille St-Antoine was a defensive fortress with eight immense towers and a wide moat. It was built by Charles V in the late 14th century and transformed into a prison during the reign of Louis XIII (1610–43). Famous occupants included Voltaire, the Marquis de Sade, and the Man in the Iron Mask. On July 14, 1789, it was stormed by an angry mob that dramatically freed all of the remaining prisoners (there were only seven), thereby launching the French Revolution. The roots of the revolt ran deep. Resentment toward Louis XVI and Marie-Antoinette had been building amid a severe financial crisis. There was a crippling bread shortage, and the free-spending

GETTING HERE

To access Oberkampf, hop on métro line 3 to the Parmentier stop or take line 9 to the namesake Oberkampf stop. If you don't mind braving the bus, lines 20, 56, 65, and 96 all stop in the neighborhood, but the routes can be trickier to navigate than the more streamlined métro system. For Bastille, take line 8 to République, Bastille, or Ledru-Rollin.

monarch was blamed. When the king dismissed the popular finance minister, Jacques Necker, enraged Parisians took to the streets. They marched to Les Invalides, helping themselves to stocks of arms, then continued on to the Bastille. A few months later, what was left of the prison was razed—and 83 of its stones were carved into miniature Bastilles and sent to the provinces as a memento (you can see one of them in the Musée Carnavalet, when it re-opens). The key to the prison was given to George Washington by Lafayette and has remained at Mount Vernon ever since. Today, nearly every major street demonstration in Paris—and there are many—passes through this square. ✉ *Bastille* Ⓜ *Bastille.*

🛍 Shopping

★ Amélie Pichard

You'll feel positively cinematic sporting the shoes of this wildly creative young designer, whose career was jump-started in 2014 by a collaboration with her idol

Pamela Anderson. Whether in zebra stripe, scarlet suede, or pink patent leather, the shoes, boots, bags, and small leather goods are always thrilling, showing loads of glamour and more than a hint of daring. You'll also find tartan, faux fur or crocodile, and basket weave. Pichard's adorable boutique is on a cobbled street just off the lucrative shopping fields of the Rue de Charonne. ✉ *34 rue de Lappe, 11e, Bastille* ☎ *01-71-20-94-08* ⊕ *www. ameliepichard.com* Ⓜ *Bastille, Charonne, Ledru-Rollin.*

Caravane

Split into two shops—La Maison and La Table—and just steps from favorite neighborhood restaurant Dersou, this shop knows high-quality home goods. The price tags may be a bit elevated for the linen and percale cotton fabrics, earthy pottery and ceramics, timeless light fixtures, and the like, but even if you walk out empty-handed, browsing is a pleasure. ✉ *19 and 22 rue St-Nicolas, Bastille* ☎ *01-53-02-96-96* ⊕ *www.caravane.fr/en* Ⓜ *Ledru-Rollin.*

Isabel Marant

This rising design star is a honeypot of bohemian rock-star style. Her separates skim the body without constricting: layered miniskirts, loose peekaboo sweaters ready to slip from a shoulder, and super fox-fur jackets in lurid colors. Look for the secondary line, Étoile, for a less expensive take. ✉ *16 rue de Charonne, 11e, Bastille* ☎ *01-49-29-71-55* ⊕ *www.isabelmarant.com* Ⓜ *Ledru-Rollin.*

Les Fleurs

This shop's name may mean flowers, but the only petals you'll find for sale here are of the dried variety. Succulents and plants line stacked tables and cabinets, with an array of ceramics and hanging macramé serving as chic planters. Antique trunks and brass-lined glass cases artfully display home goods and straight-from-the-atelier accessories. Perfect for picking up a host or hostess gift (or outfitting your apartment Parisian-style), Les Fleurs is the kind of specialty shop that quickly becomes a neighborhood go-to, particularly if you're seeking design inspiration. ✉ *5 rue Trousseau, Bastille* ⊕ *www.boutique-lesfleurs.com* ⊘ *Closed Sun. and Mon.* Ⓜ *Charonne, Ledru-Rollin.*

★ L'Épicerie du Verre Volé

Around the corner from Le Verre Volé's wine shop, this haute épicerie, or grocer, is where you'll find the perfect French souvenirs for your foodie friends back home. While you're stocking up on homemade tapenades and jams, order a sandwich to go from the deli counter, taking your pick of specialty European meats and cheeses. One must-try: the épicerie's signature "Le Prince de Paris" cured ham. ✉ *54 rue de la Folie Méricourt, Oberkampf* ☎ *01-48-05-36-55* ⊕ *www.leverrevole.fr* Ⓜ *Parmentier, St-Ambroise, Oberkampf.*

Sessùn

Designer Emma François's main inspiration is traveling to faraway places, where she picks up ideas for the textures, prints, and colors for

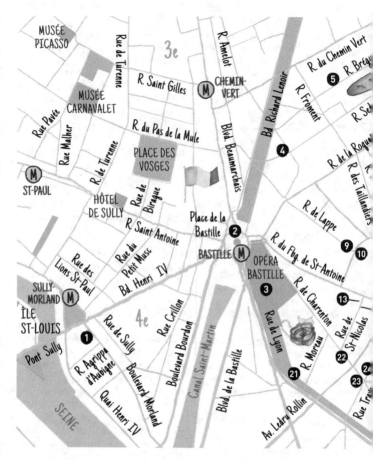

her versatile collection of fashion staples. Separates range from neutral basics—a lace inset top or camisole, a wraparound jumpsuit, a knitted cape—to brilliantly colored or natty print sweaters, trousers, blouses, and blazers. The collection is completed with a gently priced line of shoes, boots, scarves, and accessories. The Rue de Charonne concept store, the largest of the three Paris shops, also has a gallery featuring the work of French artists and artisans and a selection of handmade textiles, housewares, and jewelry. ⌂ *34 rue de Charonne, 11e, Bastille* ☎ *01–48–06–55–66* ⊕ *boutique.sessun.com/fr* Ⓜ *Bastille.*

Vintage Clothing Paris

It's worth a detour to the Marais's outer limits to visit Vintage Clothing Paris, where the racks read like an A-list of designer greats—Yves Saint Laurent, Margiela, Valentino, Comme des Garçons, and Mugler, just to name a few. Brigitte Petit's minimalist shop is the fashion insider's go-to spot for rare pieces that stand out in a crowd, like a circa-1985 Alaïa suede skirt with peekaboo grommets and a jaunty Yves Saint Laurent Epoch Russe hooded cape. ⌂ *10 rue de Crussol, 11e, Marais Quarter* ☎ *06–03–00–64–78* ⊕ *www.vintageclothingparis.com* Ⓜ *Filles du Calvaire, Oberkampf.*

☕ Coffee and Quick Bites

The Beans on Fire

$ | Café. The Beans on Fire is one of Paris's first collaborative roasters, meaning it opens up its facilities for other top names to come and roast their beans. Founders Maria and Andrés hand-source the namesake beans themselves from farms in Colombia, and the same goes for the café fare, with ingredients hailing from specialty grocer Le Zingham two blocks away. **Known for:** American-style brunch; relaxed terrace seating; seasonal soups and salads. *Average main: €9* ⌂ *7 rue du Général Blaise, Oberkampf* ☎ *01–43–55–94–73* ⊕ *www.thebeansonfire.com* Ⓜ *St-Ambroise.*

Broken Biscuits

$ | Café. You may recognize Broken Biscuits by name, since the bakery supplies pastries to some of the top coffee shops around the city. Take a seat in the small corner bar and see where the magic happens in the open kitchen-slash-pastry shop that feels more like you're visiting a friend's apartment for coffee than sitting in a stuffy old-school café. **Known for:** pretty pastries; Anglophone bakers; coffee and scones with homemade jam. *Average main: €4* ⌂ *10 passage Rochebrune, Oberkampf* ⊕ *broken-biscuits.fr* ☾ *Closed Mon. and Tues.* Ⓜ *Rue St-Maur.*

Café Chilango

$ | Mexican. Once you bite into the street-food-style tacos at Café Chilango, you'll understand why there's always a crowd gathered outside. It's hard to find Mexican food in Paris, let alone something authentic, but the duo behind Café Chilango (who both hail from the motherland) have nailed the concept, offering a seasonal menu and a vibe that transitions from low-key café to lively, mezcal-centric cocktail bar come nightfall. **Known for:** homemade tortilla chips and guacamole; seasonal cocktails; weekend brunch. *Average main: €13 ⊠ 82 rue de la Folie Méricourt, Oberkampf* ☎ *01–47–00–78–95* ⊕ *www.cafechilangoparis.com* Ⓜ *République, Parmentier.*

Café Méricourt

$ | Café. After successfully launching the shoebox-size Café Oberkampf, the all-day brunch spot expanded with its second—and much larger—locale in the *quartier* , Café Méricourt. The minimalist chic space nods to brunch capitals like Melbourne, with a menu of home-made fare (including Israeli-style *shakshuka* , eggs poached in a spicy tomato-based sauce, an Instagram favorite) and coffee brewed by a roster of guest roasters. **Known for:** breakfast rolls; sweet and savory pancakes; French beer, juice, and coffee. *Average main: €14 ⊠ 22 rue de la Folie Méricourt, Oberkampf* ☎ *01–43–38–94–04* ⊕ *www.cafemericourt.com* Ⓜ *Oberkampf.*

★ Café Oberkampf

$ | Café. When Café Oberkampf opened in 2015, it filled a niche in the neighborhood: an airy, all-day café where good coffee is a guarantee and you can get simple (yet beautifully prepped) brunch fare past Paris's traditional lunch hours. Bloggers and influencers helped give its shakshuka star status, but now the café has passed this specialty on to its sister restaurant, Café Méricourt, focusing

instead on a selection of super fresh and creative sandwiches and salads streaming from the small kitchen. **Known for:** set lunch menu; specialty coffee; "Lost in Cheeseland" grilled cheese. *Average main: €12 ⊠ 3 rue Neuve Popincourt, Oberkampf* ☎ *01–43–55–60–10* ⊕ *www.cafeoberkampf.com* Ⓜ *Parmentier, Oberkampf.*

Chambelland

$ | Bakery. In a city where bakeries dot every street corner, Chambelland offers something different: a sleek assortment of gluten-free bread, biscuits, and pastries baked with rice, buckwheat, and other alternative flours. Grains are organic and ground in the boulangerie's Provence-based mill before they're kneaded and baked in the on-site oven, and—unlike most Parisian bakeries—you can have your bread and eat it there, too, posting up at a table on the al fresco terrace. **Known for:** vegetarian salads and sandwiches; artisanal focaccia; lactose- and sugar-free cake. *Average main: €5 ⊠ 14 rue Ternaux, Oberkampf* ☎ *01–43–55–07–30* ⊕ *www.chambelland.com*

🕙 *Closed Sun. and Mon.* Ⓜ *Parmentier, Oberkampf.*

Louie Louie

$ | **Pizza.** Part pizzeria, part craft cocktail bar, Louie Louie fits perfectly in place on the corner of the buzzing Rue de Charonne. Warm lighting, exposed stone, and sleek Scandinavian tables add a contemporary feel to the 17th-century maison, which serves up whimsical libations and adventurous, wood-fired pizzas, topped with truffle-infused *burrata* (creamy mozzarella) and habanero pepper honey. **Known for:** cocktails and natural wine; set lunch menu; salade du moment. *Average main: €15* ⊠ *78 rue de Charonne, Paris* ☎ *09–73–58–14–36* ⊕ *www.louielouie.paris* Ⓜ *Charonne.*

⭐ Mokonuts

$$ | **Café.** Initially intended to be a coffee shop and bakery—the multithousand-dollar espresso machine in the corner a telltale sign—Mokonuts instead became a hybrid. It now doubles as a high-end café with delectable pastries and an intimate restaurant with Lebanese-inspired, daily changing plates. **Known for:** locally sourced vegetables; creative cookie flavors; L'Arbre à Café coffee. *Average main: €20* ⊠ *5 rue St-Bernard, Paris* ☎ *09–80–81–82–85* 🕙 *Closed weekends* Ⓜ *Faidherbe–Chaligny.*

Paperboy

$$ | **Café.** Taking a cue from the café scene in Brooklyn's Williamsburg, American-inspired Paperboy has quickly become a brunch fave in Paris, where you can order staples like pancakes, *pain perdu* (aka French toast), and eggs Benedict as well as more off-the-wall sandwiches. As if the white subway-tiled counter (where a bike remains permanently propped up) wasn't hipster enough, coffee and beer are of the craft variety, and chai and matcha are just a few of the twists on tea. **Known for:** brunch; weekday sandwiches and bagels; fresh juices. *Average main: €23* ⊠ *137 rue Amelot, Oberkampf* ☎ *01–43–38–12–13* ⊕ *www.paperboyparis.com* Ⓜ *République, Filles du Calvaire, Oberkampf.*

Passager

$ | **Café.** It would be easy to walk straight past this unmarked coffee shop if a stream of hip twenty-somethings weren't hovering out front waiting for a seat to open. Cofounded by blogger Fanny B (of *Play Like a Girl*), the exposed-brick and concrete space is about as Instagrammable as can get. **Known for:** filtered coffee; baked treats; beans from Berlin's Five Elephant. *Average main: €12* ⊠ *107 av. Ledru-Rollin, Oberkampf* 🕙 *Closed Sun. and Mon.* Ⓜ *Ledru-Rollin, Charonne, Bastille.*

Ten Belles Bread

$ | **Bakery.** An offshoot of the Canal St-Martin coffee shop, Ten Belles Bread is a full-fledged boulangerie that not only supplies its sister spot with the sourdough for its sandwiches, but also provides loaves to some of the top eateries in town (Septime, a favorite restaurant in the neighborhood, is one of many fans). Order at the counter and head to the barista behind the coffee bar, where your specialty coffee of choice is whipped up on the spot from locally roasted Belleville Brûlerie beans. **Known for:** classic café crème; terrace seating; freshly prepped sandwiches and salads. *Average main:* €15 ⊠ 17–19 rue Breguet, Bastille ☎ 01-42-40-90-78 Ⓜ Bréguet–Sabin.

Utopie

$ | Bakery. The line never seems to get shorter as people patiently wait for jewel-colored pastries and loaves of bread at Utopie— but they're worth the wait. The boulangerie once earned the title of Best Bakery in France, which is no surprise, given the bakers' backgrounds at some of the country's most prestigious patisseries. **Known for:** charcoal baguette; signature "l'authentic" made with organic flour and Guérande salt; sesame tart. *Average main:* €5 ⊠ 20 rue Jean-Pierre Timbaud, Oberkampf ☎ 09-82-50-74-48 ⊙ Closed Mon. Ⓜ Oberkampf.

Wild & The Moon

$ | Vegetarian. Wild & The Moon is spearheading the city's superfood movement with its Los Angeles–style, plant-based fare. Here, the juices are cold-pressed, milk is of the nut variety, and bowls bear names like "Blue Magic" and "Earth." Grab lunch to go from the fridge, or take a seat and savor the hot dish du jour alongside one of the seasonal (and locally sourced) tonics. **Known for:** açai bowls; superfood smoothies; raw (and sugar-free) desserts. *Average main:*

€12 ⊠ 138 rue Amelot, Oberkampf ☎ 01-43-20-50-01 ⊕ www.wildandthemoon.com Ⓜ Oberkampf.

🍴 Dining

Boucherie Les Provinces

$$ | French. After working up an appetite at the nearby Marché d'Aligre, carnivores should head to this butcher shop that doubles as a restaurant. Simply choose your cut of beef, veal, lamb, or pork, and have a seat as it's prepared. **Known for:** entrecôte (thin, boneless rib eye); lively market atmosphere; warm staff. *Average main:* €24 ⊠ 20 rue d'Aligre, Bastille ☎ 01-43-43-91-64 ⊕ www.boucherie-lesprovinces.fr ⊙ Closed Mon. Ⓜ Ledru-Rollin.

Café Charbon

$ | Contemporary. This ultracool café is a neighborhood institution that stays open late every night of the week. *Average main:* €14 ⊠ 109 rue Oberkampf, Oberkampf ☎ 01-43-57-55-13 ⊕ www.lecafecharbon.fr Ⓜ Parmentier, Menilmontant.

Café du Coin

$$ | Bistro. Café du Coin (literally "neighborhood café") lives up to its name as a hot spot for the hipster set, where half the appeal is that the decor doesn't try too hard: the walls aren't finished and the faded floor tiles are original. Foodies flock here for a leisurely French lunch, indulging in Instagram-famous mini flatbread pizzas, the most popular being the Taleggio cheese, Italian *guanciale* (pork cheek), and egg yolk. **Known for:** pizzetta du jour; daily desserts, including the house standard chocolate ganache and fromage blanc ice cream; three-course lunch menu. *Average main: €19* ⊠ *9 rue Camille Desmoulins, Oberkampf* ☎ *01-48-04-82-46* ⏱ *Closed weekends* Ⓜ *Voltaire.*

Chez Justine

$ | **Brasserie.** Groups gather at this old-world bistro for drinks and wood-fired barbecue before catching a show across the street at the Nouveau Casino. The vibe is lively and the banquette-style seating allows you to mix and mingle as you would at a house party. **Known for:** Neopolitan-syle pasta and pizza; sharing plates; late-night menu. *Average main: €15* ⊠ *96 rue Oberkampf, Oberkampf* ☎ *01-43-57-44-03* ⊕ *www.justineparis.fr* Ⓜ *Parmentier.*

⭐ Clamato

$$$ | **Seafood.** Finding a restaurant open on a Sunday can be quite a feat, which makes Septime's seafood-centric sister restaurant, Clamato, a popular hangout that heats up early. The eatery doesn't take reservations, so arrive early and snag a seat at the bar, where you can watch the action as oyster platters and plates of ceviche pass by, each prettier than the next. **Known for:** seafood platters with wild oysters and urchin (during season); natural wine; daily changing menu determined by deliveries from the Basque coast and Brittany (the ceviche is always a winner). *Average main:*

€25 ⊠ *80 rue de Charonne, Paris* ☎ *01-43-72-74-53* ⊕ *www.clamato-charonne.fr* ⏱ *Closed Mon. and Tues.* Ⓜ *Charonne.*

Dersou

$$$$ | **French Fusion.** The narrow room housing this wildly popular restaurant is about as understated as can be (think wooden bar stools and exposed concrete walls), placing all of the emphasis on the carefully curated plates emerging from the open kitchen. Dinners revolve around a five- to seven-course tasting menu, but instead of the typical wine pairing, each plate is accompanied by a cocktail crafted to perfection. **Known for:** Asian-inspired brunch; seasonal menus; fine dining minus the fuss. *Average main: €95* ⊠ *21 rue St-Nicolas, Bastille* ☎ *09-81-01-12-73* ⊕ *www.dersouparis.com* ⏱ *Closed Mon. No dinner Sun.* Ⓜ *Bastille, Ledru-Rollin.*

Double Dragon

$$ | **Asian.** Modern dishes with Asian influence abound at this popular restaurant from the sisters that founded another local favorite, Le Servan; no reservations are accepted, so it's best to squeeze in at lunch. A former pizzeria, the restaurant has a domino-tile-lined bar and beautifully painted frescoes on the ceiling that are cool without trying too hard—and the same goes for the food. **Known for:** natural wine; sharing plates; lunch specials. *Average main: €19* ⊠ *52 rue St-Maur, Oberkampf* ☎ *01-71-32-41-95* ⏱ *Closed Mon. and Tues.* Ⓜ *Rue St-Maur.*

Fulgurances

$$$$ | Contemporary. Start at the wine bar across the street before heading over to Fulgurances, where young chefs who have done stints in top eateries around the world (Copenhagen's Noma and Mexico City's Pujol to name a couple) run the kitchen during short-term residencies. These sous chefs are given the opportunity to craft a menu (and restaurant) of their own for six-month spans. **Known for:** changing tasting menus; unique wine pairings; inventive, seasonal cuisine. *Average main: €58 ⊠ 10 rue Alexandre Dumas, Bastille* ☎ *01-43-48-14-59* ⊕ *www.fulgurances.com* ⊙ *Closed Sat.–Mon.* Ⓜ *Rue des Boulets.*

Jeanne A

$ | Wine Bar. This six-table épicerie–bistro–wine bar–traiteur on a pretty cobbled street is just the thing for an uncomplicated lunch, dinner, or afternoon snack. Whether you desire a great glass of wine and a plate of charcuterie and cheese or a full meal, the classic French fare here is always excellent. **Known for:** rotisserie chicken; good breakfast spot; secluded table great for large parties. *Average main: €16 ⊠ 42 rue Jean-Pierre-Timbaud, 11e, Canal St-Martin* ☎ *01-43-55-09-49* ⊕ *www.jeanne-a-comestibles.com* Ⓜ *Parmentier, Oberkampf.*

Jouvence

$$$ | Bistro. You might assume you've stumbled back in time and onto a lovely Parisian bistro at this reimagined apothecary, now one of the more elegant eateries around Bastille. The contemporary French menu is an ode to Chef Romain Thibault's childhood and travels, with food and drink served the way he'd prefer. **Known for:** tasting menu; old-fashioned, romantic setting; reimagined classics. *Average main: €29 ⊠ 172 bis rue du Faubourg St-Antoine, Bastille* ☎ *01-56-58-04-73* ⊕ *www.jouvence. paris* ⊙ *Closed Sun. and Mon.* Ⓜ *Faidherbe—Chaligny.*

★ Le Baron Rouge

$ | Wine Bar. This proletarian wine bar near the Place d'Aligre market is a throwback to another era, with a few tables and giant barrels along the walls for filling and refilling your take-home bottles. A fun time to come is Sunday morning (yes, morning) when it's packed with locals who have just been to the market and want to linger over good food and that first glass of the day. **Known for:** wine by the barrel with refills to take home; authentic neighborhood atmosphere; oysters on a winter evening. *Average main: €11 ⊠ 1 rue Théophile Roussel, 12e, Bastille* ☎ *01-43-43-14-32* Ⓜ *Ledru-Rollin.*

Le Chateaubriand

$$$$ | Modern French. A chef who once presented a single, peeled apple pip (really) on a plate (at the museum restaurant Le Transversal outside Paris) has no ordinary approach to food. Self-taught Basque cook Inaki Aizpitarte is undeniably provocative, but he gets away with it because (a) he's young and extremely cool and (b) he has an uncanny sense of which unexpected ingredients go together, as in a combination of oysters and lime zest in chicken stock. **Known for:** inventive but approachable cuisine; lively and hip crowd; one-Michelin star. *Average main: €45 ⊠ 129 av. Parmentier, 11e, Canal St-Martin* ☎ *01–43–57–45–95* ⊕ *www.lecha-teaubriand.net* ⊗ *Closed Sun., Mon., and 1 wk at Christmas. No lunch* Ⓜ *Goncourt.*

Le Dauphin

$$ | Wine Bar. Avant-garde chef Inaki Aizpitarte transformed a dowdy café into a sleek, if chilly, all-marble watering hole for late-night cuisinistas. Honing his ever-iconoclastic take on tapas, the dishes served here are a great way to get an idea of what all the fuss is about. **Known for:** late-night revelry; superb wines by the glass; tapas by a star chef. *Average main: €20 ⊠ 131 av. Parmentier, 11e, Canal St-Martin* ☎ *01–55–28–78–88* ⊕ *www. restaurantledauphin.net* ⊗ *Closed Sun., Mon., and 1 wk at Christmas. No lunch Tues.* Ⓜ *Parmentier.*

★ Le Rigmarole

$$$$ | Barbecue. Although Japanese-style yakitori is the highlight here, the team also strums up inspiration from French and American cuisine, empha-sizing seasonal produce and hand-selecting veggies from local markets. Ceramic light fixtures hover above the counter seats, creating a refreshing atmosphere more inviting of conversation than photo taking. **Known for:** chef's choice of off-menu items; natural wines; grilled dessert. *Average*

main: €49 ⊠ 10 rue du Grand-Prieuré, Oberkampf ☎ *01–71–24–58–44* ⊕ *www.lerigmarole.com* ⊗ *Closed Mon. and Tues.* Ⓜ *Oberkampf.*

Le Servan

$$$ | Bistro. Le Servan is one of the forerunners in the city's wave of neo-bistros—think Brooklyn cool sans the pretension. The staff will happily guide you through the à la carte menu that takes classic French training (co-owner and chef Tatiana Levha cut her teeth at Michelin-starred L'Arpège and L'Astrance) and adds a more playful—and slightly Asian—twist, a reflection of the chef's Filipino roots. **Known for:** whimsical desserts; natural wine list; prix-fixe lunch menu. *Average main: €25 ⊠ 32 rue St-Maur, Oberkampf* ☎ *01–55–28–51–82* ⊕ *www.leservan.com* ⊗ *Closed weekends. No lunch Mon.* Ⓜ *Voltaire, Rue St-Maur, St-Ambroise.*

Mio Posto

$$ | Italian. An offshoot of Belleville's Il Posto, this spacious Neopolitan pizzeria and cocktail bar is cooking up some of the area's most solid quick-Italian options— and rivaling nearby East Mamma. Start with a creamy burrata (mozzarella made with cream) or salumi selection, continue with a Crudo or Tartufo (truffle) pizza, and wrap with a copious homemade tiramisu. **Known for:** Tartufo pizza; Spritz Agrumes cocktail; homemade tiramisu. *Average main: €18 ⊠ 24 rue Keller, Bastille* ☎ *01–48–05–47–23* ⊕ *www.mioposto.fr* Ⓜ *Voltaire.*

Ober Mamma

$$ | **Italian.** Notorious for its no-reservation policy, Ober Mamma draws a crowd before doors even swing open, and the line wraps around the block until closing. If you can squeeze your way into *aperitivo* (a drink/light meal before dinner), one of the most famous in Paris, put your name on the list and nibble on Italian charcuterie and cheese while waiting for a table to open. **Known for:** wood-fired pizza; Italian-sourced ingredients; craft cocktails in quirky glassware. *Average main: €18* ⊠ *107 bd. Richard Lenoir, Oberkampf* ☎ *01-58-30-62-78* ⊕ *www.bigmammagroup. com* Ⓜ *Ledru-Rollin, République, Oberkampf, Parmentier.*

Passerini

$$$ | **Italian.** After making waves as chef at now-closed Rino, Italian import Giovanni Passerini opened the doors of his eponymous Italian eatery. This resto is all about à la carte, so options abound at both lunch and dinner: think lamb meatballs with aioli, or chili pepper and garlic linguine with monkfish and crusco peppers. **Known for:** fresh pasta dishes; solid wine list; Franco-Italian cuisine. *Average main: €27* ⊠ *65 rue Traversière, Bastille* ☎ *01-43-42-27-56* ⊕ *www. passerini.paris* Ⓜ *Ledru-Rollin.*

Pierre Sang Signature

$$$$ | **Korean Fusion.** The Korean-born chef who rose to fame as a *Top Chef* finalist opened his third eatery in 2018 to create a more intimate—and gastronomic—experience than his other two tasting-menu spots offer. Korean street food bibimbap is available for takeaway in the front, while the 12-seat fine dining restaurant is tucked away in the back by the vaulted-ceiling wine cellar. **Known for:** French fare with a Korean twist; selection of the chef's signature dishes, such as langoustine jelly with cucumber and dashi gazpacho; ingredients sourced at the Boulevard Richard Lenoir market. *Average main: €59* ⊠ *8 rue Gambey, Oberkampf* ☎ *09-67-31-96-80* ⊕ *www.pierre-sang.com* ☏ *Closed Mon. and Tues.* Ⓜ *Parmentier.*

Robert

$$$$ | **Bistro.** Mid-century-modern light fixtures hang above the handful of pale wood tables in this airy bistro. Italian influences weave their way onto the menu in the form of ravioli and tortellini, but the rest of the dishes proudly proclaim which French farms and producers supply the seasonal fare. **Known for:** natural and organic wines; kitchen-counter seating perfect for solo diners; lunch specials. *Average main: €50* ⊠ *32 rue de la Fontaine au Roi, Oberkampf* ☎ *01-43-57-20-29* ⊕ *www.robert-restaurant.fr* ☏ *Closed Sun.-Tues.* Ⓜ *Goncourt.*

Septime

$$$$ | **Modern French.** Septime makes fine dining approachable and young in a contemporary space that's just as cool as its cuisine, its look a mix of French country chic meets industrial loft (and no white tablecloths in sight). The menu highlights seasonal and sustainably sourced ingredients in dishes that play with texture. **Known for:** one Michelin star; tasting menu; hard-to-score reservations opening three weeks in advance. *Average main: €80* ⊠ *80 rue de Charonne, Oberkampf* ☎ *01-43-67-38-29* ⊕ *www.septime-charonne.fr* ۞ *Closed weekends, No lunch Mon.* Ⓜ *Faidherbe–Chaligny, Ledru-Rollin, Voltaire, Charonne.*

Tannat
$$$$ | Modern French. Exposed brick, an oval-shape bar, and mirror-lined walls add a contemporary touch to the light-filled neo-bistro launched by friends Simon Auscher and Ariane Stern. With the duo's experience at Shangri-La and chef Olivier Le Corre's background at Le Bristol, you can expect a parade of well-crafted plates served in a setting that's the opposite of stuffy. **Known for:** Asian influence; affordable set menus; organic French produce. *Average main: €45* ⊠ *119 av. Parmentier, Oberkampf* ☎ *09-53-86-38-61* ⊕ *www.tannat.fr* ۞ *Closed weekends* Ⓜ *Parmentier.*

Unico
$$$ | Modern Argentine. An architect and a photographer, both Parisians born in Argentina, teamed up to open one of Bastille's hottest restaurants—literally hot, too, because the Argentinean meat served here is grilled over charcoal. Whichever cut of beef you choose (the ultimate being *lomo,* or fillet), it's so melt-in-your-mouth that the sauces served on the side seem almost superfluous. **Known for:** tender Argentinian

beef, aged and grilled; chic retro atmosphere; excellent value prix-fixe menus. *Average main: €30* ⊠ *15 rue Paul-Bert, 11e, Bastille* ☎ *01-43-67-68-08* ⊕ *www.resto-unico.com* ۞ *Closed Sun. No lunch Mon.* Ⓜ *Faidherbe–Chaligny.*

🍸 Bars and Nightlife

Au Passage
Masquerading as a wine bar, Au Passage has a changing list with nearly 200 biodynamic and natural bottles crafted by some of the team's vetted *vignerons* (winemakers), and its small plates go well beyond charcuterie and cheese (although you can find those here, too). Take your pick of market-inspired tapas off the chalkboard and squeeze into a seat in the bustling dining room that has an Austin-esque feel with its young crowd, tatted-up servers, and secondhand-chic furniture. ⊠ *1 bis, passage St-Sébastien, Oberkampf* ☎ *01-43-55-07-52* ⊕ *www.restaurant-aupassage.fr* Ⓜ *St-Sébastien–Froissart.*

Aux Deux Amis
Locals and tourists vie for a seat in this perpetually packed neighborhood bar, so your best bet is to sidle up to the counter and order a glass of wine (or better yet, a bottle) and wait to snag a table on the terrace. At first glance, the wine bar could be any old-school Parisian brasserie with its fluorescent lighting and weathered, pastel-color paint, but its stand-out natural wine list and spruced-up

THE LOW-DOWN ON NATURAL WINE

In a country where wine is as abundant as water, it's no surprise the capital is paving the way for a new wave of wine bars that are turning up their nose at social norms. The trend: natural wine, often deemed funky, fizzy, and fruity. These are the kombucha of the wine world, fermenting sans additives with lower sulfites (or none at all). Think pre–Industrial Revolution with as little mechanization as possible. In the same way organic fruit may show more blemishes than its pesticide-sprayed counterparts, a large number of natural wines are defective, or faulty. But instead of chalking the bottles up to being corked, some sommeliers and oenophiles are praising these "flaws" and heralding the wine's flavor. "You often hear people say they only drink natural wine because 'it is closer to how wine used to be,'" says American Sommelier president Andrew Bell. "Wine has lost its soul over the last 25 years, and bottles have become carbon copies looking for points [from experts like Wine Advocate's Robert Parker]. People may embrace defect as uniqueness and virtue." More restaurants are popping up around town with a wine list heavy (or based entirely) on natural vino, but if you want to get your palette prepped, Eastern Paris's dedicated natural wine bars like La Buvette, Septime La Cave, and Aux Deux Amis will offer up a crash course with each glass swirled.

small plates have earned it a cult following. ✉ *45 rue Oberkampf, Oberkampf* ☎ *01-58-30-38-13* Ⓜ *Oberkampf, Parmentier*.

Badaboum

Techno and house music pump until sunrise at this neon-light-filled nightclub. For the full experience, start in the cozy cocktail bar up front where libations change with the seasons and the ambience is vibrant and easygoing. Then head to the back for the first round of music, usually live rock and pop concerts, before you dance to electronic music until dawn. ✉ *2 bis, rue des Taillandiers, Bastille* ☎ *01-85-09-74-87* ⊕ *badaboum.paris* Ⓜ *Ledru-Rollin*.

Bataclan

This chinoiserie-style dance hall has been a neighborhood institution since opening its doors in 1865, transitioning with the times and reinventing itself Madonna-style. From vaudeville to postpunk, Bataclan has welcomed everyone from Lou Reed to Jane Birkin to Prince, who popped in to perform his after-shows while in Paris. Though the terror attack that happened here in 2015 was cause for international headlines, the venue has since reopened its doors and continues to bring together the community with music. ✉ *50 bd. Voltaire, Oberkampf* ⊕ *www.bataclan. fr* Ⓜ *Oberkampf, Filles du Calvaire*.

Chambre Noire

While this natural wine bar may be buzzing in the evenings, it's nothing close to a party scene. The narrow space looks like something out of a New Wave movie set, which makes sense given it's run by filmmaker Oliver Lomeli. Order a glass from the menu above the bar and take a seat at one of the cozy, candlelit tables where you can have a proper *apéro* (aperitif)—charcuterie and fromage included. ⊠ *82 rue de la Folie Méricourt, Oberkampf* ☎ *06–51–47–85–36* Ⓜ *Oberkampf, Parmentier.*

Favela Chic

This popular Latin cocktail bar took the scene early, forging Oberkampf's hip reputation. Back behind courtyard gates you'll find caipirinhas and mojitos, guest DJs presenting an eclectic mix of samba, soul, and hip-hop, and a nonstop dance scene. ⊠ *18 rue du Faubourg du Temple, 11e, Oberkampf* ☎ *01–40–21–38–14* ⊕ *favelachic.com* Ⓜ *République.*

Fréquence

Brooklynites would feel right at home at this cocktail bar made for music lovers. A vast collection of vinyls line the back wall, taking up as much prime real estate as the alcohols beneath, and a DJ mixes everything from soul to funk, Afro to disco. The cocktails and bites are equally appealing: enjoy a chicken Caesar bagel and cold brew for weekend brunch, homemade ricotta and lamb pita for an evening bite, or a smoky Fernando Sancho cocktail (mezcal, aquavit, orange syrup, lime). ⊠ *20 rue Keller, Bastille* ☎ *01–71–32–40–35* Ⓜ *Voltaire.*

Ici-même

One of the early adopters of Paris's now-booming natural wine movement, this *cave à vins* (wine bar) is a must for any aficionado. But newcomers fear not: the knowledgeable and engaging staff will gladly help you navigate their impressive selection. Sit at one of the cozy wood tables that dot the interior and sidewalk space, and don't forget to pop into the gallery space next door. ⊠ *68 rue de Charenton, Bastille* Ⓜ *Ledru-Rollin.*

L'Attache

For a well-conceived small bite and glass of tasty natural wine in the 11e arrondissement, L'Attache is the spot. Nestle into one of the few unassuming vintage wooden tables or snag a seat at the bar, and sip an Abbazia San Giorgio orange bianco or Lestignac cabernet sauvignon. They go nicely with the pollock rillettes (similar to pâté) or a slow-cooked egg with asparagus cream and spicy *'nduja* (spicy pork salumi). ⊠ *52 rue Basfroi, Bastille* ☎ *01–45–31–01–22* Ⓜ *Voltaire.*

★ La Buvette

A small neon sign scrolled with "la buvette" glows in the window of this *cave-à-manger*, beckoning in a hipster crowd seeking its top-notch natural wine selection. Start here before dinner with a few small plates (the signature white beans sprinkled with lemon zest are a must-try) and sample a selection of vinos while the owner gives you the run-down on the wine. ✉ *67 rue St-Maur, Oberkampf* ☏ *09-83-56-94-11* Ⓜ *Rue St-Maur, St-Ambroise.*

Le Bluebird

Inspired by a Bukowski poem, this cocktail bar is full-blown '50s—everything from the neon-lit aquarium to the kitsch sconces is reminiscent of a Don Draper hangout. Have a seat at the dimly lit bar and order one of the expertly crafted, gin-heavy cocktails. ✉ *12 rue St-Bernard, Paris* Ⓜ *Faidherbe–Chaligny.*

Le China

Step into 1930s Shanghai at Le China, where subdued red lighting faintly illuminates leather chesterfield sofas, checkerboard flooring, and a dark-wood bar. The cocktails are a mix of classics and custom creations, such as the Little Italy (bourbon, Carpano red vermouth, amaretto, orange bitters, orange zest). The upstairs "smoking room," lined with books and adorned with a fireplace, is the ideal spot to sip a quality cognac. The basement level offers something a bit more vibrant: live jazz, soul, pop, and more plays each evening. ✉ *50 rue de Charenton, Bastille* ☏ *01-43-46-08-09* ⊕ *www.lechina.eu* Ⓜ *Ledru-Rollin.*

Le Nouveau Casino

You'll find this concert hall and club tucked behind the Café Charbon. Pop and rock concerts prevail during the week, with revelry on Friday and Saturday from midnight until dawn. Hip-hop, house, disco, and techno DJs are the standard. ✉ *109 rue Oberkampf, 11e, Oberkampf* ☏ *01-43-57-57-40* ⊕ *www.nouveau-casino.fr* Ⓜ *Parmentier.*

Moonshiner

In true speakeasy fashion, Moonshiner is tucked behind the fridge door of pizzeria Pizza Da Vito. Grab a slice before heading into the saloonlike bar, where groups gather around low-lying cocktail tables and sip libations such as seasonal punch or one of the many variations of the Old Fashioned. In winter, this place can take on more of a party vibe, but one of the mustached bartenders will still take the time to help you choose a whiskey from the well-curated collection lining the shelves. ✉ *5 rue Sedaine, Bastille* ☏ *09-50-73-12-99* Ⓜ *Bréguet–Sabin, Bastille.*

Pasdeloup

Bartenders here hail from some of the city's top cocktail spots like Candelaria, so if you're debating what to have, a cocktail is a given. But don't think that means you'll be stuck sipping simple standards. Pasdeloup reinvents classics with off-the-wall ingredients and playful twists that pair perfectly with the menu of gastronomic small plates. ✉ *108 rue Amelot, Oberkampf* ☏ *09-54-74-16-36* Ⓜ *Filles du Calvaire.*

Pop In

On any given night you'll find one or two new acts from around the globe performing in the crowded basement at this pop rock spot, its atmosphere reminiscent of London's punk scene. Drinks are cheap, the mood is relaxed, and the music is free, making it a popular place during happy hour. ✉ *105 rue Amelot, Oberkampf* ☎ *01–48–05–56–11* ⊕ *www.popin.fr* Ⓜ *Oberkampf, St-Sébastien–Froissart*.

Red House

American-run Red House feels like a chilled-out, Texas-inspired watering hole, complete with a horned skull looming above the bar. Young expats come for the hip DJ, retro arcade games, and on autumn Sundays, wings and NFL games. The best part? They also make killer cocktails at reasonable prices. Wild West Side (tequila, mint, lime, cucumber, and hot pepper) is a regular favorite. ✉ *1 bis, rue de la Forge Royale, Bastille* ☎ *01–43–67–06–43* Ⓜ *Ledru-Rollin*.

★ Septime La Cave

This is the kind of spot where you could start or end the night—and it's guaranteed to be packed at all hours, every day of the week. If you couldn't snag a seat at Septime around the corner, Septime La Cave is your next best bet, with small plates that are a toned-down version of its sister eatery's starred cuisine, plus a collection of natural wines to help wash everything down. ✉ *3 rue Basfroi, Bastille* ☎ *01–43–67–14–87* ⊕ *www.septime-lacave.fr* Ⓜ *Charonne, Ledru-Rollin*.

🎭 Performing Arts

★ Opéra Bastille

Sure, the city's Opéra Garnier is second to none in opulence and classic architecture, but the more modern Opéra Bastille is arguably the better opera experience, because the building is newer and the seating is more comfortable. What the building lacks in history (it was built in 1989 for the bicentennial of the French Revolution) it makes up for in modern design savvy. The same transparent materials are used on both the exterior and interior, and the amphitheater's 2,745 seats all enjoy the same acoustic excellence. Whether Bizet or Berlioz, Bastille's operas are genuinely world-class. ✉ *Pl. de la Bastille, Bastille* ☎ *08–92–89–90–90* ⊕ *www.operadeparis.fr/en* Ⓜ *Ledru-Rollin*.

12

Belleville and Ménilmontant

LES PUCES

CLIGNAN-COURT

ÉPINETTES

LA VILLETTE

LES BATIGNOLLES

LA CHAPELLE

MONTMARTRE

TERNES

MONCEAU

PIGALLE

BELLEVILLE

CANAL ST-MARTIN

CHAILLOT

LES GRANDS BOULEVARDS

CHAMPS-ÉLYSÉES

SENTIER

BOIS DE BOULOGNE

PASSY

TROCADERO

PALAIS-ROYAL

LES HALLES

LE MARAIS

OBERKAMPF

MÉNILMONTANT

PÈRE-LACHAISE

AUTEUIL

LES INVALIDES

LES ÎLES

BASTILLE

CHARONNE

VAUGIRARD

ST-GERMAIN-DES-PRÉS

QUARTIER LATIN

BERCY

BEL-AIR

JAVEL

MONTPARNASSE

BUTTE-AUX-CAILLES

SEINE

BOIS DE VINCENNES

ST-LAMBERT

AUSTERLITZ

MONTROUGE

MAISON BLANCHE

Belleville's name may mean "beautiful city," but for years, this former town on the outskirts of Paris, today in the 19e and 20e arrondissements, had a less-than-stellar reputation. When Père-Lachaise Cemetery was built here in the early 19th century, the area was held in such low esteem that no one wanted to be buried there. More than a century later, when Edith Piaf was born here, it was seen as a low-class and very undesirable neighborhood. But times have changed. In the 1980s, Belleville attracted a large Chinese population as well as hoards of artists, drawn here by charming cobbled streets, low housing prices, and plentiful workshop space. Today, Belleville has become an international enclave for alternative and hipster culture, complete with an active street art scene and several spoken-word and music venues. Along with its neighboring district of Ménilmontant, once a hamlet within Belleville itself, this outlying area of Paris has become a multicultural—if gentrified—haven for people looking for a truly different side of Paris.—*by Emily Monaco*

◉ Sights

Cité des Sciences et de l'Industrie *(Museum of Science and Industry)*

Occupying a colorful three-story industrial space that recalls the Pompidou Center, this ambitious science museum in Parc de la Villette is packed with things to do—all of them accessible to English speakers. Scores of exhibits focus on subjects like space, transportation, and technology. Hands-on workshops keep the kids entertained, and the planetarium is invariably a hit. Temporary exhibitions, like a recent exploration of cinematic special effects, are always multilingual and usually interactive. ⊠ *Parc de la Villette, 30 av. Corentin-Cariou, Eastern Paris* ☎ *01-40-05-70-00, 01-85-53-99-74 interactive voice response* ⊕ *www.cite-sciences.fr* ✉ *Permanent and temporary exhibitions and planetarium €12* ⊗ *Closed Mon.* Ⓜ *Porte de la Villette.*

Jardin Naturel

This public garden in the 20e arrondissement, just steps from Père-Lachaise Cemetery, stands apart from the well-manicured parks you'll find in other parts of the city. With a design that tends toward the wild rather than the ordered, the park truly has biodiversity preservation at its core. Keep an eye out for the local frogs who live here. ⊠ *120 rue de la Réunion, Père Lachaise* ☎ *01-43-28-47-63* ✉ *Free* Ⓜ *Alexandre Dumas.*

Le 104

Le Cent Quatre takes its name from its address in a rough-around-the-edges corner of the 19e arrondissement, not far from the top of the Canal St-Martin. The former site of the city morgue, this cavernous art hub is home to an offbeat collection of performance venues, shops, and studios (artists of all genres compete for free studio space, and sometimes you can get a peek of them at work). Contemporary art exhibits, some of which charge admission, are staged here, as are concerts. On-site you'll also find a restaurant, a café, a bookstore, a secondhand shop, and a play area for children. Check the website before going to see what's on. ⊠ 104 rue d'Aubervilliers, Eastern Paris ☎ 01-53-35-50-00 ⊕ www.104. fr ☞ Free, prices for exhibits and concerts vary ⊗ Closed Mon. Ⓜ Stalingrad.

Musée de la Musique

Parc de la Villette's music museum contains four centuries' worth of instruments from around the world—about 1,000 in total, many of them exquisite works of art. Their sounds and stories are evoked on numerous video screens and via commentary you can follow on headphones (ask for a free audioguide in English). Leave time for the excellent temporary exhibitions, like the recent one on the life and music of French chanteuse Barbara. On the plaza adjacent to the museum, the outdoor terrace at Café des Concerts (☎ 01-42-49-74-74 ⊕ www.cafedesconcerts.com)

is an inviting place to have a drink on a sunny day. ⊠ Parc de la Villette, 221 av. Jean Jaurès, Eastern Paris ☎ 01-44-84-84-84 ⊕ www.philharmoniedeparis.fr/fr/musee-de-la-musique ☞ From €8 ⊗ Closed Mon. Ⓜ Porte de Pantin.

Musée Edith Piaf

Edith Piaf's Belleville apartment has been converted into this off-the-beaten-path museum in honor of the neighborhood's most famous daughter. The two-room apartment, which Edith lived in at the beginning of her career, is filled with objects from the singer's life, including her famous black dress. Reservations are required to visit the diminutive apartment, so be sure to call in advance. Photos are not allowed, and tours are given only in French. ⊠ 5 rue Crespin du Gast, Ménilmontant ☎ 01-43-55-52-72 ⊗ Closed Thurs.–Sun. Ⓜ Ménilmontant.

★ Parc de Belleville

This park on top of the hill of Belleville affords one of the best panoramic views of Paris, with the focal point on Notre-Dame Cathedral but also including Montparnasse and the Eiffel Tower. The park also boasts playground areas for children, gorgeous flowerbeds that are planned and planted anew every year, and more than 100 grapevines, a testament to the winemaking past of the area. ⊠ 47 rue des Couronnes, Belleville Ⓜ Couronnes.

SIGHTS

22,48 m² 23
Cité des Sciences et
de l'Industrie 4
Jardin Naturel 44
Le 104 1
Musée de
la Musique 7
Musée Edith Piaf 27
Parc de Belleville 22
Parc de la Villette 5
Père Lachaise
Cemetery 43

SHOPPING

Estelle Ramousse 24
Le Coffre 32
L'Épicerie Vintage ... 34
Librairie Galerie
Le Monte-en-l'air ... 33
Vintage 77 35

COFFEE & QUICK BITES

Belleville Brûlerie 8
Café la Laverie 36
Cô My Cantine 30
The Hood 25
Le Barbouquin 17
Les Pères
Populaires 42
Pavillon
des Canaux 2

DINING

Dong Huong 16
La Cave de
Belleville 10
La Fine Mousse 29
Le Baratin 12
Le Comptoir 40
Le Grand Bain 15
Mensae 9
Wenzhou 14
Yard 41

BARS & NIGHTLIFE

Aux Folies 13
La Commune 18
Le Floréal
Belleville 21
Le Perchoir 28
Les Trois 8 31
Mama Shelter 45
Paname Brewery
Company 3
Triplettes 19

PERFORMING ARTS

Ateliers d'Artistes
de Belleville 20
Culture Rapide 11
La Bellevilloise 39
La Maroquinerie 37
L'International 26
Philharmonie
de Paris 6
Théâtre de
Ménilmontant 38

Parc de la Villette

This former *abattoir* (slaughter-house) is now an ultramodern, 130-acre park. With lawns and play areas, an excellent science museum, a music complex, and a cinema, it's the perfect place to entertain exhausted kids. You could easily spend a whole day here.

The park itself was designed in the 1980s by postmodern architecture star Bernard Tschumi, who melded industrial elements, children's games (don't miss the dragon slide), ample green spaces, and funky sculptures along the canal into one vast yet unified playground. Loved by picnickers, the lawns also attract rehearsing samba bands and pickup soccer players. In summer there are outdoor festivals and a free open-air cinema, where people gather at dusk to watch movies on a huge inflatable screen.

In cold weather you can visit an authentic submarine and the Espace Chapiteaux (a circus tent featuring contemporary acrobatic theater performances) before hitting the museums. The hands-on one at the Cité des Sciences et de l'Industrie is a favorite stop for families and a must for science fans; its 3-D Omnimax cinema (La Géode) is housed in a giant mirrored ball. Arts-oriented visitors of all ages will marvel at the excellent, instrument-filled Musée de la Musique. The park has even more in store for music lovers in the form of the Philharmonie de Paris, a striking

GETTING HERE

Métro line 2 services Belleville and Ménilmontant; stop at Philippe Auguste for the closest access to Père-Lachaise Cemetery's primary entrance on 8 bd. de Ménilmontant. You can also use line 11 to access Belleville to the north. Be aware that Rue Ménilmontant affords a bit of a steep climb!

2,400-seat concert hall designed by Jean Nouvel.

All that's left of the slaughterhouse that once stood here is La Grande Halle, a magnificent iron-and-glass building currently used for exhibitions, performances, and trade shows. ⊠ *Parc de la Villette, 211 av. Jean Jaurès, Eastern Paris* ☎ *01–40–03–75–75* ⊕ *www.lavillette.com* Ⓜ *Porte de Pantin, Porte de la Villette.*

★ **Père-Lachaise Cemetery**
(Cimetière du Père-Lachaise)
Père-Lachaise Cemetery is worth a trip for the beautiful grounds alone, and even more so if you're seeking out the tomb of an idol. The cemetery was originally built as the Eastern Cemetery, one of four commissioned on the outskirts of Paris at each of its cardinal points in the 19th century. The largest of these four, at more than 100 acres, Père-Lachaise is home to such illustrious residents as Jim Morrison, Gertrude Stein, Edith Piaf, Oscar Wilde, Honoré de Balzac, Frédéric Chopin, and Molière. Grab a map at the main entrance before exploring; it's easy to get lost along

the cemetery's winding paths.
✉ 16 rue du Repos, Ménilmontant
☎ 01-55-25-82-10 ⊕ www.pere-lachaise.com Ⓜ Philippe Auguste.

22,48 m²

If you want to take in Paris's truly contemporary art scene, head to this gallery near the Parc de Belleville, where works are displayed on stark white walls. In addition to its regular exhibitions, the gallery also organizes performances, debates, screenings, and activities for families. ✉ 30 rue des Envierges, Belleville ☎ 09-81-72-26-37 ⊕ www.english.2248m2.com ⊘ Closed Sun.-Tues. Ⓜ Pyrénées, Jourdain.

🛍 Shopping

Estelle Ramousse

This hat maker got her start creating headdresses for a children's show. Today, her one-of-a-kind *chapeaux* are just as bright and innovative, sporting feathers and sometimes even lights. Her shop, where she also sells simpler hats for everyday wear, doubles as her workshop, so you may see the master at work. ✉ 64 rue de la Mare, Belleville ☎ 01-77-11-29-04 ⊕ www.chapeausurmesure.com ⊘ Closed Sun. Ⓜ Pyrénées.

★ L'Epicerie Vintage

This ultra-unique shop combines two things you might never consider seeking out in the same place: organic food and vintage home goods. Somehow, it works—the shop gives off a French country vibe, with loads of local produce

and tons of funky items like wicker baskets, earthenware crockery, and even furniture. ✉ 4 rue Sorbier, Ménilmontant ☎ 07-70-42-78-78 ⊘ Closed Tues. Ⓜ Ménilmontant.

Le Coffre

Le Coffre is a secondhand specialist, with a variety of clothing for both men and women. An impressive selection of Levi's jeans is on offer, as well as a combination of discounted French designer clothes and vintage style. Here, pricing for cheaper items is denoted by color: different stickers signal the cost of each item, between €2 and €10. ✉ 26 rue de Ménilmontant, Ménilmontant ☎ 01-43-15-54-70 ⊕ www.lecoffreshop.fr ⊘ Closed Sun. Ⓜ Ménilmontant.

Librairie Galerie Le Monte-en-l'air

This atypical bookshop combines its collection of books with a small art gallery. Each exhibit is linked to an editorial news item or trend, and regular readings and other events forge a true sense of community here. The shop also publishes books under the imprint Belles Lettres. ✉ 71 rue de Ménilmontant, Ménilmontant ☎ 01-40-33-04-54 ⊕ montenlair.wordpress.com Ⓜ Ménilmontant.

Vintage 77

Fashionistas will find everything they could possibly want in this boutique that combines vintage style with a handful of newer items, including shoes and accessories. The shop has a mainly '50s focus, but there's a good blend of items hailing from the 1940s through to the 1970s. The shop also accepts items on consignment. ✉ 77 rue de Ménilmontant, Ménilmontant ☎ 01-47-97-77-17 ⊘ Closed Sun. Ⓜ Ménilmontant.

☕ Coffee and Quick Bites

Belleville Brûlerie
$ | Café. One of the first great coffee roasters in Paris, Belleville Brûlerie has made its mission to share great-quality coffee with the masses. While this flagship shop in Belleville is fading into the background in favor of the second location, situated a bit closer to the Canal and boasting a full brunch menu, the Pradier address remains an essential Belleville institution. **Known for:** cupping classes (reservations online); single-origin coffees; bags to take home. *Average main: €15* ✉ 10 rue Pradier, Belleville ☎ 09-83-75-60-80 ⊕ www.cafesbelleville.com Ⓜ Pyrénées.

Café la Laverie
$ | Modern French. Located in a former laundromat, Café la Laverie has been able to balance the trendiness of this neighborhood with an authentic local charm. Lunch and coffee during the day give way to drinks and assorted heavy snacks in the evening. **Known for:** bagel sandwiches and cheesecake; craft brews; amazingly terrible (or terribly amazing?) wallpaper. *Average main: €13* ✉ 70 rue de Ménilmontant, Ménilmontant ☎ 01-43-66-39-64 ⊕ www.cafelalaverie.fr Ⓜ Ménilmontant.

Cô My Cantine
$ | Vietnamese. This casual Vietnamese joint in the heart of Ménilmontant offers a no-nonsense approach to dining: a plain, exposed-wood dining room and a short-and-sweet menu. Portions here are quite large for Paris, and the prices make these dishes a steal. **Known for:** classic bo bun; savory, aromatic pho; chicken loc lac with red rice and a fried egg. *Average main: €11* ✉ 18 rue de Ménilmontant, Ménilmontant ☎ 01-43-66-94-10 ⊕ www.comycantine.fr Ⓜ Ménilmontant.

The Hood
$ | Asian Fusion. The Hood combines great coffee and small plates, Asian-inspired food, and cultural events in one community-building locale. Regular live music nights are a popular event in the neighborhood. **Known for:** banh mi and rice bowls; natural wine; white sesame scones. *Average main: €13* ✉ 80 rue Jean-Pierre Timbaud, Ménilmontant ☎ 01-43-57-20-25 ⊕ www.thehoodparis.com ⊘ Closed Tues. Ⓜ Couronnes.

Le Barbouquin
$ | Café. This cozy coffeeshop and secondhand bookstore hybrid is decorated in bright colors that reflect the street-art-adorned Rue Dénoyez just outside. Often, it's music that takes center stage in regular jam sessions and evening concerts. **Known for:** foreign books to borrow or buy; fresh-pressed juices; cheesecake. *Average main: €13* ✉ 1 rue Dénoyez, Belleville ☎ 09-84-32-13-21 Ⓜ Belleville.

★ Les Pères Populaires

$ | **Eclectic.** This divey café-bar is as close as you'll ever get to being back in your parents' basement in high school. Convivial and cheap, Les Pères Populaires serves up tasty lunches, inexpensive drinks, and lots of spirit. **Known for:** strange hodgepodge of chairs; innovative, inspired lunch; cheese and charcuterie plates to accompany your beer. *Average main: €13* ⊠ *46 rue de Buzenval, Nation* ☎ *01–43–48–49–22* Ⓜ *Buzenval.*

★ Pavillon des Canaux

$ | **Café.** This bar and event space is organized like a home: Dining rooms decorated like a kitchen, a library, and a bedroom are each filled with tables and chairs where you can sit and enjoy a coffee, cake, or brunch. The bathroom is a fan favorite; sit in the bathtub and enjoy your meal on a plank of wood placed across it. **Known for:** cooking classes, literary evenings, and concerts; inexpensive coffee from Parisian favorite Lomi; €24 weekend brunch. *Average main: €11* ⊠ *39 quai de la Loire, La Villette* ☎ *06–81–55–57–39* ⊕ *www.pavillond-escanaux.com* Ⓜ *Laumière.*

⑪ Dining

Dong Huong

$ | **Vietnamese.** This Vietnamese standby just steps from the Belleville métro might not look like much from the outside, but inside, three dining rooms are filled with the aromatic smells of pho broth. The vast menu understandably includes a few misses, but stick to

**WORTH A TRIP:
PARC DES BUTTES-CHAUMONT**

Not far from Père-Lachaise Cemetery, the Parc des Buttes-Chaumont stands atop one of Paris's highest hills and thus affords beautiful views of the rest of the city, particularly Montmartre and its starkly white Sacré-Coeur Basilica. Don't miss the Temple de la Sibylle; it is from this structure that you'll get the best views. You can access the park from the Buttes-Chaumont or Botzaris stops on métro line 7b.

classics, and it's hard to be disappointed. **Known for:** giant bowls of flavorful pho; spiced sate soup (a variation of pho); mini spring rolls with glazed pork (weekends only). *Average main: €10* ⊠ *14 rue Louis Bonnet, Belleville* ☎ *01–43–57–42–81* ⊗ *Closed Tues.* Ⓜ *Belleville.*

La Cave de Belleville

$$ | **Wine Bar.** La Cave de Belleville is just the type of establishment that's quickly becoming popular in the French capital: the *cave à manger*. A perfect blend of wine bar, wine shop, and épicerie, the vast, light-filled space is the ideal spot to have dinner and enjoy a bottle of natural wine, or take one to go. **Known for:** charcuterie, cheese, and seafood platters; natural wines; shared tables. *Average main: €19* ⊠ *51 rue de Belleville, Belleville* ☎ *01–40–34–12–95* ⊕ *www.lacavede-belleville.wordpress.com* ⊗ *Closed Mon. lunch* Ⓜ *Pyrénées.*

La Fine Mousse

$$$ | Modern European. Beer can be just as wonderful an accompaniment to food as wine; if you're skeptical, let La Fine Mousse convince you. At once a beer bar and a beer-driven restaurant, La Fine Mousse pairs modern French cuisine with artisanal brews. **Known for:** 20 beers on draft; weekend tasting menu; young professional crowd. *Average main: €27* ✉ *4 av. Jean Aicard, Ménilmontant* ☎ *01–48–06–40–94* ⊕ *www.lafinemousse.fr* ☉ *Closed for lunch weekdays* Ⓜ *Rue St-Maur.*

Le Baratin

$$$ | Modern French. If you want to eat where Parisian chefs eat, Le Baratin is the place to be. Chef Raquel Carena's ever-changing menu of daring, creative dishes and natural wines is more than enough to make up for the somewhat frigid service. **Known for:** marinated fish appetizers; natural wines; excellent offal, from calf's brains to sweetbreads. *Average main: €30* ✉ *3 rue Jouye-Rouve, Belleville* ☎ *01–43–49–39–70* ☉ *Closed Sun. and Mon., Sat. lunch* Ⓜ *Pyrénées.*

★ **Le Comptoir**

$ | Modern French. Le Comptoir (The Counter) lives up to its name: The counter running through this cozy dining room certainly evokes a traditional French brasserie. The fresh cuisine made with local, seasonal products is the real draw here, as are the reasonable prices. **Known for:** new menu every week; surprising sweet-and-savory pairings like melon with sausage or octopus with sweet potato; vegan

menu every Monday evening. *Average main: €14* ✉ *30 rue Villiers de l'Isle Adam, Belleville* ☎ *09–84–55–25–63* ☉ *Closed Sun. and Mon. in summer* Ⓜ *Gambetta.*

★ **Le Grand Bain**

$$$ | Modern French. This Belleville hot spot has become as beloved as the star of the Paris dining scene who founded it, former Au Passage chef Edward Delling-Williams. Take a seat in the tightly packed dining room and try the small plates that dominate this menu. **Known for:** fresh fish crudos; exquisitely roasted meats; modestly priced natural wines. *Average main: €30* ✉ *14 rue Dénoyez, Belleville* ☎ *09–83–02–72–02* ⊕ *www.legrandbainparis. com* ☉ *No lunch* Ⓜ *Belleville.*

★ **Mensae**

$$$$ | Modern French. At this bistro on a quiet Belleville street, former *Top Chef* contestant Thibault Sombardier has composed a menu of seasonal produce and perfectly cooked meats. The sidewalk terrace is particularly lovely in warm weather, and the lunchtime prix fixe on weekdays (€20) is one of the best deals in the city. **Known for:** revisited classic bistro fare; seasonal soups; praline chocolate mousse. *Average main: €36* ✉ *23 rue Mélingue, Belleville* ☎ *01–53–19–80–98* ⊕ *www.mensae-restaurant. com* ☉ *Closed Sun. and Mon.* Ⓜ *Pyrénées.*

Wenzhou

$ | Chinese. For more than 20 years, this Chinese restaurant has been a local favorite in Belleville.

FAMOUS LOCALS: PÈRE-LACHAISE CEMETERY

When Napoléon I commissioned Père-Lachaise Cemetery, his vision was for a burial ground where anyone could be interred, regardless of creed, nationality, race, or sex. Today, the cemetery is home to a vast cross section of people, including many noteworthy celebrities.

Edith Piaf
The beloved singer was a native of Belleville, so it's only appropriate that "the Little Sparrow," be buried here. You'll find her tomb not far from the entrance at Rue de la Réunion, just before the wall of monuments honoring those who perished during World War II.

Oscar Wilde
The tradition has long been to kiss Oscar Wilde's imposing tomb, but ever since a glass partition was installed to keep lipstick from degrading the stone, most people kiss the glass instead. Wilde can be found at the eastern side of the cemetery, not far from the Crematorium.

Jim Morrison
The Doors' lead singer is one of the cemetery's most famous inhabitants, but some claim that his tombstone sits atop an empty grave and that Jim was laid to rest in Los Angeles. You can find Morrison's tomb not far from the Casimir Perier roundabout, where many a rock fan has left a memento.

Gertrude Stein
"America is my country, and Paris is my hometown," said Stein, who midwifed many a writing career in the 1920s. Her life partner, Alice B. Toklas, is buried with her on the southeastern side of the cemetery; you can read Alice's name on the other side of the stone.

The food is made for sharing, and the casual atmosphere keeps folks coming back again and again. **Known for:** steamed pork buns; inexpensive dumplings; vegetarian choices. *Average main: €9 ⊠ 16 rue de Belleville, Belleville* ☎ *01–47–97–70–01* ⊕ *www.lacantinechinoise.fr* ⊗ *Closed Tues.* Ⓜ *Belleville.*

Yard
$$$ | Modern European. Just steps from Père-Lachaise, this restaurant gets its name from its former life as a construction yard. After changing hands several times, Yard has established itself as a no-nonsense modern bistro, and the open kitchen makes for a very exciting view indeed. **Known for:** inexpensive, simple prix fixe; open kitchen; excellent natural wine selection. *Average main: €30 ⊠ 6 rue de Mont-Louis, Père Lachaise* ☎ *01–40–09–70–30* ⊗ *Closed weekends* Ⓜ *Alexandre Dumas.*

🍸 Bars and Nightlife

★ Aux Folies
The café vibe of this Belleville institution (and former cabaret) evaporates in the evening, when it becomes one of the most animated spots in the area. The divey decor and bright neon sign reflect the laid-back, hipster atmosphere here, and the giant sidewalk seating area is the perfect place to enjoy some of

the cheapest drinks in the capital. Don't miss the street art on Rue Dénoyez just around the corner. ⊠ *8 rue de Belleville, Belleville* ☎ *06–28–55–89–40* ⊕ *www.aux-folies-belleville.fr* Ⓜ *Belleville.*

La Commune

This greenhouse-like bar (from the team behind another winning bar, Le Syndicat) is known for their giant silver punch bowls, filled with fruity concoctions to share with friends. ⊠ *80 boulevard de Belleville, Belleville* ☎ *01–42–55–57–61* ⊕ *syndicatcocktailclub.com/la-commune* Ⓜ *Belleville, Couronnes.*

Le Floréal Belleville

At once a bar, restaurant, and cultural space, this new hangout is a great way to experience Belleville's signature low-key, convivial nightlife. Have a drink at the bar, watch videos in the projection room, or grab a bite to eat. The Art Nouveau space is located at the foot of the Parc de Belleville. ⊠ *43 rue des Couronnes, Belleville* Ⓜ *Couronnes.*

★ Le Perchoir

You won't find a sign out front, but the line waiting to take the elevator to the seventh-floor rooftop bar is a quick giveaway you've come to the right spot. Reserve a table at the industrial chic sixth-floor eatery or order upscale bar fare on the roof, an urban garden with a very Berlin (read: trendy) vibe. The best part? Its 360-degree views of Paris's skyline. ⊠ *14 rue Crespin du Gast, Ménilmontant* ☎ *01–48–06–18–48* ✎ *reservation@leperchoir.fr* ⊕ *leper-*

The charming cobbled streets of Belleville and Ménilmontant are filled with immersive wall murals. Wander down Rue Dénoyez in Belleville, or seek out the impressive murals of Geneviève de Gaulle-Anthonioz and Germaine Tillion on the corner of Rue de Tourtille and Rue Ramponeau; the portraits of the résistantes were added in 2014.

choir.tv ☞ *Closed Sun. and Mon. in winter* Ⓜ *Ménilmontant.*

Les Trois 8

A destination for beer lovers, Les Trois 8 has an ever-revolving selection of beer on tap from all over the world. If you're not a beer fan but are still craving the bar's rock-and-roll spirit, there's also a selection of wine and other drinks, as well as simple, delicious food such as charcuterie and cheese platters. ⊠ *11 rue Victor Letalle, Ménilmontant* ☎ *01–40–33–47–70* ⊕ *www.lestrois8.fr* Ⓜ *Ménilmontant.*

Mama Shelter

Hip Parisians make the pilgrimage to visit the Island Bar at this hotel, the happeningest spot around. Beautiful people flock in for solid cocktails, foosball, and even an adjacent pizza bar. It's always packed, but lines are out the door Thursday through Saturday, when DJs and other international artists perform. ⊠ *109 rue de Bagnolet, 20e, Eastern Paris* ☎ *01–43–48–48–48* ⊕ *www.mamashelter.com* Ⓜ *Alexandre Dumas.*

★ Paname Brewery Company

This brewery, with a phenomenal view over the Canal de l'Ourcq, offers five house-brewed beers year-round and a host of seasonal varieties, with a perfunctory food menu to go with them. Service is sometimes less than perfect, but the laid-back locale is still the ideal place to stop for a drink after wandering along the Canal. ⊠ *41 quai de la Loire, La Villette* ☎ *01-40-36-43-55* ⊕ *www.panamebrewing-company.com* Ⓜ *Ourcq.*

Triplettes

Hipsters and students flock to this bright, retro bar, whose decor is inspired by the animated film *Triplets of Belleville*. There's a reasonably priced happy hour, and you can also order a bite to eat from a small but satisfactory bistro menu. ⊠ *102 bd. de Belleville, Belleville* ☎ *01-43-15-09-54* Ⓜ *Belleville.*

🎭 Performing Arts

Ateliers d'Artistes de Belleville

Comprising more than 250 Belleville artists, this association was formed with the goal of both protecting and publicizing their work and workspaces. The gallery hosts temporary exhibits of local artists year-round and an "open studios" event every May. ⊠ *1 rue Francis Picabia, Belleville* ☎ *01-73-74-27-67* ⊕ *www.ateliers-artistes-belleville.fr* Ⓜ *Belleville.*

Culture Rapide

Self-dubbed a "bar and poet-house," this dive is *the* place to hear spoken-word poetry. Thursday nights are Anglophone open mike nights, and concerts and French slam poetry nights round out the calendar nicely. The reasonably priced bar menu features beers, simple cocktails, and wines by the glass, as well as platters of charcuterie and cheese. Just outside is one of the best sidewalk terraces in Belleville, beneath an imposing and apt sign reading "il faut se méfier des mots" or "one must beware of words." ⊠ *103 rue Julien Lacroix, Belleville* ☎ *01-46-36-08-04* ⊕ *www.culturerapide.com* Ⓜ *Belleville.*

L'International

This concert venue is one of the most eclectic, affordable places to hear live music in the capital, with no cover charge and an inexpensive happy hour until 9 pm. Its variety attracts all: In one week, the stage might welcome hip-hop groups, metal bands, electro-funk, or experimental soul. ⊠ *5 rue Moret, Ménilmontant* ☎ *09-50-57-60-50 only from 4 pm to 9 pm* ⊕ *www.linternational.fr* Ⓜ *Ménilmontant.*

La Bellevilloise

This Belleville staple is at once a restaurant, bar, and concert venue welcoming musicians from all over the world. Originally founded in 1877 with the goal of allowing all people access to culture, no matter their means, La Bellevilloise of today still creates an active sense of community in the neighborhood, hosting occasional ping-pong tournaments, jazz brunches, and even hummus-themed garden parties. ⊠ *19–21 rue Boyer, Belleville* ☎ *01–46–36–07–07* ⊕ *www.labellevilloise.com* Ⓜ *Gambetta.*

★ La Maroquinerie

Known affectionately as La Maroq' to regulars, this concert hall hosts an eclectic offering of artists in an intimate setting; in fact, it's not uncommon to grab a drink with the band at the bar once the show is over. There's something for everyone on the schedule, from classic French to indie to punk to electro. An on-site restaurant with an ever-evolving menu caters quite nicely to vegetarians and omni-vores alike, with Buddha bowls, burgers, salads, and more. ⊠ *23 rue Boyer, Ménilmontant* ☎ *01–40–33–36–05* ⊕ *www.lamaroquinerie.fr* Ⓜ *Ménilmontant.*

Philharmonie de Paris

Designed by French architect Jean Nouvel, this is one of the world's finest and most expensive audito-riums. It can accommodate 2,400 music lovers, and the adjustable modular seating means you'll be able to see the stage no matter where you sit. Because the hall is home to the Orchestre de Paris, concerts are mostly classical; however, programming includes guest artists and, on weekends, pop, jazz, and world music performances appeal to patrons with more diverse tastes—and smaller budgets. Part of the same complex (formerly known as the Cité de la Musique), **Philharmonie 2** features a 1,000-seat concert hall and a 250-seat amphitheater. Designed by Christian de Portzamparc, they present an eclectic range of concerts (some of which are free) in a postmodern setting. The Philharmonie de Paris is a 45-minute métro ride from downtown. If you're driving, there are 600 parking spaces available. ⊠ *221 av. Jean Jaurès, 19e, Eastern Paris* ☎ *01–44–84–44–84* ⊕ *www.philhar-moniedeparis.fr* Ⓜ *Porte de Pantin.*

★ Théâtre de Ménilmontant

This historic theater's roots were born in the 19th century, and today, it's home to three stages from three different periods: 1929, 1980, and 2005. These stages host a variety of shows, festivals, and art exhibits, favoring avant-garde, offbeat works. Plays specifically for children are sometimes on the schedule, including the occasional puppet show. ⊠ *15 rue du Retrait, Ménilmontant* ☎ *01–46–36–98–60* ⊕ *www.menilmontant.info* Ⓜ *Gambetta.*

LES
PUCES

ÉPINETTES   CLIGNAN-
COURT   LA   LA VILLETTE

LES   CHAPELLE
BATIGNOLLES   MONTMARTRE

TERNES   MONCEAU   PIGALLE

LES GRANDS   CANAL   BELLEVILLE
CHAILLOT   BOULEVARDS   SENTIER   ST-MARTIN

CHAMPS-
ÉLYSÉES   MÉNILMONTANT

BOIS DE   PASSY   TROCADÉRO   PALAIS-   LES   LE   OBERKAMPF   PÈRE-
BOULOGNE   ROYAL   HALLES   MARAIS   LACHAISE

LES
INVALIDES   LES ÎLES

AUTEUIL   VAUGIRARD   ST-GERMAIN-   BASTILLE   CHARONNE
DES-PRÉS

QUARTIER   BEL-AIR
JAVEL   MONTPARNASSE   LATIN   BERCY

ST-LAMBERT   BUTTE-AUX-   BOIS DE
CAILLES   SEINE   VINCENNES

MONTROUGE   MAISON   AUSTERLITZ
BLANCHE

P icture the charming streets of Montmartre, but remove all the tourists (not to mention the tough-on-the-legs steep climbs), and you've got Butte-aux-Cailles, a little village within the city walls. Here, half-timbered houses and cobbled streets beg to be the backdrop for artsy photos, while co-op cafés and restaurants, street art, and unique historical sights invite you to soak up the neighborhood's eccentric ambience, held over from its days as a stronghold of the Revolutionary 1871 Paris Commune. Journey a bit to the east, and you'll discover a hodgepodge of dim sum, pho, and Thai joints (not to mention some of the city's best Asian grocery stores). Moving north toward the Seine in Bercy, you'll encounter cultural behemoths including the Bibliothèque Nationale François Mitterrand and the Cinémathèque Française, an organization devoted to French cinema, as well as a quaint pedestrian shopping area, massive concert hall, and art venues all begging to be explored.—by Emily Monaco

◉ Sights

Bibliothèque Nationale François Mitterrand

The National Library of France, across the sleek Simone de Beauvoir footbridge from Bercy Park, is a stark complex comprising four 22-story L-shape buildings representing open books. Commissioned by President Mitterrand, the €1-billion library was said to be the world's most modern when it opened in 1998—a reputation quickly sullied when it was discovered that miles of books and rare documents were baking in the glass towers, unprotected from the sun (movable shutters were eventually installed). Some of the most important printed treasures of France are stored here, though the majority of them are available only to researchers. Visitors can see the impressive 17th-century Globes of Coronelli, a pair of 2-ton orbs made for Louis XIV. There's a sunken center garden with tall trees (open to the public the first weekend in June) ringed by low-ceilinged reading rooms, which are nothing special. A first-floor gallery hosts popular temporary exhibitions on subjects such as the life of Casanova. Enter through the easternmost tower. ⊠ Quai François Mauriac, Eastern Paris ☎ 01–53–79–59–59 ⊕ www.bnf.fr ⊠ Globes gallery free; all other entries from €4 ۞ Closed Mon. Ⓜ Bibliothèque, Quai de la Gare.

Bois de Vincennes

Like the Bois de Boulogne to the west, this much-loved retreat on the city's eastern border was landscaped by Napoléon III. Its roots, however, reach back to the 13th century, when Philippe Auguste created a hunting preserve in the shadow of the royal Château de Vincennes, which once ranked as the largest château in Europe. In 1731 Louis XV created a public park here, and the *bois* (or wood) now features lush lawns, a flower garden, and summertime jazz concerts. Rowboats are for hire at a pair of lakes: Lac Daumesnil, which has two islands, and Lac des Minimes, which has three. For the kids, there are pony rides, a miniature train, and numerous play areas. Here, too, you'll find the stunning Palais de la Porte Dorée (home to an immigration museum and a tropical aquarium), the Parc Zoologique, the Hippodrome de Vincennes racetrack, two cafés, and, in spring, an amusement park. Bikes can be rented at the Château de Vincennes métro stop. ⊠ *Bois de Vincennes, Eastern Paris* Ⓜ *Château de Vincennes, Porte Dorée.*

Château de Vincennes

This imposing high-walled château, on the northern edge of the Bois de Vincennes, was France's medieval answer to Versailles. Built and expanded by various kings between the 12th and 14th centuries, it is now surrounded by a dry moat and dominated by a 170-foot keep (the last of nine original towers). The royal residence eventually became a prison holding, notably, convicts of both sexes—and "the doors did not always remain closed between them," as one tour guide coyly put it. Inmates included the philosopher Diderot and the Marquis de Sade.

Both the château and its cathedral, Ste-Chapelle (designed in the style of the Paris church of the same name) have undergone a spectacular restoration, returning them to their previous glory. If you speak French, the free 90-minute tour is worthwhile; otherwise, consider spending €3 for the English audioguide. ⊠ *Av. de Paris, Eastern Paris* ☎ *01-43-28-15-48* ⊕ *www. chateau-vincennes.fr* ⊡ *€9* Ⓜ *Château de Vincennes.*

★ Cinémathèque Française

This French organization has one of the largest collections of film archives in the world, thanks to a private collection started by Henri Langlois in the mid-1930s. After German authorities in France ordered the destruction of all films made before 1937, Langlois, in cooperation with his friends, smuggled vast quantities of films out of the country to protect them. Today, the Cinémathèque not only houses one of the most extensive museums of cinematic artifacts in the world, but it also hosts exhibits and film retrospectives, with screenings from the archives nearly every day. ⊠ *51 rue de Bercy, Bercy* ☎ *01-71-19-33-33* ⊕ *www.cinema-theque.fr* ⊡ *Museum €5, screenings extra* Ⓜ *Bercy.*

★ Cité de la Mode et du Design

(City of Fashion and Design)
This imposing ultramodern building is home to a museum, design school, and several exhibition spaces where fashion and design are at the forefront. The green tubelike building (sometimes

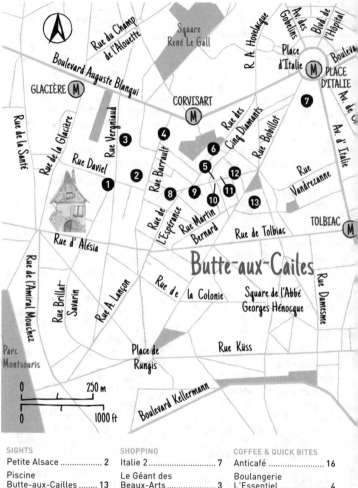

DINING

BARS & NIGHTLIFE

dubbed "that green thingy") was designed by architects Dominique Jakob and Brendan MacFarlane. Inside, within former storehouses, visitors will find the Art Ludique Museum and French fashion institute, as well as temporary events and exhibits each year: fashion photography in spring, a themed, interactive exhibit in summer, and each winter, a temporary discovery of a different country through its culture. ⊠ 34 quai d'Austerlitz, Bercy ☎ 01-76-77-25-30 ⊕ www.citemod-edesign.fr ⊗ Closed Tues. Ⓜ Gare d'Austerlitz.

Les Amies et Amis de la Commune de Paris 1871

History nerds will appreciate the library of books, videos, songs, and images documenting the Paris Commune, a Revolutionary government that took control of Paris for just a few months in 1871 but that left an indelible mark on the area. The association is dedicated to the Commune's history, including its link to the Butte-aux-Cailles neighborhood, where a bloody battle took place on May 24 right before the Commune fell. The association also holds regular events and conferences. ⊠ 46 rue des Cinq-Diamants, Butte-aux-Cailles ☎ 01-45-81-60-54 ⊕ www.commune1871.org ⊗ Closed weekends Ⓜ Corvisart.

★ Les Frigos

Not far from Austerlitz train station, this former refrigerated hangar once used to stock products to be transported by train (its name is French for "fridges") has been converted into studios for working

GETTING HERE

The closest stop to Butte-aux-Cailles is Corvisart on métro line 6. The closest to Bercy is the stop of the same name on lines 6 and 14. Your métro ticket will also allow you access to the tram (line 3), which travels along the outer limit of Paris. Mostly used by locals, it has useful stops at Porte d'Italie (a lovely walk from Butte-aux-Cailles), Porte de Choisy (for Chinatown), and Porte Dorée for easy access to the Bois de Vincennes.

artists in Paris. While the Frigos are not open to the public every day, regular exhibits allow visitors to explore the building, meet the artists, and discover the street art installations that cover the space. ⊠ 19 rue des Frigos, Bibliothèque ☎ 01-44-24-03-40 ⊕ www.les-frigos. com ⊠ Free Ⓜ Bibliothèque François Mitterrand.

Parc Floral de Paris

A lake, a butterfly garden, and seasonal displays of blooms make the Bois de Vincennes's 70-acre floral park a lovely place to spend a summer afternoon. Kids will also enjoy the minigolf and game areas. The park hosts jazz concerts most weekends from April through September, but other months many attractions are closed. ⊠ Rte. de la Pyramide, Eastern Paris ☎ 01-49-57-24-81 ⊕ www.vincennes-tour-isme.fr/Decouvrir/Parc-Floral ⊠ €3 May-Oct.; free rest of year Ⓜ Château de Vincennes.

★ **Pavillons de Bercy** (*Musée des Arts Forains*)

This unique museum is devoted entirely to carnivals and fairs, with a good number of the exhibits devoted to the *foires* (fairs) of Paris's Belle Époque. You must reserve tickets in advance, so be sure to plan ahead if you want to discover centuries-old merry-go-rounds, see carnival costumes of yore, and witness actors bring the exhibits to life. ✉ *53 av. des Terroirs de France, Bercy* ☎ *01–43–40–16–22* ⊕ *www.arts-forains.com* ✇ *€16* Ⓜ *Cour St-Émilion.*

Petite Alsace

Take a stroll down Rue Daviel and you may feel you're in Germany, not the capital of France. The ensemble of 40 half-timbered houses added here in 1912 were dubbed "Petite Alsace" or "Little Alsace" for the houses' resemblance to those typical of France's Alsace-Lorraine region, which takes strong architectural influences from neighboring Germany. The result? A large dose of charm in an already charming neighborhood. As families still live here, visitors are not encouraged to enter the courtyard, but rather to admire the structure from the outside. ✉ *10 rue Daviel, Butte-aux-Cailles* Ⓜ *Corvisart.*

Piscine Butte-aux-Cailles

Do as the locals do and take a dip at this swimming complex with three pools, two of which are outdoors and open all year long (heated, of course, to a comfy 82ºF). The high vaulted ceilings of the indoor pool are evocative

of the Art Nouveau style. As with all Parisian pools, men are not permitted to swim in trunks (only Speedo-style swimwear), and all swimmers must wear a bathing cap. ✉ *5 pl. Paul Verlaine, Butte-aux-Cailles* ☎ *01–45–89–60–05* ⊕ *www.paris.fr/equipements/piscine-de-la-butte-aux-cailles-2927* ✇ *€4* Ⓜ *Tolbiac.*

Piscine Josephine Baker

This modern aquatic center, which floats on the Seine and is named after the much-beloved American entertainer, features a pool with a retractable glass roof, two solariums, a steam room, Jacuzzis, and a gym. Check the opening hours and schedule of classes online. ✉ *Porte de la Gare, 21 quai François Mauriac, Eastern Paris* ☎ *01–56–61–96–50* ⊕ *www.piscine-baker.fr* ✇ *Pool €4 (€7 in summer), fees may apply for other activities* Ⓜ *Quai de la Gare, Bibilothèque.*

Street Art 13 (*Galerie Itinerrance*)

The 13e arrondissement is home to one of Paris's most active street art scenes, and Street Art 13, a project envisaged by Galerie Itinerrance, has brought 34 wall paintings by 25 street artists of 12 nationalities to the area. You can find a proposed organized walk to see them all on the project's website. Within the walls of its brick-and-mortar structure, Street Art 13's gallery also hosts more traditional art shows. ⊠ *24 bd. du Général Jean Simon, Bibliothèque* ☎ *01-44-06-45-39* ⊕ *www.streetart13.fr* Ⓜ *Bibliothèque François Mitterrand.*

🛍 Shopping

Bercy Village

Not far from the Bercy train station, this "village" is made up of 42 warehouses that once played host to the largest wine market in the world. The 19th-century warehouses have since been converted into a pedestrian area of shops and cafés, with a cinema, beauty parlors, clothing shops, and more. The village also hosts events such as live music performances, free yoga classes, and temporary exhibits, especially in summer. ⊠ *Cour St-Émilion, Bercy* ☎ *08-25-16-60-75* ⊕ *www.bercyvillage.com* ⊙ *Some shops closed Sun.* Ⓜ *Cour St-Émilion.*

Italie 2

This shopping mall is the largest within the city limits of Paris. With three levels and more than 130 stores, it's a great place to shop for clothing, home goods, and beauty products. Food options within the mall include bakeries, a pan-Asian takeaway, and an Italian restaurant with pizzas, panini, and salads. ⊠ *30 av. d'Italie, Bibliothèque* ☎ *01-45-80-72-00* ⊕ *www.italiedeux.com* Ⓜ *Pl. d'Italie.*

La Boutique Sans Argent

Quite literally "The Shop without Money," this boutique is the physical manifestation of the idea that one man's trash is another man's treasure. Bring items you no longer need and pick up items that have been dropped off. You need nothing to gain the right to "shop." Rather, the boutique encourages shoppers to become aware of the importance of reusing items rather than tossing them. ⊠ *2 rue Edouard Robert, Bois de Vincennes* ☎ *09-53-42-23-66* ⊕ *laboutiquesansargent.org* ⊙ *Closed Sun. and Mon., 1st Sat. of every month, 3 wks in summer* Ⓜ *Michel Bizot.*

Le Géant des Beaux-Arts

If spending time in the city that was once home to Monet, van Gogh, and Picasso is giving you inspiration, this art supply store might be worth a peruse. Oil, watercolor, and acrylic paints as well as canvases and crafting supplies are all sold here. ⊠ *15 rue Vergniaud, Butte-aux-Cailles* ☎ *01-40-78-00-80* ⊕ *www.geant-beaux-arts.fr* ⊙ *Closed Sun.* Ⓜ *Corvisart.*

★ Les Abeilles

This store specializes in one thing and one thing only: honey. Dozens of single-origin honeys from all over France—and the world—inhabit these shelves, and the manager is an urban beekeeper himself. Feel free to ask for tastes before you make your final decisions. A few basic honeys are available on tap; the selection changes fairly regularly. ⊠ *21 rue de la Butte aux Cailles, Butte-aux-Cailles* ☎ *01-45-81-43-48* ⊕ *www.lesabeilles.biz* ☉ *Closed Sun. and Mon.* Ⓜ *Corvisart.*

Tang Frères

Since the '70s, Tang Frères has brought all sorts of Asian grocery products to Paris. Fresh produce, meats, and a huge variety of shelf-stable goods like sauces, snacks, and sodas are available here. The Avenue d'Ivry store in the heart of Chinatown also has a Tang Gourmet Paris shop, where you can grab steamed pork buns, sautéed noodles, and Vietnamese banh mi sandwiches for lunch on the go. ⊠ *48 av. d'Ivry, Chinatown* ☎ *01-45-70-80-00* ⊕ *www.tang-freres.fr* ☉ *Closed Mon.* Ⓜ *Porte d'Ivry.*

🍵 Coffee and Quick Bites

Anticafé

$ | Café. Unlike traditional French cafés, Anticafé charges not by the drink or snack, but by the hour (€5 per hour or €24 per full day). With several locations throughout the city, it's evidence of a larger coworking movement happening in Paris—meaning there's ample chance to meet locals who come to cafés to work. **Known for:** unlimited coffee, tea, and snacks; free high-speed Wi-Fi; board games and books. *Average main: €5* ⊠ *59 rue Nationale, Bibliothèque* ☎ *01-53-82-57-06* ⊕ *www.anticafe.eu* ☉ *Closed weekends, July and Aug.* Ⓜ *Olympiades.*

★ Boulangerie l'Essentiel

$ | Bakery. Baker Anthony Bosson's hard work—and choice to use top-quality organic flours—is apparent at his 13e arrondissement bakery. His *flûte*, a slow-fermented baguette with a slightly nutty aroma, was even recognized by Paris's best baguette competition, a well-deserved honor. **Known for:** award-winning flûte; rich, buttery brioche of the month; sweet Versot bread. *Average main: €2* ⊠ *73 bd. Auguste Blanqui, Butte-aux-Cailles* ☎ *01-40-21-69-22* ⊕ *boulangerie-lessentiel.com* ☉ *Closed Mon.* Ⓜ *Corvisart.*

Laurent Duchêne

$ | Bakery. This shop from Laurent Duchêne, holder of the prestigious Meilleur Ouvrier de France distinction, is a wonderland of bright, colorful pastries. Classics and unique creations coexist side by side, but in some cases, the simplest looking cakes are the best choices. **Known for:** buttery, almond-based financier, voted one of the best in Paris; award-winning butter croissant; surprising flavor combos. *Average main: €2* ⊠ *2 rue Wurtz, Butte-aux-Cailles* ☎ *01-45-65-00-77* ⊕ *www.laurent-duchene.com* ☉ *Closed Sun., Aug.* Ⓜ *Corvisart.*

Les 400 Coups *(Les 400 Coups à la Cinémathèque Française)*

$ | Café. This café within the Cinémathèque Française gets its name from one of François Truffaut's most famous cinematic masterpieces. The eco-friendly café serves an array of French- and Franco-Japanese-inspired bites and also has a corner for kids to play.

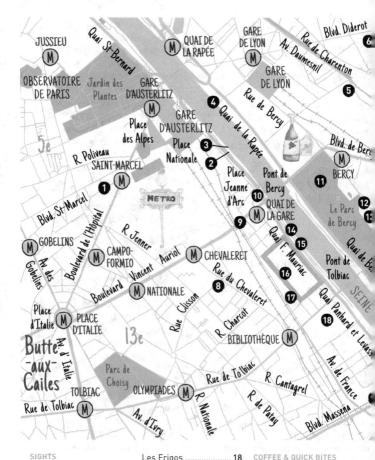

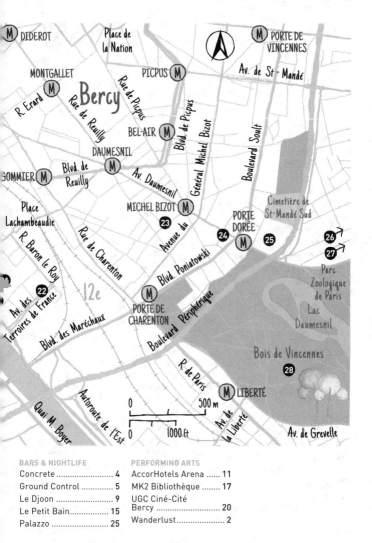

Known for: local, seasonal vegetables; quiches and Buddha bowls; charcuterie from the Auvergne region. *Average main: €10 ⊠ 51 rue de Bercy, Bercy* ☎ *01-43-44-18-72* ⊕ *www.les400coupsalacinematheque. fr* ☉ *Closed Tues. No dinner (drinks and light snacks available)* Ⓜ *Bercy.*

L'OisiveThé

$ | Café. There are cat cafés and coworking cafés—and then there is L'OisiveThé, the first knitting café in Paris. Cozy up at a table in the homey teahouse, where a vast selection of both yarns and teas are on offer and patrons range widely in age and expertise. **Known for:** handdyed yarns from the United States and Britain; 70 types of tea; brunch on weekends. *Average main: €12 ⊠ 8 rue de la Butte aux Cailles, Butte-aux-Cailles* ☎ *01-53-80-31-33* ⊕ *www. loisivethe.eatbu.com* ☉ *Closed Mon., Aug. No dinner* Ⓜ *Corvisart.*

★ Vandermeersch

$ | Bakery. Dubbed "the pastry chef of bakers," Stéphane Vandermeersch is the Parisian master of Alsatian specialties like the *kouglof* (with hazelnuts, raisins, and a sprinkling of sugar on top) as well as flaky classics like croissants. Pick up some pastries on your way to the nearby Bois de Vincennes. **Known for:** award-winning Epiphany galette; chocolate-almond croissant; Alsatian kouglof. *Average main: €2 ⊠ 278 av. Daumesnil, Bois de Vincennes* ☎ *01-43-46-21-66* ⊕ *www. boulangerie-patisserie-vandermeersch.com* ☉ *Closed Sun. and Mon., 1 month in summer* Ⓜ *Porte Dorée.*

BACK IN THE DAY

Butte-aux-Cailles was originally founded as a tannery district thanks to its location near the now-extinct Bièvre River, and while the industry couldn't have been olfactorily pleasant, the smell may well have been what preserved the neighborhood's charm. In the 18th century, when new city limits were being drawn, Butte-aux-Cailles was deliberately kept outside the city. This meant that when Georges-Eugène Haussmann drew up plans to revitalize Paris in the 19th century, Butte-aux-Cailles escaped the redesign and was thus kept much as it had been for centuries.

🍴 Dining

Chez Gladines

$ | Basque. This Basque minichain's Butte-aux-Cailles outpost is a local favorite thanks to its generous portions of Basque specialities, inexpensive versions of bistro classics, and familial atmosphere. Low in price and high in energy, the restaurant unites students, locals, and visitors alike—often in such tight quarters that folks leave with a new friend or two. **Known for:** piquillo peppers with salt cod; cassoulet; foie gras with flavors like rum, mango, or ginger. *Average main: €15 ⊠ 30 rue des Cinq-Diamants, Butte-aux-Cailles* ☎ *09-67-31-96-46* ⊕ *www. chezgladines-butteauxcailles.fr* ☞ *No reservations* Ⓜ *Corvisart.*

Chez Lili et Marcel

$ | Bistro. This neighborhood restaurant not far from the Bercy train station certainly plays into the French bistro tropes, with gingham napkins and a menu printed on an imitation newspaper. The dining room can get a bit packed, but portions are generous and prices are far cheaper than in much of the capital. **Known for:** "Cocotte de Lili," served in a cast-iron cocotte; tiramisu; wide sidewalk terrace, perfect for people-watching. *Average main: €15* ⊠ *1 quai d'Austerlitz, Bercy* ☎ *01–45–85–00–08* Ⓜ *Quai de la Gare.*

L'Alchimiste

$$ | Bistro. The diminutive L'Alchimiste is a homey iteration of the classic French bistro. With just a handful of tables, a handwritten menu that changes regularly, and hearty, unfussy dishes, it's an authentic meal from aperitif to dessert. **Known for:** (free!) spreads and dips served with aperitif; braised lamb; friendly service. *Average main: €23* ⊠ *181 rue de Charenton, Bercy* ☎ *01–43–47–10–38* Ⓢ *Closed Sun.* Ⓜ *Montgallet.*

★ L'Aubergeade

$$$ | French. French country cooking is on the menu at L'Aubergeade, which takes its name from the French word for "inn." Convivial and friendly, the no-nonsense bistro offers generous portions of honest food. **Known for:** steak tartare and fries; changing seasonal menu; reasonable lunchtime prix fixe. *Average main: €27* ⊠ *17 rue de Chaligny, Bercy* ☎ *01–43–44–33–36* Ⓢ *Closed Mon.* Ⓜ *Reuilly–Diderot.*

Le Temps des Cerises

$$ | Bistro. Serving hearty French classics, this restaurant is closely linked with the Paris Commune (as one of the last holdouts of the *Communards* , Butte-aux-Cailles still reverberates with the spirit of this period). The restaurant was inspired by the Commune, not only in choosing its name, which refers to a song composed by a Communard and strongly associated with the uprising and its philosophy, but in its operation style: Le Temps des Cerises is owned and run not by one person or chef, but by a cooperative team. **Known for:** strict no-telephone policy; stews and steaks; €13.50 lunch deal. *Average main: €21* ⊠ *18 rue de la Butte aux Cailles, Butte-aux-Cailles* ☎ *01–45–89–69–48* ⊕ *www.letemps-descerisescoop.com* Ⓢ *Closed Sun.* Ⓜ *Corvisart.*

★ Sellae

$$$$ | Bistro. This buzzed-about restaurant is just the type of neo-bistro that is taking Paris by storm; here, elevated bistro classics are served with contemporary flair, at affordable prices. The Italian chef draws inspiration from his home, but you'll find all the French staples here, from escargots to frog legs to *mousse au chocolat* for dessert. **Known for:** excellent prix-fixe menu; mousse au chocolat; wine list. *Average main: €36* ⊠ *18 rue des Wallons, Bercy* ☎ *01–43–31–36–04* Ⓢ *Closed Sun.* Ⓜ *Saint-Marcel.*

⭐ Tempero

$$ | Modern French. French and Brazilian cuisines marry with a light Asian touch at this creative restaurant, perhaps one of Paris's best-kept secrets. The chef, originally from Brazil, spent time working at some of the city's most illustrious restaurants before opening the spot, which is a great stop after visiting the nearby Bibliothèque Nationale François Mitterrand. **Known for:** Japanese-inspired fish dishes; good-value lunch prix fixe; excellent desserts. *Average main: €20 ⊠ 5 rue Clisson, Bibliothèque* ☎ *09-54-17-48-88* ⊕ *www.tempero.fr* ⊗ *Closed weekends, No dinner Mon.–Wed.* Ⓜ *Chevaleret.*

Tricotin

$ | Chinese. This local favorite for dim sum and Thai, Cambodian, Laotian, and Vietnamese specialties is just steps from the tram line in one of Paris's Chinatowns, sometimes referred to as the Choisy Triangle. This inexpensive spot gets quite crowded—and loud—on weekends, but it's worth it for the quality food at low prices. **Known for:** fried turnip cakes; chewy rice pancakes with shrimp; unsweetened iced tea (a rarity in Paris). *Average main: €13 ⊠ 15 av. de Choisy, Chinatown* ☎ *01-45-84-74-44* Ⓜ *Porte de Choisy.*

🍸 Bars and Nightlife

⭐ Concrete

On a barge moored in the Seine, superhip Concrete is one of Paris's preeminent hard-core dance venues and a trailblazer on the techno scene. The club goes full tilt until the wee hours on Friday and Saturday nights; it also opens on alternate Sundays, when you can party from 7 am to 2 am accompanied by live acts—heavy on the techno—and Paris's hottest DJs. ⊠ *69 port de la Rapée, Bastille* ☎ *No phone* ⊕ *www.concreteparis.fr* Ⓜ *Gare de Lyon, Gare d'Austerlitz.*

Folie en Tête

Folie en Tête or "Crazy in the Head," is a former mainstay of Paris's '70s punk scene. The comfortable interior is decorated with percussion instruments, comic books, and old skis. It's known for world music and jazz, not to mention the traffic light in the toilet that lets you know when it's safe to enter. ⊠ *33 rue de la Butte aux Cailles, 13e, Eastern Paris* ☎ *01-45-80-65-99* ⊕ *lafolieentete.wix.com/lesite* Ⓜ *Corvisart, Place d'Italie.*

★ Ground Control

This former rail depot, filled with old train carriages converted into street-food stalls and biodynamic wine and craft beer bars, has become one of the hottest places to hang in Paris. Catch one of its regular events, including DJed dance parties, an organic food market, and art exhibits, and be sure to sample the food at La Résidence, where refugee chefs are invited to cook the food from their homelands. ⊠ 81 rue du Charolais, Bercy ⊕ www.groundcontrolparis. com ⋐ Free Ⓜ Reuilly–Diderot.

Le Djoon

This is not the place to stand around. Le Djoon attracts a devoted dance crowd, and DJs (inspired by the '80s New York house scene) mix afro, disco, and funk. It's a taxi-ride away from everywhere, but a fun diversion from the normally cramped clubs. It's open Friday and Saturday from 11:30 to 5 am, Thursday from 10 to 1 am. ⊠ 22 bd. Vincent Auriol, 13e, Eastern Paris ☎ 01–45–70–83–49 ⊕ www.djoon. com Ⓜ Quai de la Gare.

Le Merle Moqueur

There's perhaps nowhere better to experience the true Butte-aux-Cailles ambience than Le Merle Moqueur, a small, inexpensive bar on the Rue de la Butte aux Cailles. Drinks are inexpensive, and the warmth of the locals will surely make you a friend or two. In the heat of summer, don't be surprised if the crowd pours out of the small bar into the street. ⊠ 11 rue de la Butte aux Cailles, Butte-aux-Cailles ☎ 01–45–65–12–43 Ⓜ Corvisart.

★ Le Petit Bain

There's something about dancing on the water that gets this cool, casual crowd revved up for the live concerts and DJ nights set on a huge barge moored on the Seine. Eclectic sounds include alternative, electro, rock, and folktronica plus a program of cultural events. It's also great place to go just for watching the sun set on the river over a nice drink. ⊠ 7 Port de la Gare, 13e, Bercy ☎ 01–43–49–68–92 ⊕ www.petitbain. org Ⓜ Quay de la Gare.

★ Palazzo

Whether you get to visit Palazzo will depend entirely on when you visit Paris; this pop-up terrace complete with bar, snack hut, beanbag chairs, and covered semi-private tables is only open from mid-May to early October. The festive hot spot located just across from the Art Deco Palais de la Porte Dorée also features special events like yoga and meditation, DJed dance evenings, and even massages. ⊠ 293 av. Daumesnil, Bois de Vincennes ☎ 07–51–59–86–32 ⊕ www.palazzo-portedoree. fr ⋐ Closed Mon. and Tues. Ⓜ Porte Dorée.

Sputnik

This Butte-aux-Cailles dive is a local favorite for students, an after-work crowd, and those waiting for a table at Le Temps des Cerises just across the street. Simple and unpretentious, this is a great place to play foosball and enjoy a playlist of classics. ✉ 14–16 rue de la Butte aux Cailles, Butte-aux-Cailles ☎ 01-45-65-19-82 ⊕ www.sputnik.fr Ⓜ Corvisart.

🎭 Performing Arts

AccorHotels Arena (Palais Omnisports de Paris-Bercy) The concert venue and indoor sports arena formerly known as Bercy underwent a major renovation in 2014, renewing the original 1984 structure's pyramid shape and sloping green lawn. The arena often welcomes musical stars such as Nicki Minaj and Florence + the Machine to Paris and has also been used for many sporting events including tennis, show jumping, and handball. The 2024 Summer Olympics are scheduled to take place in part at this arena. ✉ 8 bd. de Bercy, Bercy ⊕ www.accorhotel-sarena.com Ⓜ Bercy.

MK2 Bibliothèque This slick, 20- salle cineplex in the shadow of Mitterrand's National Library has trademark scarlet-red chairs—they fit two people without a divider, so the experience is sort of like watching a movie at home on your couch. MK2 Bibliothèque also contains two restaurants, plus shops selling gifts and DVDs. ✉ 128–162 av. de France, 13e, Eastern Paris ☎ 08-92-69-84-84 €0.60 per min ⊕ www.mk2.com Ⓜ Quai de la Gare, Bibliothèque.

UGC Ciné-Cité Bercy This mammoth 18-screen complex is in the Bercy Village shopping area. For sound and seating, it's one of the best. ✉ 2 cour Saint Emilion, 12e, Bastille ☎ 01-76-64-79-64 ⊕ www.ugc.fr Ⓜ Cour Saint Emilion.

Wanderlust This cultural space at the Cité de la Mode et du Design plays host to a variety of musical guests, mainly in dancehall and hip-hop genres. Regular events on the outdoor terrace overlooking the Seine are scheduled in the summer and early fall, including hip-hop classes and dance evenings. Inside, Wanderlust is home to a nightclub and restaurant. ✉ 32 quai d'Austerlitz, Bibliothèque ☎ 06-33-09-89-28 ⊕ www.wanderlustparis.com Ⓜ Quai de la Gare.

INDEX

Photo Credits

Chapter 4: Le Marais: Jérôme Galland (99). **Chapter 5:** Quartier Latin: Kiev.Victor/Shutterstock (107). **Chapter 6:** St-Germain-des-Prés and Les Invalides: Jodi Nasser (129). **Chapter 9:** Montmartre and Pigalle: kavalenkau/Shutterstock (181).

Fodor's PARIS

Editorial: Douglas Stallings, *Editorial Director*; Margaret Kelly, Jacinta O'Halloran, *Senior Editors*; Kayla Becker, Alexis Kelly, Amanda Sadlowski, *Editors*; Teddy Minford, *Content Editor*; Rachael Roth, *Content Manager*

Design: Tina Malaney, *Design and Production Director*; Jessica Gonzalez, *Production Designer*

Photography: Jill Krueger, *Senior Photo Editor*

Maps: Rebecca Baer, *Senior Map Editor*; Mark Stroud (Moon Street Cartography) and Andrew Murphy, Cartographers

Production: Jennifer DePrima, *Editorial Production Manager*; Carrie Parker, *Senior Production Editor*; Elyse Rozelle, *Production Editor*

Business & Operations: Chuck Hoover, *Chief Marketing Officer*; Robert Ames, *General Manager*; Stephen Horowitz, *Director of Business Development and Revenue Operations*; Tara McCrillis, *Director of Publishing Operations*

Public Relations and Marketing: Joe Ewaskiw, *Manager*; Esther Su, *Marketing Manager*

Illustrator: Jessica Gonzalez

Writers: Erin Dahl, Lily Heise, Georgette Moger, Emily Monaco, Lane Nieset

Editorial Contributors: Jennifer Ladonne, Linda Hervieux, Virginia Power, Jack Vermee

Editor: Kayla Becker

Production Editor: Jennifer DePrima

Designers: Tina Malaney, Chie Ushio

Production Design: Jessica Gonzalez

1st Edition

ISBN 978-1-64097-200-1

ISSN 2379-8076

SPECIAL SALES

This book is available at special discounts for bulk purchases for sales promotions or premiums. For more information, e-mail SpecialMarkets@fodors.com.

PRINTED IN THE UNITED STATES OF AMERICA

10 9 8 7 6 5 4 3 2

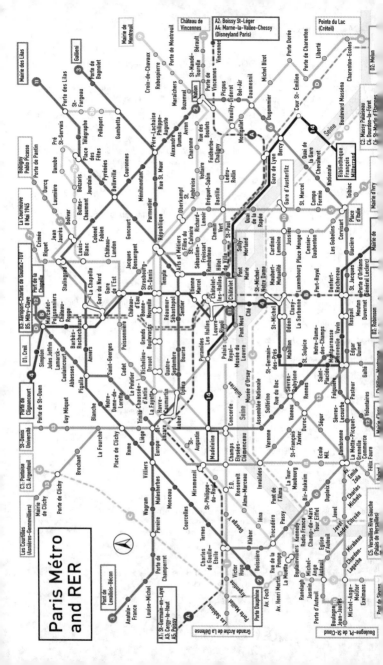

Paris Métro and RER

RESOURCES

Paris's Métro system (⊕ *www.ratp.fr/ en*) is the easiest and cheapest way to get around the city. Tickets cost €1.90 each; a *carnet* (10 tickets for €14.90) is a better value. The *Carte Navigo* system is the daily, monthly, and weekly subscription plan, with reusable cards available at automatic ticket machines and ticket windows. All métro tickets and passes are valid not only for the métro but also for all RER, tram, and bus travel within Paris.

Métro service starts at 5:30 am and continues until the last trains reach their terminus at 1:15 am Sunday through Thursday, and until 2:15 am on Friday, Saturday, and some national holidays. For itineraries, maps, and realtime tips on delays and closings, download the RATP transit system's Vianavigo or Citymapper for a trove of handy info like which end of the métro platform gets you closest to your exit on the other end of your journey.

Biking is another great way to see Paris. You'll spot self-service, bike-rental stations by Velib' Métropole throughout the city. There are two ways to rent a Velib': sign up on the website or buy a ticket from a machine at each docking station (major credit cards accepted). First, select the amount of time you wish to rent (€5 per day, up to 3 rentals; €15 per week, unlimited rentals), then tap the code you're given on the bike's keypad to unlock it.

If you're traveling from Paris to another city, you'll likely use the SNCF, France's rail system, which is fast, punctual, comfortable, and comprehensive—when it's not on strike. There are various options: local trains, overnight trains with sleeping accommodations, and the high-speed TGVs (or Trains à Grande Vitesse), which average 320 kph.

VISITOR INFORMATION

The regional tourism board—with multiple Arrivals-level kiosks at both Charles de Gaulle and Orly airports— can provide you with maps, brochures, and more the moment you touch down. Once you're in Paris, you can turn to the civic tourist information office. The main one is centrally located on Rue des Pyramides (near the Opéra), and four branch offices are stationed at the city's most popular tourist sights. Most are open daily; the Gare de Lyon and Gare de l'Est branches, however, are open Monday through Saturday only.

ONLINE RESOURCES

Besides the official tourist office websites ⊕ *en.parisinfo.com* and ⊕ *www. visitparisregion.com*, there are several other helpful government sponsored sites. The Paris mayor's office site, ⊕ *www.paris.fr*, covers all kinds of public cultural attractions, student resources, parks, markets, and more.

ABOUT OUR WRITERS & ILLUSTRATOR

Erin Dahl is an American writer and brand consultant based in Paris. Her work has appeared in publications like *Nylon, Coveteur,* and *HiP Paris*. She is also co-founder of the English content agency, Content Coopérative. Erin wrote the Marais, Bastille, Sentier and Les Grands Boulevards chapters of this guide.

Lily Heise is a Paris-based freelance writer who has been exploring the city's best secrets since 2000. Her writing has been appeared in The Huffington Post, CondeNastTraveler. com, Business Insider, Playboy.com, and other publications. She is also the author of two books on searching for romance in Paris and shares further travel tips on her blog www.jetaimeme-neither.com. Lily wrote the Les Halles and Palais-Royal, St-Germain-des-Prés and Les Invalides, and Les Batignolles and Les Puces chapters.

Georgette Moger is a New Yorker splitting her time between Los Angeles and Paris. Her travel writing on food, wine, and spirits can be found in the pages of *Wine Enthusiast* and sites such as *Liquor.com, Departures, Tasting Table* as well as in her monthly column, *Bar Imaginaire,* for the online publication, *Spirits Hunters*. Her best-selling book, *Regarding Cocktails,* has been translated into French and German. Georgette wrote the Montmartre and Pigalle chapter.

Emily Monaco is an American writer based in France. Her writing on food, wine, and culture shock has been featured in publications including the *Wall Street Journal, EatingWell,* and the BBC. Emily wrote the Experience, Quartier Latin, Belleville and Ménilmontant, and Butte-aux-Cailles and Bercy chapters.

Lane Nieset is a freelance writer from Miami who has called France home for the past five years. From her base in Nice (and frequent visits to Paris), she covers a mix of travel, lifestyle, wine and food for publications such as *National Geographic Travel, Travel + Leisure, Vogue.com,* and *Food & Wine*. She has also appeared as a guest host in the Cannes episode of BBC Travel's *RSVP Abroad* series. Lane has eaten and sipped her way around more than 50 countries on all seven continents, trying everything from snowshoeing in Antarctica to glacier trekking in the French Alps. Lane took on the Canal St-Martin, Oberkampf and Bastille, and Trocadéro and Champs-Élysées chapters.

Jessica Gonzalez is a Los Angeles-based graphic designer and illustrator. Her past work as a freelance artist includes creating art and merchandise for various artists in the LA music industry. As a graphic and production designer for the Fodor's Travel team, she has worked on redesigns of Fodor's guides and 25 Best series. Jessica plans to launch a personal line of creative apparel, prints, and pins in 2019.